Social Fairness in a Post-Pandemic World

Hikari Ishido • Jiro Mizushima
Masaya Kobayashi • Xiaofang Zhang
Editors

Social Fairness in a Post-Pandemic World

Interdisciplinary Perspectives

palgrave
macmillan

Editors
Hikari Ishido
Graduate School of Global and Transdisciplinary Studies
Chiba University
Chiba, Japan

Masaya Kobayashi
Graduate School of Social Sciences
Chiba University
Chiba, Japan

Jiro Mizushima
Graduate School of Social Sciences
Chiba University
Chiba, Japan

Xiaofang Zhang
Institute for Advanced Academic Research/
Graduate School of Social Science
Chiba University
Chiba, Japan

ISBN 978-981-19-9653-5 ISBN 978-981-19-9654-2 (eBook)
https://doi.org/10.1007/978-981-19-9654-2

This Palgrave Macmillan imprint is published by the registered company Springer Nature Singapore Pte Ltd.
The registered company address is: 152 Beach Road, #21-01/04 Gateway East, Singapore 189721, Singapore

Preface

This is an interdisciplinary collection of scholarly works concerning the initial and future impacts of COVID-19, a truly worldwide pandemic, on our global society. The main focus of this book is the urgent need to re-examine the concept of social fairness or justice in light of the COVID-19 crisis that has been manifesting itself since the end of 2019. For example, there is a large disparity in the response to the COVID-19 pandemic (e.g., stance on the fair distribution of vaccines) of organizations for "regional integration" such as the European Union (EU), the Association of Southeast Asian Nations (ASEAN), and the Asia-Pacific Economic Cooperation (APEC), Western countries, and "sovereign nations" located in the Asia-Pacific region, including Japan and China, in addition to the "various regions and actors" within sovereign states, and the situation moves forward without a consensus on "fairness."

In the COVID-19 crisis, in particular, there is a conflict between liberalism (respect for individual rights over and above the interests of the state and society) and nationalism (a tendency to emphasize the interests of the state and society over individual rights). It is necessary for actors to cooperate with each other in the face of the common challenge of COVID-19 infections. This book combines political, economic, historical, philosophical, and cultural aspects to examine whether it is possible to envision a "fair society" after COVID-19.

The book is structured as follows. **Chapter 1, Introduction: Multi-layered and multi-dimensional viewpoints towards a Fair Society,** makes a philosophical discussion of the "fairness" as a conceptual framework underlying this book. This is then followed by three parts, Part I: Global Perspective (Chaps. 2, 3, 4, and 5), Part II: Regional Focus (Chaps. 6, 7, 8, 9, and 10), and Part III: Thematic Issues (Chaps. 11 and 12). Finally, there is a brief overall Conclusion to the book.

Part I (Global Perspective) is organized as follows. **Chapter 2, "Fairness in the Global Allocation System for the COVID-19 Vaccine COVAX: Limits to Affected Parties' Participation in Decision-Making"** (Iwao Fujisawa), points out the limits of fair vaccine allocation and its future prospects from the perspective of international law, in light of the fact that the COVID-19 crisis has resulted in international disparities in vaccine supply and vaccination status. **Chapter 3, "Environment and Economy after COVID-19: Focusing on Global Warming Issues"** (Xiaofang Zhang), extracts a specific concept of fairness regarding the environment and discusses its feasibility, based on the fact that the COVID-19 crisis and global environmental issues are linked through economic activities. **Chapter 4, "An Investigation Through Philosophy and Case Studies on Regional Integration, Migrants and Refugees, and the COVID-19 Crisis"** (Gerald Moshammer, Natanaree Posrithong and Hikari Ishido), discusses the response to the COVID-19 crisis by the regional integration of a collective of nations by comparing philosophies and cases.

Chapter 5, "Challenges and Possibilities for Global Economic Cooperation after COVID-19: a Focus on East Asia" (Kuihua Han), gives a future-oriented discussion on how economic cooperation can be promoted while avoiding conflicts among sovereign nations in the post-COVID world.

Part II (Regional Focus) has the following five chapters. **Chapter 6, "Social Justice and the Response to the COVID-19 Crisis in European Countries"** (Jiro Mizushima), focuses on the response of European countries to the COVID-19 pandemic, based on an original typology of the various countries, and analyzes in detail how the concepts of "fairness" and "unfairness" appear. **Chapter 7, "Well-being and Fairness in the COVID-19 Crisis in Japan: Insights from Positive Political**

Psychology" (Masaya Kobayashi), discusses the impact of well-being on situational changes in the lives of citizens in the COVID-19 crisis from a quantitative and ideological perspective. **Chapter 8, "COVID-19 Policy Response and Citizens' Well-Being in Australia"** (by Lindsay Oades, translated from English to Japanese by Xiaofang Zhang, and reviewed by the editors), uses Australia as a case study and provides an issue concerning social justice while describing the link between political systems and vaccination rates. **Chapter 9, "Mexico Facing the COVID-19 Pandemic: Ineffective Societal and Governmental Responses in a Country with a High Level of Socioeconomic Inequality and a Precarious Health System"** (Alfonso Torrero), makes a point on the need for social fairness with a focus on the health system in Mexico. **Chapter 10, "APEC's Response to the COVID-19 Crisis and Social Justice"** (Hikari Ishido), discusses the international framework of the Asia-Pacific Economic Cooperation's "concept of fairness," which sounds like a contradiction in terms of "open regionalism," and the specific circumstances of conflicts among nations.

Part III (Thematic issues) covers the following two schematically important chapters. **Chapter 11, "Vicious Cycle of Gender Disparity: COVID-19 and Impact on Women and Gender"** (written by Afsana Begum, translated from English to Japanese by Xiaofang Zhang, and content reviewed by the editor), is a case study of South Asia and Japan that proactively discusses gender issues and fairness in the COVID-19 crisis. Finally, **Chapter 12, "Modern Japanese Literature and Infectious Diseases: Representations of Infectious Diseases and Social Fairness in Literary Works"** (Yongjiao Zhang), discusses how modern Japanese literary works have represented infectious diseases from the perspective of literary history, and gives a perspective on whether the so-called "disaster" of infectious diseases can be accepted as "value".

Since social events do not occur within the boundaries of academic disciplines, this search must be interdisciplinary. At the time of writing, the COVID-19 crisis is not yet under control, and major institutional changes, such as an agreement (treaty) on the fair distribution of vaccines among nations, are being envisioned.

One thing that emerges from the chapters of this book is that the concept of "fairness" should ideally be universal, transcending the concept of "justice" for sovereign states and individual citizens (which can change depending on the subject), and that its achievement should involve a certain amount of "self-sacrifice." As a concept of "fairness," we can see a social situation (at least in Japan) in which the assertion of rights is regarded as fact, but as a crew member of Spaceship Earth, we should also fulfill our duties. Specifically, there are many areas that require research as well as concrete action, including voluntary responses to emergencies such as the spread of infection, distribution of vaccines, citizen-level activities to resolve inter-state conflicts, and efforts to improve the well-being of the general public and vulnerable groups. It would be a great encouragement to all the authors if this small book can give us some perspective on how to lead the future society in terms of ideology and activities, while looking back constructively on what has happened (the global spread of COVID-19).

This study was supported by the Institute for Global Prominent Research of Chiba University, and was conducted under the leadership of Professor Jiro Mizushima, with contributions from the fellow researchers. These chapters (with the exception of Chap. 9) have preceding versions in Japanese (published by Akashi Shoten), and we wish to thank the publisher for the permission to publish this English version (after significant revisions and updates).

We also wish to thank Ms. Yuki Tashiro (research consultant) and Ms. Maki Nishino (Secretariat of the fair society research group for their invaluable contributions.

Chiba, Japan — Hikari Ishido
Chiba, Japan — Jiro Mizushima
Chiba, Japan — Masaya Kobayashi
Chiba, Japan — Xiaofang Zhang
December 2022

Contents

Notes on Contributors

Afsana Begum is a Ph.D. Candidate at Graduate School of Humanities and Studies on Public Affairs, Chiba University. Her major works are *Brave Girl Diary* (co-authored, UNDP and National Human Rights Commission, 2014) and *Empowerment of Women and the Scope of Triple Burden* (2014).

Iwao Fujisawa is Professor of Graduate School of Social Sciences, Chiba University; His major works are: "The Non-Interference Principle and Freedom of Information" (*Quarterly Jurist,* 37: 9–15, 2021.) and "A Review of the Approximate Application of Treaties: One Aspect of the Effect of Purpose in Treaty Regimes" (*International Journal of Law and Diplomacy*, 119(2): 273–299, 2020).

Kuihua Han is Research Fellow of Graduate School of Social Sciences, Chiba University; Her major work is (co-authored by Kika Kan, Sogoku Yin, and Byoung-sop Han), "The Possibility of Trilateral Economic Partnership," in *Global Relations*, Vol. 3, *Diversification of Regional Integration*, January 14, 2021.

Hikari Ishido is Professor of International Economics at the Graduate School of Global and Transdisciplinary Studies, Chiba University; director of Chiba University Bangkok Campus (in Thailand); and director general of the APEC Study Center Japan.

Masaya Kobayashi is Professor of Political Philosophy, Public Philosophy, Positive Psychology, and Comparative Politics at the Graduate School of Social Sciences (he currently serves as Dean), Chiba University, Japan. He heads Chiba University's Research Center on Public Affairs and represents multiple academic networks related to his specializations above.

Jiro Mizushima is Professor of History of European Politics and Comparative European Politics at the Graduate School of Social Sciences, Chiba University, Japan. He heads the university's flagship research project "New Frontiers of Studies on Fair Society: Values and Public Vision in the Age after COVID-19."

Gerald Moshammer is Assistant Professor at Mahidol University International College; His major work is: "Moving People and Shifting Technologies: A Socioethical Heuristic Approach," *Journal of Population and Social Studies* (*JPSS*), 28 (Special): 27–48.

Lindsay G. Oades is Professor in Positive Psychology at the Melbourne Graduate School of Education (he currently serves as Dean), The University of Melbourne. He has published numerous journal articles, (with J.A. Taylor et al., "Wellbeing Literacy as an Emancipatory and Transformative Capability," *Wellbeing and Resilience Education: COVID-19 and Its Impact on Education*, 209–231, 2021.

Natanaree Posrithong is Assistant Professor at Mahidol University International College. Her major work is: "The Siamese 'Modern Girl' and Women's Consumer Culture, 1925–35," *Journal of Social Issues in Southeast Asia*, 34(1), March 2019.

Alfonso Torrero Russo is a Ph.D. Candidate at Universidad Autónoma Metropolitana, Mexico. His contribution in this volume considers regional development, poverty, and communities in Mexico, from the perspective of fairness.

Xiaofang Zhang is Assistant Professor from China at the Institute for Advanced Academic Research/Graduate School of Social Sciences, Chiba

University, Japan. She specializes in environmental policy and conducts multiple research projects under the university's flagship research project "New Frontiers of Studies on Fair Society: Values and Public Vision in the age after COVID-19."

Yongjiao Zhang is Lecturer at the School of Foreign Languages, Shanghai University and Research Fellow at Graduate School of Social Sciences, Chiba University. Her major work "Re-reading Miyazawa Kenji's Literature on Infectious Disease: Representations of Epidemics, War, and Medical Care" was published in *Showa Literary Studies*, 84: 51–65, 2022.

List of Figures

List of Tables

1

Introduction: Multi-Layered and Multi-Dimensional Viewpoints towards a Fair Society

Masaya Kobayashi and Hikari Ishido

1 What Is Fairness? The Relationship between Justice and Fairness in Political Philosophy

This introduction addresses the basic concept of fairness, the focus of this volume for a post-pandemic era. Fairness is one of the most important concepts in both politics and society. Although there has been a substantial amount of philosophical discussions around this concept, comparatively few of them have been fairness studies with practical applications.

As the theory of justice has gained attention in political and legal philosophy (discussed later), the concept of fairness has often been

M. Kobayashi
Graduate School of Social Sciences, Chiba University, Chiba, Japan
e-mail: masaya_kobayashi@nifty.com

H. Ishido (✉)
Graduate School of Global and Transdisciplinary Studies, Chiba University, Chiba, Japan
e-mail: ishido@faculty.chiba-u.jp

H. Ishido et al. (eds.), *Social Fairness in a Post-Pandemic World*,
https://doi.org/10.1007/978-981-19-9654-2_1

mentioned in relation to it. Thus, in considering a fair society through the experience of COVID-19, let us first clarify a number of related concepts such as fairness, fair society, justice, equality, and equity. What does "fairness" mean? Does "fair society" have any special meaning beyond "fair"? Fairness and justice are often used synonymously: However, do these concepts have different meanings and nuances? Do equality and fairness mean the same thing as justice? Are there any differences between these two concepts?

Originally, there was little discussion of fairness in political philosophy. This situation changed when John Rawls raised the idea of "justice as fairness." If we consider the concepts of fairness or justice in the literature, we almost always find references to this concept. In contemporary political philosophy, it is so difficult to discuss fairness without Rawls' concept of "justice as fairness." In an early paper "Justice as Fairness," he wrote as follows: "It might seem at first sight that the concepts of justice and fairness are the same, and that there is no reason to distinguish them, or to say that one is more fundamental than the other. I think that this impression is mistaken. In this paper, I wish to show that the fundamental idea in the concept of justice is fairness" (Rawls, 1958: 164, 1999: 47).

Since Rawls' work, fairness has become central to the discussion of justice. Rawls himself discussed "justice as fairness" while using the two concepts differentially, yet his influence has led to the use of fairness and justice as a set in the same discussions. As Rawls himself stated, however, the idea that the two concepts are the same is not self-evident.

For example, Michael Sandel's well-known interactive lecture series at Harvard University is called "Justice." (Sandel 2009). "Can we say that the title of this lecture series could have been 'fairness'?" We believe that the title of his lecture cannot be "fairness." There are some philosophical differences between Rawls (1971) and Sandel (1982), and these are reflected in the title of the lectures (by Sandel). For liberals from Rawls onward, there is an equation between "justice ≒ fairness," but for Sandel and other communitarians, justice cannot be equated with fairness.

Most arguments around these concepts are based on English usage. Nevertheless, as it is crucial to examine these in other cultural concepts, let us consider them both from the English and the Japanese perspective. For example, an English dictionary (Cambridge Academic Content Dictionary) explains fairness and justice as follows:

Fairness: 1. The quality of treating people equally or in a way that is right or reasonable.
Justice: 1. The condition of being morally correct or fair; 2. The system of laws by which people are judged and punished; 3. A judge, esp. of one of the higher courts of law.

The Corresponding Japanese dictionary-style explanations are:

Fairness: 1. Fair and free from wickedness and perversion; 2. To be clear and righteous.
Justice: 1. The right course, the right path one should follow; 2. Right meaning or commentary; 3.1. To achieve and maintain an order that compensates for the well-being of society as a whole; 3.2. The moral character of an individual that enables him or her to act in a way that is just in society.

Thus, in both the English and Japanese definitions, the concept of fairness is similar to justice, as Rawlsian usage suggests. A synonym of English fairness is impartiality; fairness in both languages means impartiality, or the absence of favoritism or bias. On the other hand, justice is particularly related to law or order. Justice includes justice with respect to social order and justice as a personal characteristic, whereas fairness is associated chiefly with the way in which we treat people.

In the everyday sense, it is right that there is no impartiality or favoritism, but what is right may not be limited to the absence of favoritism. For example, a school teacher may grade students uniformly harshly, discouraging everyone from learning. This would be bad grading, though not biased because there is no partiality. Alternatively, if the government makes people suffer by imposing uniformly heavy taxes, and depriving all people of liberty, this would be wrong, if fair, politics. These are not education or politics that are just, even if they can be called fair and impartial.

On the other hand, there can be cases of justice but not of fairness. Special favors for only a few people around the government or for the supporting and wealthy classes, known as patronage (clientelism) or nepotism, is political corruption, which is neither right nor fair in a democracy. However, what if, as a result of a power struggle within the government, only the political corruption of the (potential) losers is exposed and busted, while the winning faction continues to enjoy its clientelistic interests. In this case, the exposure itself is just, but it is not fair concerning the winner-loser equity or parity.

Put differently, as Rawls suggested, the two concepts of fairness and justice are not necessarily the same. In this perspective, however, "justice" is used in a particularly narrow sense. In everyday language, there is a sense in which unfairness is unjust because it is not right: this usage of justice is in the broadest sense. In this case, as both English and Japanese dictionaries indicate, fair means virtually the same thing as just or "right." Since "good deeds" in moral right and wrong may be said to be right in general, "right" or justice in the broad sense includes moral goodness, including fairness, in addition to justice and fairness in the narrow sense. This "justice ≒ right" in the broad sense (almost synonymous) includes good deeds along with justice in the fair and narrow sense.

This relationship may be illustrated in Fig. 1.1. As shown, fairness and justice in the narrow sense overlap, but there is a difference in meaning. Since justice in the broad sense encompasses both, we can say that justice (broad sense) ⊃ justice (narrow sense)/fairness (Kobayashi 2021a, b, c). Thus, the relationship between justice and fairness is an intricate one and not necessarily straightforward. Moreover, it is not necessarily in line with Rawls' usage. So then, in what follows, let us first examine Rawls' argument.

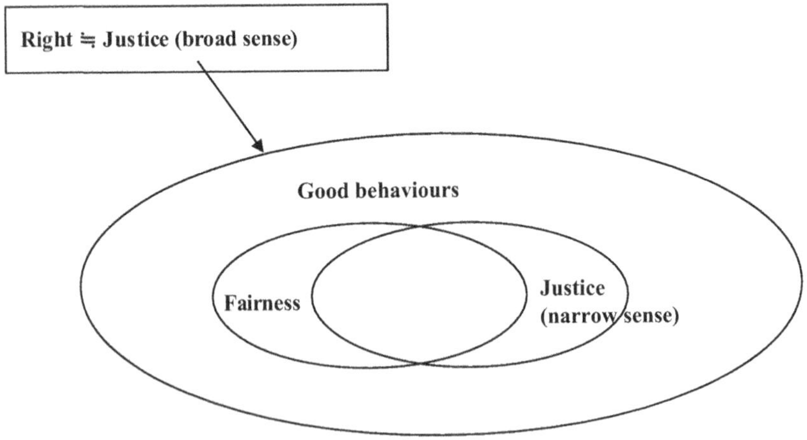

Fig. 1.1 The relationship between justice and fairness

2 The Concept of Fairness and the Origination of "Fair Society" Theory

According to Rawls, fundamental to justice is the concept of fairness, as in the expressions fair game, fair competition, and bargaining, which relate to the right dealing between people who are cooperating or competing with each other (Rawls [1956] 1999: 59). It is a mutual recognition among people without hierarchical relationships: if they accept that the rules are fair with respect to their acts of practice, and if they have no grievances with them, they have a self-evident obligation (and corresponding rights) to be obeyed: this is the duty of fair play, that is, to obey the rules.

Rawls considered utilitarianism as "a kind of efficiency" to promote the general welfare of people, and, while criticizing it, he introduced the two principles of justice as the duty of fair play. This argument was refined and systematically presented in his *A Theory of Justice* (1971), in Chapter 2.18, "The Individual Principle: The Principle of Fairness," which makes reference to the legal philosopher H.L.A. Hart's treatise on natural rights. Rawls wrote, "When many people are engaged in mutually beneficial cooperative schemes according to rules, and limit their liberty in ways necessary to produce the convenience of all, then those who are obeying the restrictions have the right to be obeyed as well on the part of those who derive benefit from their obedience." From this is derived the notion of obligation (Rawls 2010).

Later, in his *Political Liberalism* (1993), Rawls states (in Chapter 1, Section 3, "The Concept of Society as a Fair System of Cooperation") that cooperation is conducted by means of publicly recognized rules and procedures, accompanied by "fair terms of cooperation" that "each participant may reasonably accept, provided that everyone else likewise accepts them" (Rawls 1993:16). These conditions are expressed by basic principles that identify fundamental rights and duties of people. At issue here is the concept of reciprocity, whereby each cooperating party gains benefits by observing rules and procedures.

The idea of reciprocity lies between the idea of altruistic impartiality and the idea of mutual advantage, in which all persons gain advantages over the present or expected future state. Reciprocity implies that everyone benefits in relation to an appropriate standard of equality. In other words, everyone gains an advantage by joining a system of cooperation compared to the case where no system of cooperation exists. However, in the current global state of nation states and societies, not everyone in the system is expected to benefit: the wealthy may have to pay more taxes than they do now (Rawls 1993:16).

In "Society as a Fair System of Cooperation" (Part 1, section 2, in his *Justice as Fairness: A Restatement* (2001)), the idea of social cooperation includes the three essential features: (a) publicly recognized rules and procedures, (b) the reciprocity and mutuality that fair conditions of cooperation specify, and (c) the idea of rational advantage or good for each participant. A reasonable person would, Rawls argues, propose and accept these conditions: Rawls distinguishes between "rational" in the sense of increasing profit taken by some people and "reasonable" for reasonable people.

Thus, Rawls' "principle of justice" has developed from fair play (in which ① free and equal people ② accept and obey rules) to the explicate statement of ③ reciprocity in cooperation and ④ advantage for all participants.

Based on these considerations, Rawls proposed the following two principles of Justice. The final formulation (Rawls 2001: 42) is:

1. First principle (*Greatest Equal Liberty Principle*): each person has the same indefeasible claim to a fully adequate scheme of equal basic liberties, which scheme is compatible with the same scheme of liberties for all; and
2. Second principle: Social and economic inequalities are to satisfy two conditions: first (2.1:*Fair Equality of Opportunity Principle*), they are to be attached to offices and positions open to all under conditions of fair equality of opportunity; and second (2.2: *Difference Principle*), they are to be to the greatest benefit of the least advantaged members.

Rawls established a lexical priority, in which the first principle takes precedence over the second principle, and, in the second principle, (2.1) takes precedence over (2.2). Although the specifics of the principles of justice have been refined over the years, the basic tenets of the two general principles have remained unchanged.

Of these interrelated principles of justice, the Difference principle is often noted as the basis for human welfare, which indeed is the core of his theory. At the same time, what is noteworthy in relation to the concept of fairness is the Fair Equal Opportunity Principle: when people have the same qualities and talents and the will to use them, they should have equal opportunities for achieving their goals in life, and differences in social classes should not prevent them from doing so. Thus, it is necessary to place constraints on the free market system so that concentrations of assets and wealth, as well as political domination, do not create inequalities of opportunity. Both the Fair Equality Opportunity Principle and the Difference Principle require governments to amend the related inequalities.

Rawls' political philosophy changed dramatically between his *Theory of Justice* (1971) and his *Political Liberalism* (1993). Corresponding to this change, the idea of "society as a fair system of cooperation' has increased its significance in his political philosophy: its basic idea has already appeared in the expressions of "system of cooperation" and "social cooperation" in the *Theory of Justice*, but the term and formulation of "society as a fair system of cooperation" first appeared in his later stage, *Political Liberalism*. This term signifies, in short, a fair socicty. This Rawls' perspective is the origination of the term "fair society" in contemporary academic literature. This is the prototype of the "fair society" in liberalism today.

3 Four Elements of Fairness

Nevertheless, there are other kinds of theories of fairness. In *On Fairness* (2000), Craig L. Car philosophically criticized the Kantian conception of fairness, including the Rawlsian idea, and proposed "fidelity to social practice" as an alternative explanation of fairness. This idea is based on associative morality and linked to a common purpose, specific role and responsibility, and general cooperation. So then, this can be regarded as a communitarian conception of fairness.

Thus, intending to elucidate the multiple elements of fairness, Kobayashi (2021a, b, c) has integrated representative conceptions of fairness by proposing the following four components of fairness: Rule-Compliance, Equal Impartiality, Ethical Fidelity, and Benefit Reciprocity. "Rule-Compliance" (or Law-abidingness) means whether we comply with or abide by laws or rules, as is seen in everyday language. "Equal (or Parity) Impartiality" corresponds to the Kantian or Rawlsian notion of fairness, such as equal human fundamental rights. "Ethical Fidelity" is ethical uprightness, or squareness in social practice, theorized by Car's communitarian notion. Finally, "Benefit Reciprocity" is the last (but not the least) element of fairness, indicating the important balance of giving and taking, just as Rawls later emphasized.

In the context of this book, Rule-Compliance is associated with international treaties and domestic laws or regulations, regarding the environment. Impartial Equality is related to equal respect for fundamental human rights or nation states. Ethical Fidelity is concerned with bona fide sincerity or loyalty to the ongoing legal restrictions and cultural customs (both have been high on agenda in the context of COVID-19). Finally, "Benefit Reciprocity" is witnessed in the actual giving and taking of essential goods, including facial masks, across countries; a country's support measures for another country facing natural calamities such as earthquakes and typhoons several years back, can reciprocally be remembered, and the country as a donor several years back is now receiving pandemic-related supports.

Thus, the four-dimensional fairness theory can be formally expressed as follows and also in Fig. 1.2: (Rule-)Compliance, (Equal) Impartiality, (ethical) Fidelity, and (Benefit) Reciprocity correspond to the four-dimensional axes consisting of vertical, horizontal, ethical, and benefit(or happiness) axis in this four-dimensional space.

In addition, the word equity is closely associated with fairness. As equity is defined as "equal treatment, fairness" (Cambridge Academic Content Dictionary), it indicates Equal Impartiality. Nevertheless, it frequently contains ethical or moral meaning, especially in Japanese. These

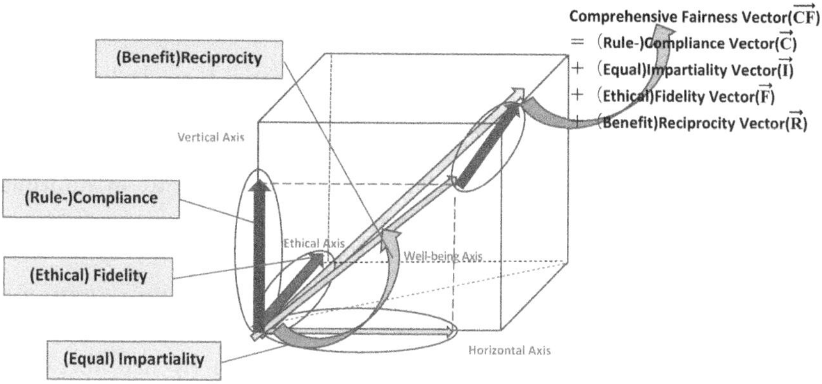

Fig. 1.2 Four-dimensional fairness concept. (Note: The Well-being axis is indicated in a curve because the fourth dimension cannot be visualized in the three-dimensional space.)

two senses are quantitative fairness (fairness as impartial equality) and qualitative fairness (fairness as ethical fidelity), and both composites equity: Equality and equity here correspond to arithmetic and geometrical equality/justice in Aristotle's political philosophy. While issue-specific descriptions prevail in the following chapters, these four elements of fairness will be our analytical focus all throughout this book. The final section (Interim Conclusion) will explicitly address this analytical framework and contextualize each chapter in the light of multi-dimensional fairness.

4 Theoretical Framework of Multiple Levels, Dimensions, and Systems

In the humanities and social sciences today, there is no longer a general theory or model addressing "the world," as we know it at least intuitively. This is one of the reasons for academic confusion as well as fragmentation. In the postwar period, modernization and development theories developed in the 1960s, mainly in the United States, and systems theory in sociology/political science and neoclassical economics and development theory in economics formed standard theories that were paradigms.

However, all these comprehensive general theories have declined since the end of the 1960s, and no paradigmatic theory has been established. In order to overcome such an academic stagnation, this monograph presents a perspective to address pandemic-stricken situations in multiple realms. In doing so, we will consider the relationships among various levels of actors.

The global market economy has upset the nation-state system and increased the gap between the rich and the poor within each country and worldwide. In the U.S., the outburst of capitalism by neo-liberalism caused the Lehman Shock in 2008, leading to a global market economic crisis. Combined with the failure of the Iraq War, this led to the birth of the Obama Administration. Nevertheless the stagnation and decline of the U.S. economy could not halt, and the Trump Administration came to office in 2017.

This administration abandoned the path of international cooperation by advocating "America First" and has upset the global political and economic system. In addition to the U.S., in the democratic homelands of France and the U.K., domestic political dissatisfaction and resentment have led to the rise of right-wing populism. Accordingly, a crisis of democracy is widely recognized, and the U.K. has withdrawn from the European Union (EU).

Thus, regional integrations such as the EU and the U.S.-led cooperative international order are seriously jeopardized. There is also a danger of increasing global conflicts between civilizations: economic conflict between the U.S. and China, and escalating tension between the U.S. and Iran. In addition, the U.S. allowed the U.S.–Russia Intermediate-Range Nuclear Forces Disarmament Treaty to expire in 2019, making it difficult for the international community to respond to rising global environmental problems such as global warming and abnormal weather.

Then the outbreak of the new coronavirus has, since 2020, caused countries and some of their regions to drastically restrict the entry of people from other countries, making international exchange difficult. This pandemic surge is the first time that the global biosphere has been threatened since the end of World War II. Furthermore, the Russian invasion of Ukraine may cause the dissolution of international order and enduring war: this can be the most serious conflict since World War II. Accordingly, it seems that a worldwide societal crisis has arrived.

There is a view that these global issues could be ideologically attributed to the dominance of atomic theory. Although atomism considers macro phenomena as a set of minimal units, it often assumes the individual as the minimal unit in domestic affairs and the state as the minimal unit in international relations. Compared to holistic theories, the greatest ideological significance of atomism is that it defends the freedom of individuals and nations.

If the individual or the nation has ethics, it leads to liberal democracy and international cooperation. Without morality, however, atomism ideologically justifies and accelerates selfishness in individuals and nations. Domestically, it enables the unstoppable domination of the market economy and politics based on egoism, and, internationally, it leads to the collapse of international cooperative relations due to self-centeredness, thereby worsening the global environment.

Therefore, to overcome pandemic-related social problems, it is necessary to go beyond unethical atomism and revive a public philosophy that respects the relationships with other subjects in individuals and nations. However, since we must not repeat the failures of past holistic theories, it is important to acknowledge their weaknesses and open a new ideological horizon that can overcome the conflict between atomism and holism.

So then, it is necessary to take into account both the freedom of the individual or the state and their relations with other subjects or the whole. The key to the dialectical integration of both atomism and holism lies in the relations between agents: this thought can be termed relationalism.

It is communitarianism (Sandel 1982) that pursues this direction in normative political philosophy or public philosophy. While many other political philosophies (utilitarianism, libertarianism, liberalism) consider the individual as the starting point or center, communitarianism respects the communal element by emphasizing the "communal" aspect of people thinking and living together.

Communitarianism is holistic in nature because it also emphasizes the communal aspect. On the other hand, the expression "liberal communitarianism" is sometimes used because it is based on modern liberalism(Etzioni 1998): this philosophy emphasizes responsibility to others and personal virtue while respecting individual freedom and human rights. The two orientations indicate that this political philosophy aims at a dialectical integration of freedom and community, both liberal and communal. Since interpersonal relations are essential for this, the communitarian public philosophy is relational.

Nevertheless, communitarianism is normative political philosophy, and it alone is insufficient for empirical analysis. Therefore, this book presents a conceptual and analytical framework inspired by public philosophy. In order to construct a relational theory, system theory is the most functional among the existing grand theory, this book utilizes a new system theory, revising Talcott Parsons' social system theory, the former paradigmatic theory in sociology(Parsons 1951): this new theory is termed positive public system theory by an editor, suggested by system-informed positive psychology proposed by Margarett L. Kern, Lindsay Oades (Ch.8) and others(2019).

As summarized in Fig. 1.3, at the center is the human system which would be composed of body and mind, and the increase of individual life well-being is to be pursued (Kobayashi and Ishido 2021). The basis of our society today is generally one of "societal communities." This concept, derived from later Parsons (2007), expresses the presence of diverse elements of society (association) as well as the community. The three circles in the middle indicate political, economic, and cultural sub-systems, all of which comprise essential human activities. These three sub-systems correspond to vertical, horizontal, and ethical axes mentioned above: these sub-systems have their origin in the Parsonian social system theory's three functions (Goal-attainment, Adaptation, Latency or Pattern Maintenance) in his AGIL paradigm. Note also that human activities can be subdivided into the public sphere (e.g., activities including both citizen's informal/voluntary activities and through formal institutions including the government and business firms) and the private sphere (e.g., informal private activities of a person and a family), as indicated in the figure. Both public and private spheres are seen to serve as essential aspects of the human system (unfortunately, both have been negatively affected by the pandemic).

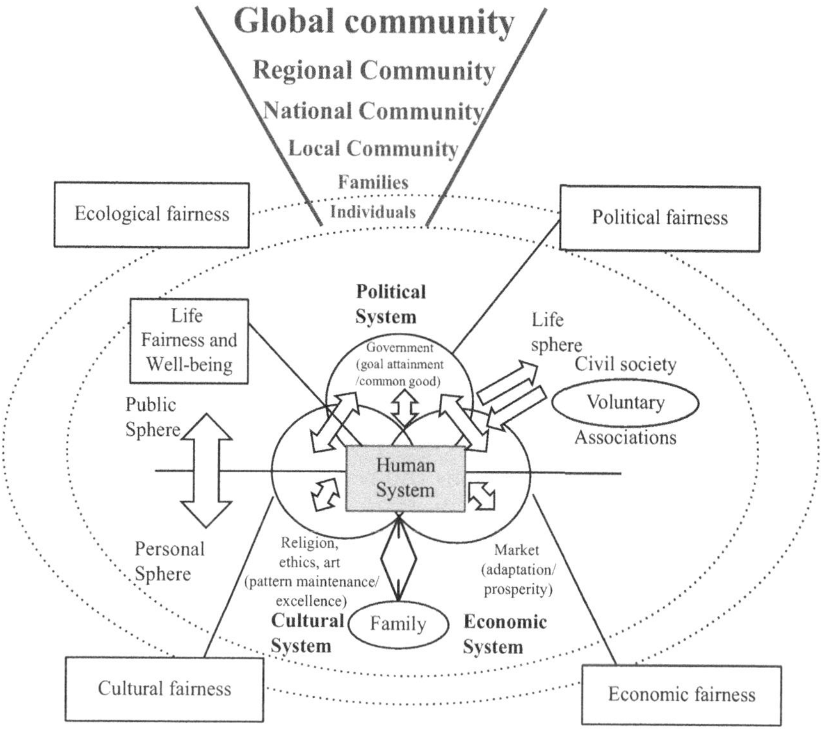

Fig. 1.3 Hierarchical and multidimensional view on society

Spatially, there are multi-layered societal communities at different levels; the figure therefore shows the multi-level layers of social communities: global (associated with natural or ecological environment), regional (e.g., European Union and the Association of Southeast Asian Nations), national and local societal communities, together with family and individuals under these societal communities.

In our life setting, overall, we pay attention to the degree of fairness (and well-being) in various public/private spheres, including political, economic, and cultural systems. Additionally, ecological fairness would subsume all of these, and gender-related fairness is built into the human system. The formal relationship between sovereign states is equal and horizontal in today's international system. In parallel with the domestic system, which has predominantly become an atomistic political and economic system, this horizontal sovereign state system is also atomistic if there is no international association or connection, and its smallest unit is the nation-state. The nation-state is formed by the national community/the people and the state apparatus as a formal institution.

While the new coronavirus problem, the focus of this book, is currently dividing countries, there is an awareness of the need for international cooperation and solidarity to deal with pandemics, and there are calls for new international integration. The future development of regional and global integration will be greatly influenced by how people view fairness after such a world-historical pandemic experience. A multi-layered and multi-dimensional analysis that includes the human body and mind can lead hopefully to normative suggestions and policies for developing international relations and regional integration in a desirable direction by at least partially analyzing intricate dynamics.

Table 1.1 places each chapter of this book in the multi-layered (i.e., global, regional and national, local, and family/individual) and multi-dimensional (i.e., political, economic, and societal-cultural) manner, in

Table 1.1 Categorization of each chapter in this book

Dimension: Main focus level:	Ecological	Political	Economic	Societal-cultural
Global (including biosphere)	Chapter 1 Chapter 3 (global warming)	Chapter 2 (COVID-19 Vaccine)		
Regional (international) and national		Chapter 6 (Europe) Chapter 8 (Australia) Chapter 9 (Mexico)		Chapter 6 (Europe) Chapter7 (Japan) Chapter 9 (Mexico)
		Chapter 4 (regional integration), Chapter 5 (East Asia), Chapter 10 (APEC)		
Sub-national (local, family, individual)		Chapter 7 (Japan), Chapter 11 (gender)		
				Chapter 12 (Japanese literature)

Source: Made by the editors based on the contents of each chapter

line with Fig. 1.2. Since fairness can have multiple connotations (as seen above), each of the chapters addresses diverse issues; there is, however, a loose categorization along this table. For example, the present Chap. 1 (Introduction: Multi-layered and Multi-dimensional Viewpoints towards a Fair Society) covers all categories, and is primarily placed in the global category because this category comprises the multi-layered human system), with political, economic and cultural aspects; Chap. 2 (Fairness in the Global Allocation System for the COVID-19 Vaccine COVAX: Limits to Affected Parties' 'Participation in Decision-Making) is placed in the "Global-Political" cell; and Chap. 3 (Environment and Economy after COVID-19: Focusing on Global Warming Issues), is placed in the "Global-Ecological" cell. Likewise, each of the chapters in this book (reproduced below) has a specific coverage in terms of the layer and dimension in the table (to be elaborated on in the Interim Conclusion).

Chapter 1 Introduction: Multi-layered and multi-dimensional viewpoints towards a Fair Society

Part I. Global Perspective

Chapter 2 Fairness in the Global Allocation System for the COVID-19 Vaccine COVAX: Limits to Affected Parties' Participation in Decision-Making.

Chapter 3 Environment and Economy after COVID-19: Focusing on Global Warming Issues.

Chapter 4 An Investigation Through Philosophy and Case Studies on Regional Integration, Migrants and Refugees, and the COVID-19 Crisis.

Chapter 5 Challenges and Possibilities for Global Economic Cooperation after COVID-19: Focus on East Asia.

Part II. Regional Focus

Chapter 6 Social Justice and the Response to the COVID-19 Crisis in European Countries.

Chapter 7 Well-being and Fairness in the COVID-19 Crisis in Japan: Insights from Positive Political Psychology.

Chapter 8 COVID-19 Policy Response and Citizens' Well-Being in Australia.
Chapter 9 Mexico facing the COVID-19 pandemic: slow and ineffective societal and governmental responses in a country with a high level of socioeconomic inequality and a precarious health system.
Chapter 10 APEC's Response to the COVID-19 Crisis and Social Justice.

Part III. Thematic issues

Chapter 11 COVID-19 and its impact on Women and Gender.
Chapter 12 Modern Japanese Literature and Infectious Diseases: Representations of Infectious Diseases and Social Justice in Literary Works.

As shown in Table 1.1, the chapter-by-chapter coverage of this book in terms of multiple levels (layers) and issue areas (dimensions) is rather wide, with the fairness concept always at the center (explicitly, or rather implicitly). We envision the concepts of fairness *emerging* from the issue areas covered in each of the chapters. In the final part of this book (Interim Conclusion), we (the editors of this book) attempt to depict a fair society in the global perspective and through the experience of COVID-19.

References

Car, Craig L. 2000. *On Fairness*. New York: Routledge.
Etzioni, A. 1998. *The New Golden Rule: Community and Morality in a Democratic Society*. New York: Basic Books.
Kern, M.L., P. Williams, C. Spong, R. Colla, K. Sharma, A. Downie, J.A. Taylor, S. Sharp, C. Siokou & L.G. Oades. 2019. Systems Informed Positive Psychology, The Journal of Positive Psychology. July. https://doi.org/10.1080/17439760.2019.1639799.
Kobayashi, Masaya. 2021a. Chapter 2 Kousei Shakai Ron no Shosouteki Tenkai: Roruzu no Seigiron kara Komyunitarianizumu made (in Japanese) [Development of Thoughts on Fair Society: from Rawls' Theory of Justice to Communitarianism]. In *Kouseishakai no bijon: Gakusaiteki Apurochi niyoru*

Riron, Shisou, Genjou Bunseki (in Japanese) [Vision for a Fair Society: Theory, Thought and the Analysis of Status Quo through Interdisciplinary Approaches], ed. Jiro Mizushima, Chiyo Yonemura, and Masaya Kobayashi. Tokyo: Akashi Shoten.

———. 2021b. Chapter 3 Tajigenteki na Tougouteki Kousei Shakai Riron: Kyouryokuteki Kokyo Sisutemu niokeru Kihanteki 4 Kijun (in Japanese) [Multi-dimensional Theory of Integrated Fair Society: Four Normative Criteria in a Cooperative Public System]. In *Kouseishakai no bijon: Gakusaiteki Apurochi niyoru Riron, Shisou, Genjou Bunseki (in Japanese) [Vision for a Fair Society: Theory, Thought and the Analysis of Status Quo through Interdisciplinary Approaches]*, ed. Jiro Mizushima, Chiyo Yonemura, and Masaya Kobayashi. Tokyo: Akashi Shoten.

———. 2021c. (in Japanese) (Chapter 11)" In Hikari Ishido and Ayame Suzuki (Eds.), (2021b), Tagenka Suru Chiiki Tougou (in Japanese) [Regional Integrations Becoming Multi-dimensional]. Tokyo: Iwanami Shoten.

Kobayashi, Masaya and Hikari Ishido. 2021. *Systems Informed Positive Psychology and Communitarianism*. The CRSGC-Chiba Essay/Conference Paper, https://www.chiba-u.ac.jp/crsgc/research/files/kobayashiPaper.pdf

Parsons, T. 1951. *The Social Systems*. University of California Libraries.

———., American Society. 2007. *A Theory of the Societal Community*. New York: Routledge.

Rawls, John. [1956] 1999. *Justice as Fairness*. Samuel Freeman ed., Collected Papers. Cambridge, Mass.: Harvard University Press.

———. 1957. Justice as Fairness. *Journal of Philosophy* 54 (22): 653–662.

———. 1958. Justice as Fairness. The Philosophical Review 67 (2): 164–194.

———. 1971. *A Theory of Justice*. Cambridge, MA: The Belknap Press of Harvard University Press.

———. 1993. *Political Liberalism: The John Dewey Essays in Philosophy, 4*. New York: Columbia University Press.

———. 2001. *Justice as Fairness: A Restatement*. Cambridge, MA: Harvard University Press.

Sandel, M.J. 1982. *Liberalism and Limits of Justice*. Cambridge, MA: Cambridge University Press.

———. 2009. *Justice: What's the Right Thing to Do?* New York: Farrar, Straus and Giroux.

Part I

Global Perspective

2

Fairness in the Global Allocation System for the COVID-19 Vaccine COVAX: Limits to Affected Parties' Participation in Decision-Making

Iwao Fujisawa

1 Introduction

Global Allocation of COVID-19 Vaccines

Few would doubt that one of the keys to curbing the explosive growth of COVID-19 infections is for people to be vaccinated. In fact, the question of how to distribute vaccines domestically and expand the vaccination process has become a political issue in many countries, including Japan. However, the biggest obstacle to ending the explosive growth of COVID-19 infections revolves around questions of global vaccine allocation and the promotion of vaccination. Unfortunately, during the early stages of the pandemic, vaccines were a scarce commodity, in that there was an insufficient supply to vaccinate everyone in the world.

I. Fujisawa (✉)
Graduate School of Social Sciences, Chiba University, Chiba, Japan
e-mail: iwaofujisawa@faculty.chiba-u.jp

H. Ishido et al. (eds.), *Social Fairness in a Post-Pandemic World*,
https://doi.org/10.1007/978-981-19-9654-2_2

It is in this context of scarcity that the "fair and equitable allocation" of vaccines across the globe was advocated (WHO 2020a).

One view of the allocation of scarce goods would be that the most efficient allocation is through trading in the market. For the COVID-19 vaccine, developed countries, especially Europe, the United States (US), and Japan, fought to secure the vaccine for their own populations and entered into bilateral agreements with pharmaceutical companies. This approach also became known as vaccine nationalism. Specifically, developed countries attempted to secure vaccines in advance through "advance purchase agreements," in which a country provides R & D funds to a pharmaceutical company in return for a vaccine candidate that is still in the R & D stage. If the vaccine is developed successfully, the country preferentially receives the vaccine from the pharmaceutical company (Phelan et al. 2020: 800).

The Problem with Vaccine Nationalism

It may not be impossible to conclude that the global allocation of vaccines based on such advance purchase agreements is an economically efficient allocation of goods, in the sense that the goods are allocated to those who pay the highest prices. Everyone has an equal opportunity to participate in market transactions, and the governments and populations of developing countries are simply being outbid by the governments and populations of developed countries in the vaccine market.

However, the allocation of vaccines by market mechanisms through advance purchase agreements between developed countries and pharmaceutical companies should still be considered problematic. First, vaccine allocation based on advance purchase agreements would disadvantage residents of low-income countries who lack financial resources. If there is no difference in human worth between residents of high-income countries and those of low-income countries, then it can be considered unfair that only people in low-income countries have no access to vaccines and are exposed to life-threatening risks from COVID-19. Second, vaccine allocation through advance purchase agreements between developed countries and pharmaceutical companies is not rational from a perspective that aims to end the explosive growth of COVID-19 infections globally and may unnecessarily prolong the global pandemic (Herzog et al. 2021). For example, even if vaccinations halt the infection in developed countries, if no vaccinations are carried out in developing countries and COVID-19 infections remain unchecked, there is a risk that a new variant that cannot be dealt with by existing vaccines will arise in developing countries and the infection will spread again to developed countries. To prevent such a situation, it is necessary to promote vaccination throughout the world. "No one is safe until everyone is safe" (WHO 2021b).

An international framework for cooperation, called COVAX, seeks to overcome these difficulties of vaccine nationalism and achieve a fair and equitable distribution of vaccines across the world. The question now is: is the COVAX allocation of vaccines fair and equitable? The following is an overview of the COVAX system and a discussion on the fairness and equity of vaccine allocation under COVAX.

2 COVAX: An Experiment to Use Market Mechanisms for Fair and Equitable Allocation

Lack of an International Legal System to Regulate Vaccine Allocation

The World Health Organization (WHO), one of the specialized agencies of the United Nations (UN), is tasked with preventing the international spread of infectious diseases such as COVID-19. The WHO is an international organization established by the Constitution of the World Health Organization (hereinafter referred to as "the Constitution"), a multilateral treaty, but the Constitution does not contain substantive rules of conduct for member states on health issues, including the prevention of infectious diseases. Instead, the World Health Assembly, composed of all WHO member states, is empowered to adopt rules on matters such as infectious diseases (Article 21 of the Constitution). The adopted rules become legally binding on all member states other than those that have notified the Secretary-General of their rejection of the rules or of their reservations against the rules within a certain period of time determined by notification by the General Assembly (Article 22 of the Constitution) (Gostin 2014: 111). Pursuant to this rule-making authority, the International Health Regulations [IHR (2005)] were adopted in 2005 with the following objective: "to prevent, protect against, control and provide a public health response to the international spread of disease in ways that are commensurate with and restricted to public health risks, and which avoid unnecessary interference with international traffic and trade" (WHO 2005). However, this regulation does not provide for the allocation of vaccines.

ACT Accelerator

Thus, the Access to COVID-19 Tools (ACT) Accelerator is an initiative launched in April 2020 by WHO, the EU Commission, France, and the Bill & Melinda Gates Foundation to promote the research and development, production, and equitable access to diagnosis, treatment, and vaccines for COVID-19. The ACT Accelerator is a time-limited framework for collaboration among existing organizations to end the COVID-19 pandemic; it is not a decision-making body and does not create a new organization. Therefore, the formal governance of the activities is carried out by the decision-making bodies of the existing organizations that co-host the ACT Accelerator. The ACT Accelerator has four areas of activity: (1) diagnostics, (2) treatment, (3) vaccines, and (4) liaison with national health systems (WHO 2021a).

COVAX

The vaccination pillar of the ACT Accelerator is a mechanism called COVAX. COVAX is a global initiative that is a collaboration of the UN Children's Fund (UNICEF), the World Bank, national governments, and vaccine manufacturers to ensure that COVID-19 vaccines are available in both high- and low-income countries worldwide. It is co-sponsored by (1) Coalition for Epidemic Preparedness Innovations (CEPI, a Norwegian association), (2) Gavi, the Vaccine Alliance (a Swiss association), and (3) WHO.

The vaccine procurement and distribution arm of COVAX, led by Gavi, a not-for-profit corporation under Swiss law, is called the COVAX Facility, and has 193 participating countries (WHO 2021b).

The COVAX Facility is a mechanism to pool demand and resources to ensure the availability of and equitable access to all vaccines. Specifically, Gavi pools a large amount of funds from funds paid by participating countries and donations from Official Development Assistance (ODA), etc., and uses these funds to conclude "advance purchase agreements" with several pharmaceutical companies for promising vaccine candidates. In return for providing R & D funding to these pharmaceutical companies, Gavi will receive a priority supply of vaccines that have been successfully developed and will distribute the supplied vaccines fairly and equitably among the participating countries. There is also an argument that the intellectual property rights for the COVID-19 vaccine should be waived in order to make the vaccine available to low-income countries, but the COVAX Facility has not taken such a position, and the intellectual property rights for the vaccines remain in place (Gavi 2020a; Kato 2021).

Thus, the COVAX Facility is no different from the vaccine nationalism method in that it uses "advance purchase agreements" to secure vaccines. However, unlike vaccine nationalism, in which each country contracts with a pharmaceutical company, (1) the risk of vaccine development failure can be hedged by Gavi through investments in multiple vaccine candidates using the large sums of money raised, and (2) the vaccines supplied are distributed among the participating countries, so that low-income countries can also have access to vaccines, which is an advantage (Phelan et al. 2020: 801).

Types of Contracts Related to the COVAX Facility

Broadly speaking, the COVAX Facility's activities are supported by three types of contracts (von Bogdandy and Villarreal 2021: 106–107).

As explained above, there is no provision for vaccines in legally binding instruments such as the WHO Constitution or the International Health Regulations, much less a provision that legally mandates participation in a vaccine allocation mechanism such as the COVAX Facility. Therefore, participation in the COVAX Facility is voluntary. Hence, countries wishing to participate need to enter into a contract with Gavi, which can be broadly divided into the following two types.

First, high-income countries enter into a Commitment Agreement with Gavi as "Self-Financing Participants." Self-financing participant countries are obligated to pay in advance the funds necessary for Gavi to enter into advance purchase agreements with pharmaceutical companies, and to pay for vaccines supplied by the COVAX Facility (Gavi 2020a; Kato 2021). At first glance, there may be no benefit to participating in the COVAX Facility for self-financing participants, as they also bear the cost of vaccines. However, as mentioned above, the COVAX Facility is able to hedge the risk of development failure by investing the large amount of funds raised in multiple vaccine candidates, thus reducing the risk in cases where a contracted pharmaceutical company fails to develop a vaccine and no vaccine is supplied.

Second, low-income countries (92 countries) enter into contracts with Gavi by submitting vaccine requests to Gavi as Advance Market Commitment (AMC)-Eligible Economies. The cost of procuring and distributing vaccines to AMC Eligible Economies is covered by ODA, private foundations, and other donations, so, unlike self-financing participants, there is no financial burden on AMC Eligible Economies (Gavi 2020b; Kato 2021).

Then, thirdly, as previously mentioned several times, Gavi pools the advance payments from self-financing participating countries and donations from ODA and other sources, and uses this pooled amount of money as the source for concluding advance purchase agreements with the manufacturers of several promising vaccine candidates.

Limited Success

The COVAX Facility aimed to supply at least 950 million doses of the vaccine to AMC Eligible Economies by the end of 2021 (Gavi 2020b). However, as of mid-November 2021, only 256.5 million doses of vaccine had been supplied to AMC Eligible Economies. As a result, as of mid-November 2021, 67% of the population in high-income countries had received both doses of the COVID-19 vaccine, whereas in low-income countries, less than 5% of the population had received the first dose (Sirleaf et al. 2021). The situation somewhat improved thereafter, because the COVAX almost reached the 950 million doses target at the end of 2021 (Open Consultants 2022). But the disparity in the vaccination coverage between high-income countries and low-income countries remains. As of November 1, 2022, only 52% of the population in the AMC countries has received two doses of the COVID-19 vaccine, whereas 80% of the population in high-income countries have got two doses (COVAX 2022b). And the scheme for self-financing participants is largely perceived as a failure, since many high-income countries bypassed the scheme and the number of doses delivered to self-financing participants has been small compared to those delivered to AMC countries (Open Consultants 2022).

Overall, the COVAX Facility has not produced the results that were hoped for. The first reason for this may be that the supply of vaccines to AMC Eligible Economies is solely dependent on donations. The G7, China, and others have pledged to donate, but there is a lack of transparency in the timeline for when the donations will actually be made. The second reason is that the conclusion of an agreement between an individual state and a pharmaceutical company, which was the origin of the problem in the first place, is not prohibited even for countries participating in the COVAX Facility (Gavi 2020a). As a result, supply to low- and middle-income countries is hampered, for example, by undisclosed contracts between high-income countries and pharmaceutical companies for a third vaccination program, known as a booster (Sirleaf et al. 2021). COVAX is aware of those flaws. So, it is now advocating for instituting in advance a mechanism that should be equipped with reliable sources of at-risk financing and ensure that volumes supplied to high-income countries are accompanied in parallel by proportionate doses for lower-income countries (COVAX 2022a).

3 Vaccine Allocation Framework in COVAX

Equity and Fairness as a Guiding Principle for the Allocation Framework

With regard to the COVAX Facility, there are institutional design problems, such as reliance on donations and neglecting the issues of bilateral advance purchase agreements. However, even if these supply issues are resolved, there is a further problem: ensuring fairness and equity in the allocation of vaccines through the COVAX Facility.

The Terms and Conditions of the agreement between Gavi and the participating countries described above stipulate that vaccine allocations will be determined based on an allocation framework to be developed by the WHO (Gavi 2020a, b).

The WHO developed a framework for the fair distribution of vaccines in September 2020. According to this framework, ethical values such as equity and fairness must guide the allocation of scarce resources such as vaccines related to COVID-19. The choice of how to allocate scarce resources must represent the objective that is being valued most, but the right objectives and choices cannot be clarified by science and evidence alone and require a value judgement. Distribution must therefore be based, first and foremost, on the assumption that all human beings are of equal moral value and have the same rights based on the fact that they are human beings. Therefore, allocations based on characteristics over which the person has no control, such as race, place of birth, gender, or ability to pay, should not be permitted (WHO 2020a).

So how do we define "equity" and "fairness" to guide the allocation framework? According to the WHO, equity requires that "similar cases be treated similarly." On the other hand, there are various competing views on what "fairness" means and requires, and each view is reasonable in itself. Therefore, the content of the fairness that guides the allocation must be clearly explained and defended, and its application must be consistent. WHO considers vaccine distribution to be fair when (1) the highest priority objective is vaccine distribution in a manner that will bring about the best possible outcome in terms of ending the pandemic, and (2) the second highest priority objective is distribution to those most in need of vaccines (WHO 2020a).

Specific Framework for Allocation

Based on these concepts of equity and fairness, the WHO has developed the following specific allocation framework (WHO 2020a).

According to the WHO, the overarching goal of vaccine distribution is to protect individuals and health systems and to minimize social and economic impacts. In the early stages, however, when vaccine supplies are expected to be scarce, the focus should be on reducing mortality and protecting health systems. From the perspective of this initial goal of reducing deaths and protecting health systems, priority targets for vaccination are identified as healthcare workers, people aged 65 years and older, and people with underlying medical conditions. For most countries, vaccine allocation to 20% of the population will cover these vulnerable groups.

Therefore, vaccine allocation will be carried out in two stages. The first phase is until vaccination of 20% of the population in all countries is achieved; in this phase, all participating countries will receive a proportional allocation of vaccine based on each country's population.

The second phase is the allocation after vaccination of 20% of the population in all participating countries has been achieved; in this phase, the allocation is not proportional, and weighted allocations will be made based on the risk assessment of each country in terms of threat (the potential impact of COVID-19 on one country based on epidemiological data) and vulnerability (consideration of national health systems and population factors for each countries).

According to the WHO, the proportional allocation in the first phase meets the basic needs of all countries simultaneously in the initial stage and is consistent with "the principle of fairness," while the weighted allocation in the second phase takes into account differences in risk situations between countries and is consistent with "the principle of equity" (WHO 2020a). As we have already seen, the WHO interprets fairness as (1) the best possible outcome vis-à-vis the end of the pandemic and (2) the distribution of vaccines to those who need them most. In the WHO's view, proportional allocation would be consistent with these criteria for fairness. The WHO also defined equity as "similar cases being treated similarly." The reverse side of this concept of equity would be that the weighted allocation in the second stage would be consistent with the proposition that countries with different risks would need to be treated differently.

Later on, in April 2022, the WHO revised the allocation framework for the second phase. In light of the changed circumstances since its first adoption in 2020, especially the "exponential increase of global production capacity" that eased the supply shortages, as well as the fact that there remained wide differences in the vaccination coverage between high-income countries and low-income countries, the second phase was revised to be "focused only on donor-funded, facilitated and donated doses" for AMC countries. Accordingly, the second phase is now based on two principles: (1) it should "move from a push, supply-driven approach to a pull, demand-driven approach", and (2) it should "continue to enhance equity by accounting for all sources of supply and prioritizing participants with lower coverage towards achieving self-defined targets, up to their limits." Apparently, the WHO considers the disparity in the vaccination coverage as inequitable because practically it means that people with a certain quality (e.g under the age of 40 years) in low-income countries will remain unvaccinated when those with the same quality in high-income countries have been vaccinated.

Criticisms

In this manner, the allocation of vaccines under the COVAX Facility is carried out in two phases. However, there is strong criticism of proportional allocation in the first phase (Herzog et al. 2021).

According to this criticism, vaccines should be allocated according to their most probable function of reducing deaths and serious economic and social damage, and the proportional allocation adopted by the WHO is not consistent with its own ethical values of human well-being, equal respect for human beings, and global equity. Consistent with these values is an allocation based on the Fair Priority Model rather than a proportional allocation.

The Fair Priority Model is based on the widely shared ethical values of benefiting people and limiting harm, prioritizing those who are disadvantaged, and equal moral concern, and specifically proposes the following three phases of vaccine distribution. In the first phase, to minimize premature deaths caused by COVID-19, the vaccine will be allocated among nations based on the degree of standard expected years of life lost (SEYLL) that can be avoided per dose. In the second phase, to reduce economic and social harm, allocations are made among countries on the basis of the improvement in gross national income (GNI) and reduction in the absolute poverty gap per dose. In the third phase, priority will be given to countries with the highest transmission rates in order to end the spread of COVID-19 in society.

Procedural Fairness

Whether the WHO allocation framework or the Fair Priority Model advocated by its critics is fair and equitable can be set aside here. This is because the WHO itself has acknowledged that there is no single standard for what is "fair" and that there can be multiple, competing, but each reasonable, positions.

Rather, the challenge, as the WHO has pointed out, is who chooses a particular position and the criteria for vaccine allocation based on that position, on what basis and how, when multiple positions on fairness exist. In this context, it is important to ensure procedural fairness or legitimacy of decision-making. In other words, for choices about the global distribution of vaccines to be legitimate and fair, (1) the choice itself, (2) the moral justification for the choice, and (3) the choice process must be publicly communicated, must be inclusive of the perspectives of those affected by the choice, and must be subject to revision based on new evidence and other relevant circumstances and information (WHO 2020a). In the words of the Strategic Advisory Group of Experts on Immunization (SAGE), the WHO's advisory body on vaccines, there is a need for "global decisions about vaccine allocation through a transparent process based on shared values, the best available scientific evidence, and appropriate representation and input from affected parties" (WHO 2020b).

Lack of Procedural Fairness in Determining the Allocation Framework

The problem is that, despite this emphasis by the WHO itself on "appropriate representation and input by affected parties" into the decision-making process for the global allocation of vaccines, there is no indication that those affected by this decision were actually involved in the process of determining the allocation framework seen above. An external evaluation report points out that the WHO determined the allocation framework without proper inputs from the eventual recipients and end users, particularly low-income and lower-middle-income countries. According to the report, that was a strategic mistake since as a result of the lack of inputs from those countries the 20% target for the first phase was announced at a time when high-income countries "aimed for the higher coverage rates (70% and more)." The reports concludes that the disparity undermined the fairness and equity of the allocation framework (Open Consultants 2022).

As the report indicates, those affected by the decision on the allocation framework include the 193 countries participating in the COVAX Facility. However, the terms and conditions of the contracts between Gavi and these participating countries only stipulate that the allocation framework "shall be developed by WHO and is subject to periodic review by self-financing participants and AMC Eligible Economies" (Gavi 2020a, b). In other words, countries participating in the COVAX Facility are not given the opportunity to participate in the decision-making process of the allocation framework but are only given the opportunity to review the allocation after a certain period of time has passed after the WHO has decided on the allocation framework, based on the results of the allocation under the previous allocation framework.

This is not the only issue. The participating countries are certainly not the only ones affected by the allocation framework. Vaccines are given to individuals to protect them from COVID-19, and it will be the individuals who are actually affected by the allocation of the vaccine. For example, in the WHO allocation framework, the first phase of vaccine allocation for 20% of the population is proportional according to each country's population, on the grounds that in most countries, vaccinating 20% of the population would cover healthcare workers, people aged 65 years and older, and people with underlying medical conditions. However, in this case, in countries where the number of people eligible for these priority vaccinations is less than 20% of the population, people other than the elderly can also be vaccinated, whereas in countries like Japan, where the elderly alone account for well over 20% of the population, there will be some elderly people who will not get the vaccine. In this case, the elderly who are unable to receive the vaccine are negatively affected by the WHO's decision on the allocation framework.

4 Participation of Affected Parties in Decision-Making and its Limitations

The WHO's decision on the vaccine allocation framework lacks procedural fairness or legitimacy, which the WHO itself places importance on, in two ways: (1) the scope of those affected is limited to participating countries, and (2) even participating countries are not allowed to participate in the decision-making process and are only given the opportunity to review it after the fact.

So, is this inadequate participation of affected persons in decision-making a mere neglect on the part of the WHO? Or is there a limit to the idea of participation in decision-making by those affected in the first place? Let us briefly consider this point.

Decision-Makers and Affected Parties

The global allocation of vaccines by the COVAX Facility comes with the ultimate goal of ending the COVID-19 pandemic. In other words, it is assumed that the future deaths and other adverse consequences of COVID-19 will depend on the decisions about the allocation framework. If vaccines are well allocated, future deaths are more likely to decrease; if they are distributed according to incorrect criteria, future deaths are more likely to increase.

The sociologist Niklas Luhmann calls this probability of future damage attributed to decisions made the present "risk," and distinguishes it from "danger," which refers to the probability of future damage not attributable to decisions made in the present. According to Luhmann, in contemporary society, what was once considered "danger" is increasingly communicated as "risk" (Luhmann 2003: 9–40). This means, for example, that the probability of a house collapsing in an earthquake in the future was not considered to be a consequence of any decision in the past, but in modern society it is considered to be a consequence of a decision in the present not to carry out earthquake-proof construction.

As a result of this attribution of the probability of future damage to decisions made in the present, the distinction between the decision-maker and the affected parties becomes prominent in modern society. There are countless decisions being made every day in the world, and it is practically impossible for everyone to participate in every decision. As a result, there is a distinction between those who make decisions and those who are likely to suffer future damage from the decisions made by others (Luhmann 2003: 111–134). For example, an electric power company that decides to build a nuclear power plant is a decision-maker, and people who do not participate in the decision but are likely to be damaged by a nuclear accident in the future are the affected parties.

The All-Affected Principle and Its Limits

In light of Luhmann's argument, the idea of the participation of affected parties in decision-making, as the WHO calls it, is an attempt to bring decision-makers and affected parties into line by involving all affected persons in decision-making.

The position that calls for the participation of all affected parties in decision-making is called the All-Affected Principle. This position is grounded in the democratic principle that anyone affected by a political decision should have the right to participate in the process of making that decision (Matsuo 2016: 356–360), in the concept of positive liberty (Ito 2020: 27–30), or from the administrative law perspective of controlling the activities of the institutions of global governance (Benvenisti 2014: 178–184).

However, even if normatively justified by these principles, there are difficulties in actually applying the "All-Affected Principle" to specific issues, such as the decision on the global allocation of vaccines, which is the issue at hand. First, there is the issue of how to determine the scope of those affected. Since, as is well known, COVID-19 has spread globally and poses a threat to the health of people all over the world, we can assume that the global allocation of vaccines aimed at ending this pandemic will affect everyone in the world to a greater or lesser extent. However, it is not realistic to expect everyone in the world to participate in the WHO's process of determining the allocation framework. In the first place, no mechanism has been devised to involve people from all over the world; even if such a mechanism existed, it would take an enormous amount of time to make a decision after listening to and discussing the opinions of everyone in the world. However, the pandemic is ongoing, and decisions on the vaccine allocation framework must be made quickly so that vaccines can be distributed as soon as they become available. In the words of the COVAX, there are "natural tensions between the need for transparency, the need to act with urgency and the need to ensure stakeholder buy-in" (COVAX 2022a).

The Drawback That It Is Only Possible to Determine Who the Affected Parties Are After the Fact

Second, the "All-Affected Principle" might not require the participation of all those who are more or less affected, and it is possible to believe that it is sufficient to allow only "those who are seriously affected" to participate in decision-making. The problem is that there is no unequivocable criterion for determining the severity of the impact, but that decision can be made through careful deliberation. In other words, deliberation is open to external objections, and the range of stakeholders to be included should be constantly revised in response to objections (Matsuo 2016: 362–364).

However, in this case, would it not be possible that the "All-Affected Principle" could ensure procedural fairness in the determination of the vaccine allocation framework? As per the above discussion that draws on

Luhmann's work, the decisions at issue in the vaccine allocation framework are those to which the probability of future harm, such as infection with COVID-19, is attributed. Therefore, who will actually be materially and significantly affected as a result of the decision is indeterminate at the time of the decision and can only be determined at a future point in time (Matsuo 2016: 359). Therefore, even if the participants in the vaccine allocation framework decision-making process are identified based on the expectation that "this person will be significantly affected," it may eventually turn out that those who should have participated did not participate or those who did not need to participate did participate. In principle, the possibility of the consequence of not being procedurally fair cannot be ruled out.

Toward Ex-Post Facto Justification

In this light, it is perhaps unavoidable that the WHO, while emphasizing the need for procedural fairness or legitimacy in its decision-making on the vaccine allocation framework, made the decision on its own without involving anyone in the decision-making process, leaving only room for participation in an ex-post facto review. If, on the one hand, it is practically impossible to include everyone in the world, and, on the other hand, even if only "those who will be seriously affected" are to be included, it is impossible in principle to determine the range of participants in advance, and it is not unreasonable to think that participation in decision-making should be abandoned and justification secured through participation in ex post procedures such as a review.

However, even if there are limits to ensuring procedural fairness through participation in decision-making, it does not mean there is no need for participation in the decision-making process at all. Even then, there is instrumental value, such as the quality of decisions being enhanced by the input of information and opinions from participants, and decisions based on broad participation are more likely to be complied with by the addressees of the decision (Benvenisti 2014: 178–184). Moreover, if the damage that may occur in the future as a result of the decision is perceived to be catastrophic (Luhmann 2003: 158–160), ex-post procedures would be too late and participation in the decision-making process would be required. If tens of millions of deaths could occur in the future depending on decisions about the vaccine allocation framework, many would consider this catastrophic. Therefore, the widest possible participation in decision-making should still be pursued, even if it does not guarantee procedural fairness.

There is also scope for further improvement with regard to the WHO's vaccine allocation framework as regards the ex-post procedures themselves. At present, the only form of ex-post procedure envisaged is a "review" of the allocation framework, and only countries participating in the COVAX Facility are eligible to participate in this procedure. However, in terms of the form of the procedure, for example, if there are those that suffer serious damage as a result of the allocation framework, it may not be sufficient to simply reconsider and revise the framework, but it may also be necessary to implement a "remedy" procedure, such as compensation or reparation for the damage. With regard to participants, it seems relatively easy for the WHO to modify the scope of participants through communication with those who raise objections about being materially affected after the fact, so it does not seem justified to limit the scope of participants to countries participating in the COVAX Facility, whether in "review" or "remedy" proceedings.

5 Conclusion

COVAX is an ambitious attempt to overcome vaccine nationalism and ensure a fair and equitable global allocation of vaccines. However, as discussed in the preceding paragraphs, COVAX has also had some problems. Improvements in COVAX and the design of vaccine allocation frameworks for future pandemics will require that at least the following three issues be addressed head-on.

First, (1) instead of relying on voluntary donations to cover the cost of distributing vaccines to low-income countries, it would be necessary to impose some kind of contribution obligation on developed countries. Next, (2) bilateral agreements between individual states and pharmaceutical companies, which are hotbeds of vaccine nationalism, should be legally prohibited.

Finally, it is of critical import to enhance the fairness and equity of vaccine allocation by (3) successfully combining the participation of the widest possible range of persons in the decision-making process with the participation of those who have actually been seriously affected in the ex-post review and remedial procedures.

References

Benvenisti, Eyal. 2014. *The Law of Global Governance*. Hague Academy of International Law.

von Bogdandy, Armin, and Pedro A. Villarreal. 2021. The Role of International Law in Vaccinating Against COVID-19: Appraising the COVAX Initiative. *Zeitschrift für ausländisches öffentliches Recht und Völkerrecht* 81: 89–116.

COVAX. 2022a. *COVAX: Key Learnings for Future Pandemic Preparedness and Response*, September 14.

———. 2022b. *COVAX Data Brief*, November 1.

Gavi. 2020a. *COVAX Facility Terms and Conditions for Self-Financing Participants*, October 19.

———. 2020b. *Vaccine Request Annex A: COVAX Facility Terms and Conditions for the AMC Group Participants*, November 18.

Gostin, Lawrence O. 2014. *Global Health Law*. Harvard University Press.

Herzog, Lisa M., Ole F. Norheim, Ezekiel J. Emanuel, and Matthew S. McCoy. 2021. COVAX Must Go Beyond Proportional Allocation of Covid Vaccines to Ensure Fair and Equitable Access. *BMJ* 2021 (372): m4853.

Ito, Kazuyori, 2020, “International Law and Constitutionalism: Is it Possible to Talk about Global Constitutional Order?", in Mori, Hajime and Iwatsuki, Naoki (eds.), Advanced Readings in International Law, Nihon Hyoronsha, 18-30.

Kato, Akiko. 2021. A Framework for Facilitating Access to Coronavirus Vaccines: COVAX, Intellectual Property Pools, and Further Patent Waivers? *Japanese Society of International Law Expert Comment*, No. 2021-5. https://jsil.jp/archives/expert/2021-5.

Luhmann, Niklas. 2003. *Soziologie des Risikos*. Walter de Gruyter.

Matsuo, Ryusuke. 2016. Let the Affected Decide: Normative Justifications for Stakeholder Democracy. *The Annuals of the Japanese Political Science Association* 2016 (2): 356–375.

Open Consultants. 2022. *External Evaluation of the Access To COVID-19 Tools Accelerator (ACT-A)*, October 10.

Phelan, Alexandra L., Mark Eccleston-Turner, Michelle Rourke, Allan Maleche, and Chenguang Wang. 2020. Legal Agreements: Barriers and Enablers to Global Equitable COVID-19 Vaccine Access. *The Lancet* 396 (10254): 800–802.

Sirleaf, H.E., Ellen Johnson, and Rt Hon. Helen Clark. 2021. *Losing Time: End this Pandemic and Secure the Future: Progress Six Months after the Report of the Independent Panel for Pandemic Preparedness and Response*, November 22.

WHO. 2005. Resolution WHA58.3, May 23.

———. 2020a. *WHO Concept for Fair Access and Equitable Allocation of COVID-19 Health Products*. Final Working Version, September 9.

———. 2020b. *WHO SAGE Values Framework for the Allocation and Prioritization of COVID-19 Vaccination*, September 14.

———. 2021a. *What is the Access to COVID-19 Tools (ACT) Accelerator, How Is It Structured and How Does It Work?*. Version, April 6.

———. 2021b. *Joint COVAX Statement on Supply Forecast for 2021 and Early 2022*, September 8.

———. 2022. *Annex 3: Phase 2 of the Allocation Mechanism: Demand-Driven Allocation for AMC-91 Participants with a Focus on Supporting Lower Coverage Participants*, April 14.

3

Environment and Economy After COVID-19: Focusing on Global Warming Issues

Xiaofang Zhang

1 Introduction

After the Industrial Revolution, which began in the United Kingdom in the middle of the eighteenth century, the concentration of greenhouse gases (GHG) increased sharply due to the increase in fossil fuel consumption and the decrease in forest area resulting from human production activities.[1] Due to the increase in GHG, the average global temperature is projected to rise by more than 1 degree Celsius compared to before the Industrial Revolution and to reach 1.5 degrees and 2.0 degrees by the end of this century (IPCC 2021). The various natural, social, and economic impacts of Climate Change associated with rising global temperatures are

[1] Japan Meteorological Agency HP: https://www.data.jma.go.jp/cpdinfo/chishiki_ondanka/p02.html (confirmed on February 15, 2021).

X. Zhang (✉)
Institute for Advanced Academic Research/ Graduate School of Social Science, Chiba University, Chiba, Japan
e-mail: zhang@chiba-u.jp

H. Ishido et al. (eds.), *Social Fairness in a Post-Pandemic World*,
https://doi.org/10.1007/978-981-19-9654-2_3

called Global Warming problems. The problem of Global Warming is one of the most demanding environmental problems related to the survival of humankind. There was also a deep-rooted skepticism about the view that Global Warming results from human factors. On the other hand, according to the Intergovernmental Panel on Climate Change (IPCC 2021: 4):

> It is unequivocal that human influence has warmed the atmosphere, ocean, and land. Widespread and rapid changes in the atmosphere, ocean, cryosphere, and biosphere have occurred.[2]

In recent years, the frequency of extreme weather, such as intense heat, warm winters, and localized torrential rains, has increased in various parts of the world. It is thought that this has been caused by Global Warming.

The global epidemic of the new coronavirus (COVID-19) from the end of 2019 has caused a global economic crisis. Due to the contraction of economic activity, carbon dioxide (CO_2) emissions in 2020 have decreased significantly Reducing CO_2 emissions is essential to prevent the progress of Global Warming, but it seems necessary to recover the economy from the effects of the economic crisis as soon as possible and to provide people with an economically stable life. Finding the balance between the economy and the environment becomes even more important. Strong measures and international cooperation are essential to avoid the effects of Climate Change on human survival, However, building an effective and fair international framework is not easy.

Therefore, this chapter first explains (in Sect. 2) the basic knowledge of the mechanics of Global Warming and the factors that cause it. Section 3 discusses the inevitable nature of concurrently attaining environmental preservation and economic growth, taking the issue of Global Warming as an example. Section 4 introduces international efforts on the issue of

[2] "The Intergovernmental Panel on Climate Change (IPCC) is the international body for assessing the science related to Climate Change. The IPCC was set up in 1988 by the World Meteorological Organization (WMO) and United Nations Environment Program (UNEP) to provide policymakers with regular assessments of the scientific basis of Climate Change, its impacts and future risks, and options for adaptation and mitigation." (https://www.ipcc.ch/site/assets/uploads/2021/07/AR6_FS_What_is_IPCC.pdf).

Global Warming and discusses the limitations of "Fairness." Then, in Sect. 5, we consider the role that more comprehensive "Environmental Fairness" plays in solving Global Warming. From the viewpoint of Behavioral economics, the section analyzes the factors that hinder the promotion of Global Warming countermeasures and consider the ideal way of fair Global Warming countermeasures. In the final section, summary and concluding remarks will be made, based on the whole discussion in this chapter.

2 Global Warming and Climate Change

Mechanism of Global Warming

The average temperature of the earth is currently maintained at about 15°C. The mechanism is that the Earth gets energy from the Sun, as shown in Fig. 3.1. This warms the ground surface. And heat is radiated into space from the ground surface in the form of infrared rays. At that

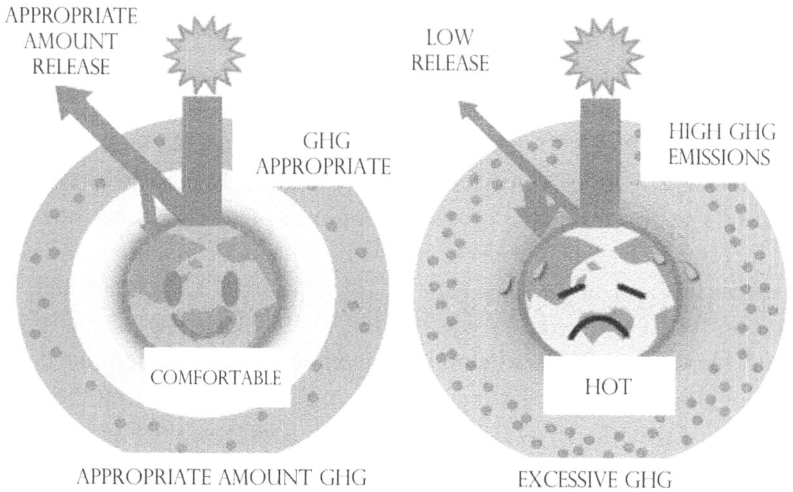

Fig. 3.1 Mechanism of Global Warming. (Source: From the Hyogo Prefecture Freon Recovery and Processing Promotion Council website http://www.hardoc.org/ondanka.html (accessed on October 3, 2021))

time, GHG in the atmosphere absorb some heat and radiate it down again to heat the ground surface and the lower atmosphere. The constant GHG on the Earth keep the temperature suitable for the survival of living things. If there are no GHG on the Earth, the average temperature is thought to be around -18°C. After the Industrial Revolution, on the other hand, a large amount of GHG are released as part of human economic activity, and the average temperature of the whole earth is rising, and this phenomenon is called "Global Warming."

Factors of Global Warming

There has long been skepticism about the fact that Global Warming and climate change are considered natural phenomena and are caused by the increase in GHG emissions due to human activities. However, in recent years, the relationship between global warming and human activities has being elucidated by accumulating scientific knowledge according to the IPCC, Fifth Assessment Report (2014: 2) that the human influence on the climate system is "clear." On the other hand, the Sixth Report (2021: 4), was evaluated using the expression "unequivocal."[3] In this way, the human influence on the climate system can no longer be denied.

Figure 3.2 shows changes in GHG emissions caused by humans by type. Of these, CO2 and Methane (CH_4) account for more than 90% of the total, of which CO_2 accounts for 76% of the total 65% of anthropogenic CO_2 emissions come from the use of fossil fuels such as coal, oil, natural gas, and industrial processes. For example, a large amount of fossil fuel is used to generate electricity that supports a convenient and comfortable life, and, at the same time, a large amount of CO_2 is emitted. The amount of CO_2 emitted by combustion varies depending on the type of fossil fuels, but it is overwhelmingly larger than that of renewable energy and nuclear power generation, which do not emit CO_2 during the power generation process. In addition to this, CO_2 is emitted during the process of burning gasoline and natural gas when riding a car. In other words, CO_2 is emitted directly or indirectly by various activities that we humans

[3] The IPCC Sixth Assessment Report referred to in this paper is a report prepared by the IPCC Working Group 1.

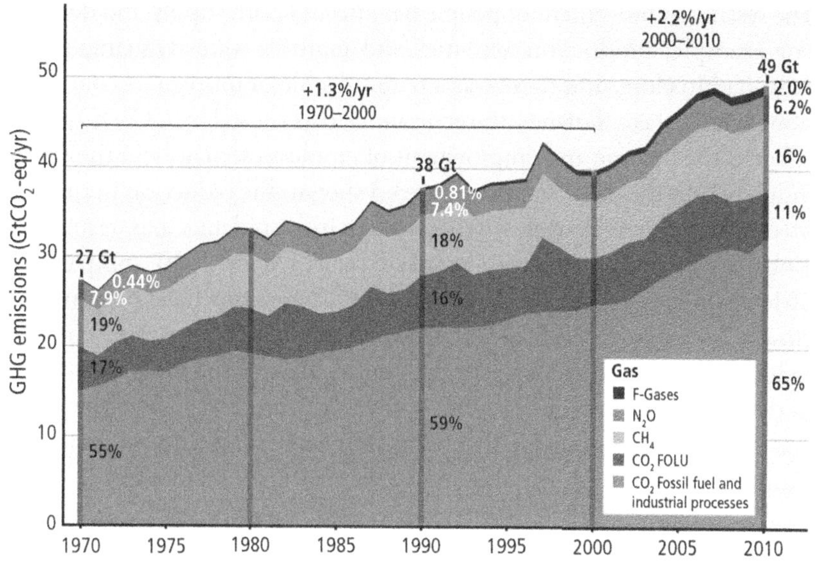

Fig. 3.2 Changes in anthropogenic GHG emissions by type (1970–2010). (Source: IPCC 2014: 5)

carry out. On the other hand, due to the decrease in forest area and land fluctuations, the increase in CO_2 resulting from the decrease in the absorption of CO_2 in the natural world accounts for 11% of the anthropogenic CO_2 emissions. CH_4 is the second-largest GHG to global warming after CO_2 accounting for 16% of the total GHG in terms of CO_2. CH_4 is generated from wetlands, paddy fields, agricultural activities, natural gas production, and waste burning.

3 Environment and Economy

COVID-19 Impact on CO_2 Emissions

After 2020, COVID-19, a global-scale pandemic, spread to the world in many countries, and to control the infection, travel restrictions and outing restrictions were enforced. As a result, the world economy is rapidly deteriorating, and a global economic crisis is occurring during COVID-19.

The restricted movement of people has affected both supply and demand. For example, production activities and logistics were stagnant, restaurants had to close, and there was a reduced scale of tourism, accommodation, aviation, etc. Further, the economic crisis caused by COVID-19 has affected the income and employment of employees, mainly in the service industry. On the other hand, as Fig. 3.3 shown, the reduction in the scale of economic activity due to the coronavirus epidemic has resulted in global CO_2 emissions being reduced by 5.3% in 2020 compared to 2019.[4] Thus, economic activities and CO_2 emissions have proven to be closely linked with each other. However, this is a short-term emission reduction that occurred at a special period. Due to the long-term nature of the pandemic, the idea of "with corona" is pervading all over the world, and the world economy is also becoming active. Global CO_2 emissions from energy combustion and industrial processes rebounded in 2021.

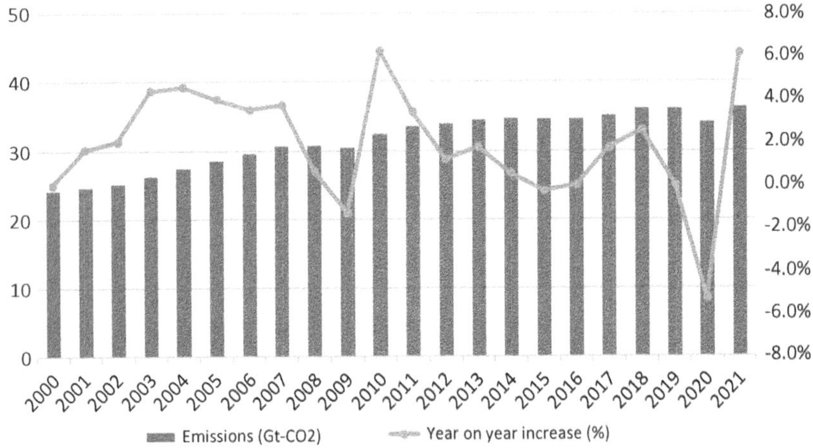

Fig. 3.3 CO_2 emissions from energy combustion and industrial processes, 1900–2021. (Source: IEA, *"GLOBAL Energy Review: CO2 Emissions in 2021"* March 2022)

[4] The absolute value of emissions has decreased, but by sector, it tends to increase in the household sector. This limits people's outings and increases their household waste and electricity consumption as they spend more time at home, leading to increased emissions from burning garbage and power generation.

The CO_2 emissions grew to 36.3Gt in 2021, a 6% increase from 2020, and a record high.

To solve the problem of Global Warming, it is essential to reduce CO_2 emissions, yet at the individual level, the impact of the COVID-19 is increasing the gap between rich and poor across the globe. The government needs to rescue citizens affected by the economic crisis caused by COVID-19. The experience of the economic crisis caused by COVID-19 suggests that curbing economic activity widens the gap between rich and poor in society in the future, we need as early as possible to find a way to balance the environment and the economy to develop our economy, and it will also be essential and indispensable for achieving the goals of the SDGs (Sustainable Development Goals). For example, prioritizing the short-term economy and overfishing because of the high demand for tuna would make it impossible to achieve the SDGs of "14 LIFE BELOW WATER" On the other hand, economic prosperity can contribute to the achievement of many SDGs goals, such as "1 NO POVERTY", "2 ZERO HUNGER", and "3 GOOD HEALTH AND WELL-BEING".

The Effects of Climate Change

Climate Change due to Global Warming has a profound effect on ecosystems, including human society. Next, let us look at its impact. The key risks that follow, all of which are identified with high confidence, span sectors, and regions (IPCC 2014: 12).

It will be difficult to remember all these effects of Climate Change; however, remembering at least the following three points will help us to understand the impacts of Climate Change. The first point is that all global populations are facing the negative effects of Climate Change. It suggests that the issue of Global Warming is not about others, but an urgent issue facing us all. The second point is that Climate Change hurts ecosystems, including human societies. If we focus solely on human societies, it will affect our lives, health, and livelihoods. In other words, avoiding Climate Change suggests protecting our lives, health, and livelihoods. And third, some regions and occupations are more susceptible to Climate

Change. The low-income groups are more affected, and there is a "Fairness" issue here.

Next, let us look at how Climate Change affects the Fairness issue between different income groups. Figure 3.4 shows the per capita absolute CO_2 consumption emissions by four global income groups for 2015. The higher-income group makes higher CO_2 emissions, and the per capita emissions of the high-income group are significantly different from other income groups. On the other hand, Fig. 3.5 shows that at the ratio of losses due to meteorological disasters to GDP per capita, the lower-income countries will be more negatively affected by Climate Change than the high-income countries. Therefore, climate disasters will further widen the gap and countries between the poor and the rich and exacerbate social inequity.

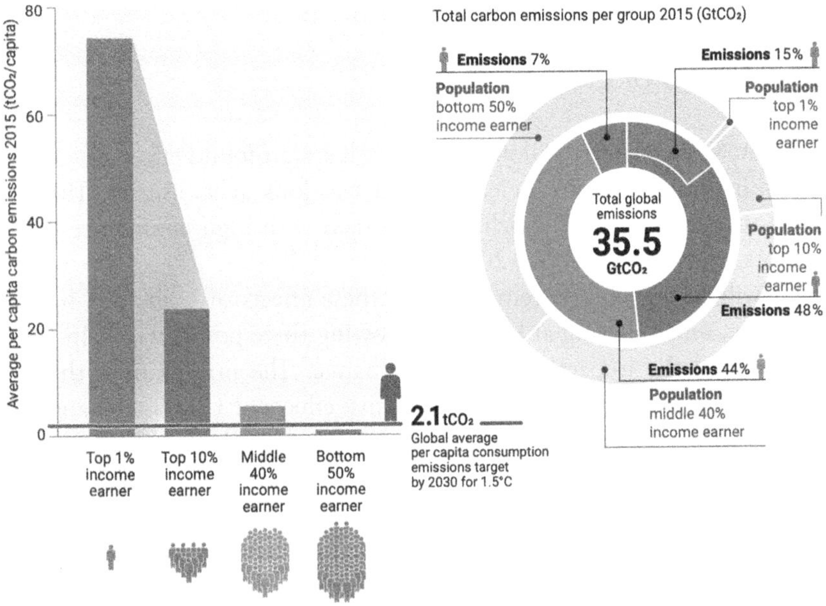

Fig. 3.4 Per capita CO_2 emissions and absolute emissions by income (2015). (Source: UNEP (2020): XV)

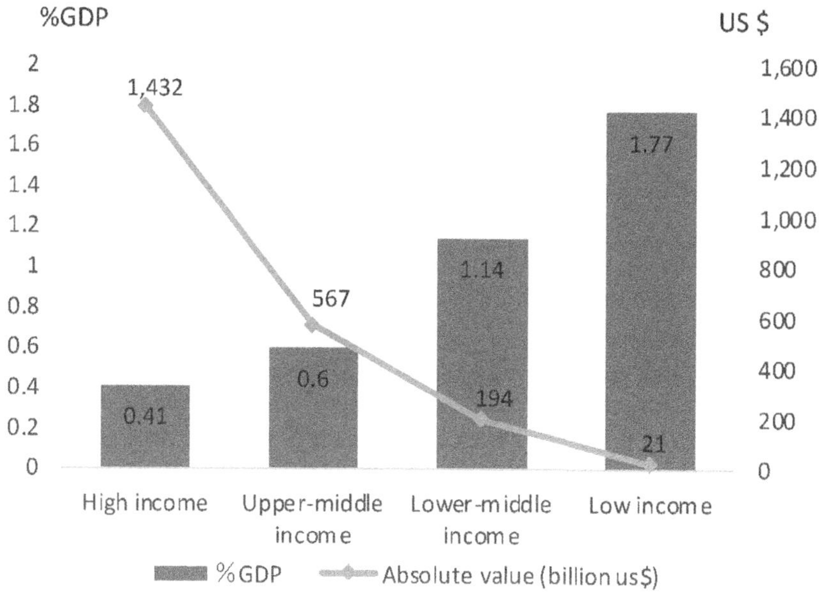

Fig. 3.5 Recorded climate-related disaster losses per income group compared to GDP losses, 1998–2017. (Source: Created by the author based on UNISDR (2018): 16)

1. *Risk of death, injury, ill-health, or disrupted livelihoods in low-lying coastal zones and small island developing states and other small islands, due to storm surges, coastal flooding, and sea level rise*
2. *Risk of severe ill-health and disrupted livelihoods for large urban populations due to inland flooding in some regions*
3. *Systemic risks due to extreme weather events leading to breakdown of infrastructure networks and critical services such as electricity, water supply, and health and emergency services*
4. *Risk of mortality and morbidity during periods of extreme heat, particularly for vulnerable urban populations and those working outdoors in urban or rural areas*
5. *Risk of food insecurity and the breakdown of food systems linked to warming, drought, flooding, and precipitation variability and extremes, particularly for poorer populations in urban and rural settings*
6. *Risk of loss of rural livelihoods and income due to insufficient access to drinking and irrigation water and reduced agricultural productivity, particularly for farmers and pastoralists with minimal capital in semi-arid regions*
7. *Risk of loss of marine and coastal ecosystems, biodiversity, and the ecosystem goods, functions, and services they provide for coastal livelihoods, especially for fishing communities in the tropics and the Arctic*
8. *Risk of loss of terrestrial and inland water ecosystems, biodiversity, and the ecosystem goods, functions, and services they provide for livelihoods*

As we have seen above, Climate Change has enormous impacts in many respects. The impact listed here is "high confidence." More scientific knowledge about the impacts of Climate Change will be accumulated in the future, and then impacts other than the above may be revealed.

In this section, we pointed out that humans are both the perpetrators of Global Warming and the victims of Climate Change. The solution to the Global Warming problem cannot only avoid the adverse effects of Climate Change, but also help us achieve SDGs. For example, "No poverty", "Zero hunger", "Good health and well-being", etc. Many of the SDGs can be achieved by developing the economy. But if we don't have a safe environment, how can we develop the economy efficiently and effectively? So, we can say that environmental protection is extremely important in building a sustainable society.

4 Global Warming and Fairness

When it costs money to resolve environmental pollution, who has a responsibility to pay? The idea of the "Polluter-pays Principle" (PPP) was proposed by the Organization for Economic Co-operation and Development (OECD) in 1972. Since OECD proposed PPP, PPP has become widely used in environmental policies (Asako et al. 2015: 136). On the other hand, as mentioned above, all countries are perpetrators and victims of Global Warming. From the standpoint of fairness, all countries will be required to take appropriate measures against Global Warming. On the other hand, what should be the criteria when considering the division of responsibilities of different countries such as emissions (past/present/future) and economic conditions (whether we can afford the cost of Climate Change measures). From the experience of the United Nations Framework Convention on Climate Change (UNFCCC), the idea of "fairness" has played an important role.

From the standpoint of developing countries, it is unfair to demand that developing countries reduce their emissions because developed countries have emitted a lot of GHG since the Industrial Revolution. For this reason developing countries insist that developed countries should take responsibility for reducing GHG first. This idea based on historical emissions is reflected in the UNFCCC. An example is the adoption of the "Kyoto Protocol," which stipulates binding reduction targets for developed countries at the 3rd Session of the Conference of the Parties (COP3) held in Kyoto in 1997.[5] In addition, the Kyoto Protocol introduced the "Kyoto Mechanism," a flexible device, to reduce the cost burden of developed countries, that is, to achieve reduction targets with more cost-effective measures.[6] In this way, the UNFCCC was devised to ensure "fairness" by considering the interests of both developed and developing countries. On the other hand, on January 20, 2001, before the Kyoto Protocol came into effect, the United States, which had the highest emissions in the world at that time, had a new Bush Administration On March 28 of the same year, Mr. Bush, then the president of the United States, announced that the United States would withdrawal from the Kyoto Protocol because "Participating in the Kyoto Protocol hurts its economy," "developing countries have not participated in the Kyoto Protocol," and "scientific uncertainty about Global Warming."[7] On the other hand, on December 12, 2011, after the Kyoto Protocol came into effect, Canada's Environment Minister announced that Canada would withdraw from the Kyoto Protocol because "major emitters such as the United States and China have not participated." In addition, Japan, Russia, and New Zealand did not participate in the Kyoto Protocol 2nd commitment period, which sets a reduction target for 2013–2020, meaning that the Kyoto Protocol 2nd has not come into effect.

[5] In 1992, the United Nations Framework Convention on Climate Change was adopted by the United Nations General Assembly with the ultimate goal of "stabilizing the concentration of GHG in the atmosphere," Effective March 2014. Based on this treaty, the Conference of Parties of United Nations Conventions (COP) has been held every year since 1995.

[6] "Kyoto Mechanics" is a general term for "Clean Development Mechanism (CDM)," "Joint Implementation (JI)," and "Emission Trading (ET)."

[7] The Kyoto Protocol meets two requirements: (1) contracts of more than 55 countries, and (2) CO_2 emissions of the developed countries (1990) that have been contracted to be 55% or more of the emissions of all developed countries Therefore, it will take effect 90 days later. The Kyoto Protocol came into effect on February 16, 2005.

The COP21 was held in France in December 2015, and the Paris Agreement was adopted as a new international framework for reducing GHG emissions after 2020, replacing the Kyoto Protocol. The new system is fairer than the Kyoto Protocol in that all countries have agreed to make efforts to reduce emissions, but there are no compulsory reduction targets for setting the most crucial reduction targets for every country. Instead, it is an effort-oriented goal. This point is the same as in the case of the Kyoto Protocol, but as a work to ensure the achievement of the reduction target, Paris Agreement stipulated that the participating countries would update and provide information on the progress every five years and receive an expert evaluation. In this respect, Paris Agreement has Higher transparency and effectiveness than the Kyoto Protocol. In addition, the Kyoto Protocol required only developed countries to provide financial support to developing countries, while the Paris Agreement required that developing countries with support capacity also provide voluntary financial support. It can be evaluated that the fairness of the Paris Agreement has become higher than the Kyoto Protocol. As a measure to prevent withdrawal seen before or after the Kyoto Protocol came into effect, a condition was set to take effect one year after the Paris Agreement withdrawal announcement. And withdrawal county can rejoin 30 days after their withdrawal. On the other hand, the Paris Agreement is legally binding but has no penalties, this point is the same as the Kyoto Protocol. Thus, in international negotiations on Climate Change, "Fairness" plays an important role in the division of responsibilities such as emission reduction and financial support. However, it is impossible to prevent the progress of Global Warming simply by clarifying the division of responsibilities. To take measures and achieve reduction targets is indispensable. As mentioned, the Kyoto Protocol and the Paris Agreement are legally binding, but legally binding refers to international law. The international law does not have clear penalties for violations, so it may not be implemented even if the government sets a reduction target. The UNFCCC is still facing the challenge of asking countries to ensure compliance reduction obligations. Furthermore, Not only in the issue of global warming but also in exchanges between nations, factors such as "politics" and "economy" often dominate over

"Fairness". In this way, it can be said that there is a limit to "Fairness" in international consultations on clime change. Next let me show you some examples.

The COP26 was held in the United Kingdom on November 1, 2021. Looking at the goals of individual fields, it is impressive that the countries that can be agreed upon differ depending on the interests. For example, in addition to the presidency of the United Kingdom, 24 countries (November 13, 2021) have agreed on the goal of turning new car sales into vehicles that do not emit emissions such as electric vehicles, by 2040. Yet three of the world's biggest automobile industries countries Japan, the United States, and Germany, have not signed this agreement (NHK NEWS 2021). Looking at the coal pledge, more than 40 countries pledge to quit coal. Major coal-using countries, including Poland, Vietnam, and Chile, are among those to make the commitment. But some of the world's biggest coal-dependent countries, including China and the United States, did not sign up (BBC NEWS 2021). Also, ten countries and regions, including Costa Rica, Denmark, France, and Ireland, participated in the international framework for oil and gas production phasing out. By contrast, most oil-producing countries, along with Japan, the United States, and China, did not sign up. This suggests that politics and the economy are still key aspects of the UNFCCC.

5 Environmental Fairness

What Is Environmental Fairness?

In the previous section, we pointed out that there is a limit to "fairness" when it comes to solving the problem of Global Warming, especially in achieving the reduction targets, so it is necessary to reconsider the normative principles required for a practical international framework in the future. Therefore, the more comprehensive concept of "fairness" can play a significant role. Before we embark on the discussion, let me explain what is intended by the term "environmental fairness.". According to Lee and Kobayashi (2021), "environmental fairness" has four requirements, "(Rule-) Compliance," "(Equal) Impartiality," "(Ethical) Fidelity," and "(Benefit) Reciprocity," and the meanings of each of these are as follows.

- *"(Rule-) Compliance" means whether or not we comply with and achieve international treaties, regulations, and promises regarding the environment and laws and goals such as domestic laws.*
- *"(Equal) Impartiality" means the environment surrounding oneself, the impact of environmental problems, and the equality of the burden for environmental conservation.*
- *"(Ethical) Fidelity" indicates the logical responsibility of integrity to work for environmental protection.*
- *"(Benefit) Reciprocity" represents the degree of reward for environmental conservation efforts and contributions.*

Since the benefits of Global Warming countermeasures are distributed all across the world, the burden of countermeasure costs in one country leads to benefits for other countries. This provides an incentive for "free-riding." However, the amount of reduction that occurs when all countries make sincere efforts to reduce emissions for their own country and other countries is far greater than the amount of reduction that would occur if some countries neglected to take reduction measures. Thus, with regard to the Global Warming issue the openness that shows the logical responsibility of working for environmental conservation plays a major role. Although recommendations have been made on reduction measures in the UNFCCC, there is considerable freedom because there are no unified and compulsory provisions about what measures to promote domestically. Additionally, as pointed out earlier, the Kyoto Protocol and the Paris Agreement are inadequate in terms of achieving reduction targets. In other words, the importance of compliance is not fully emphasized. The reason is that they are free to participate in UNFCCC; if severe penalties and regulations are set, they will not participate from the beginning. On the other hand, the results are significantly different when compared with the reduced emissions when compliance is observed and the reduced emissions when compliance is not observed. But perhaps we can expect the role of "Fidelity" and "Reciprocity" to improve this situation. Let us consider this from the perspective of behavioral economics and environmental methods.

The Obstructive Factors of Behavioral

While it has been agreed that all countries will strive to reduce GHG as the most critical environmental issue for the survival base of humankind, on the other hand, it is not easy for governments to make powerful and effective measures, from setting reduction targets to observing reduction targets, when it comes to actual reduction action. The behavior economics theory may be helpful in understanding why this is the case.

In traditional economics, human beings are assumed to be "Homo economicus" always acting rationally to maximize their self-interest. However in behavioral economics, humans are viewed as "Homo sapiens" unable to consistently make fully rational decisions due to their limited cognitive and information-processing abilities. Moreover, humans exhibit "Myopia behavior" which prioritizes the present over the future, influenced by psychological tendencies such as "Loss avoidance" and "Status quo bias." According to Thaler and Sunstein, prominent researchers in behavioral economics, the discomfort experienced from a loss shares a common characteristic. They argue that this feeling is twice as intense as the happiness derived from gaining something (Thaler and Sunstein 2009: 59). When addressing the issue of Global Warming issue, it is necessary to bear the cost of implementing countermeasures before we can experience their effects. Conversely, it may take some time for the results of these measures to become evident. This implies that the perceived loss associated with environmental improvement is estimated to outweigh the gain such as "loss avoidance," a characteristic of human psychology, which can be one of the factors contributing to the inertia in delaying global warming countermeasures.

Loss avoidance is one of the factors contributing to the Status quo bias, and lack of attention is also another factor (Thaler and Sunstein 2009: 62). For example, interest in the issue of Global Warming tends to surge following disasters resulting from abnormal weather patterns. Similarly, the hosting of international climate conferences like the COP leads to an increase in public interest. However at an individual level, except for environmental activists and researchers, most people, do not maintain consistent attention towards Global Warming. On a national scale, governments facing many social issues, such as domestic wealth disparity, income, and employment. Therefore governments may not always prioritize the resolution of Global Warming. These inherent psychological tendencies in humans may hinder compliance with reduction targets. Therefore, to address Global Warming, we should overcome the Loss avoidance and the Status quo bias.

Economic instrument-ETS

The role of "Fidelity" and "Reciprocity" in thinking about ways to overcome the loss avoidance and the Status quo bias will be helpful. Next, by focusing on environmental policy methods, especially economic instruments, information-provision methods, and supportive measures, how Fidelity and Reciprocity play a role is discussed. First, an emissions trading system (cap & trade) as an economic instrument can be taken up (Fig. 3.6).

Figure 3.6 shows the marginal abatement costs when two companies are assumed to reduce emissions. 100 t-CO_2 is assumed as a reduction target for companies A and B. In the case of the regulatory method, both Company A and Company B should reduce evenly by 50 t-CO_2. In this case, due to the difference in technology level, Company A can achieve the reduction target at a lower cost than Company B, even though the same emission is reduced. On the other hand, looking at the case of the emissions trading system (ETS), the emissions of both parties shift to the point where the reduced costs of both parties are equalized by utilizing the transactions. In the ETS case, Company A reduces emissions to 70 t-CO_2, and Company B reduces emissions to 30 t-CO_2. In the ETS case, company A can sell their 20 t-CO_2 (70 t-CO_2 -50 t-CO_2) surplus emissions to company B. Compared to the regulatory method, the cost will be lower for the area of M1-M2-M3 (shaded area). In short in the ETS there are economic benefits for both Company A, which has a relatively low reduction cost, and Company B, which has a relatively high

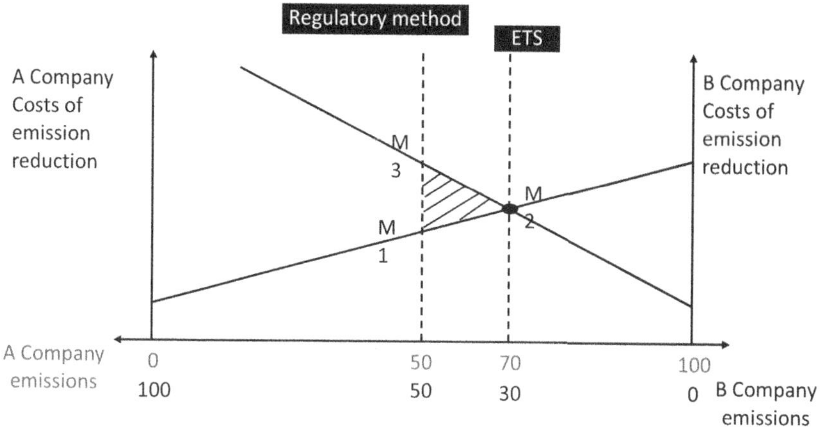

Fig. 3.6 Regulatory methods and emissions trading. (Source: Made by the author based on the Ministry of the Environment (2017) "Material 6 Quantitative Approach of the 3rd Study Group": 6)

reduction cost, and there is also an incentive to reduce emissions actively. Therefore, "loss avoidance" can be avoided, to some extent, by introducing an ETS. Further, in return for efforts to reduce emissions, it can be said that the requirement for reciprocity is also satisfied in that the sale of surplus emissions is permitted. As mentioned earlier, the ETS was introduced as one of the "Kyoto Mechanisms." However, the EU emphasized reductions within the region and does not have much interest in reductions outside the region to use the ETS. So, in 2005 EU introduced the EU-ETS in advance (Kameyama 2002: 204). Since then, countries and regions such as China and Tokyo Metropolitan, Japan, and Saitama prefecture, Japan have introduced their domestic ETS and achieved reduction effects, but the international emissions trading market has not yet been formed.

Information-provision and supportive measures effectively eliminate the "Status quo bias" caused by lack of attention. Back to Global Warming as an example, the information provision method requires the disclosure of national emission information, which informs all countries of the state of emissions and the progress of emission reductions and is under pressure from the international community. With such a mechanism, efforts to reduce emissions in one's own country will always be seen in other countries. There is a risk of being criticized by the international community for neglecting efforts to reduce emissions. In other words, building good relations with other countries is a prerequisite to making sincere efforts to reduce emissions. Today, the disclosure of emission information is not limited to the national level, and governments should oblige domestic companies that emit large amounts of GHG to disclose information. Such an informative method is low-cost and effective (Thaler and Sunstein 2009: 296). Sometimes business companies simply do not know how to reduce their GHG emission. The governments could provide practical advice to them through a range of supportive measures.

6 Conclusion

This chapter has discussed the need for a balance between the post-corona environment and the economy, with a focus on Global Warming. Due to human factors, Global Warming is progressing at an unprecedented speed. The resulting climate change is adversely affecting the survival base of humankind. As all human beings are perpetrators and victims of Global Warming, international cooperation is indispensable for solving Global Warming. However, the experience of the climate change framework so far does not lead to a solid and effective framework. The reasons for this are that the evaluation criteria for the principle of fairness differ greatly depending on the position of the country, there is an incentive for "free-riding" in the Global Warming problem, and the inherent in human being's psychological tendencies such as "loss avoidance" and "Status quo bias" is the reason of tendency to postpone emission reduction behavior. However, we cannot wait for emission reduction behavior because climate change due to Global Warming has a tremendous negative impact on the survival base of humankind. For the well-being of us and future generations, it is desirable to have a society in which environmental protection and the economy are compatible. To achieve this goal in the post-pandemic era, the idea of a fair society characterized by the aforementioned four requirements, i.e., Compliance, Impartiality, Fidelity, and Reciprocity, is indispensable.

References

Asako Kazumi, Ochiai Katsuaki, Ochiai Yukiko, 2015, *Graphic Environmental Economics*, Shinsei-sha

BBC NEWS. 2021. https://www.bbc.com/news/science-environment-59159018. Accessed 21 October 2022.

IAE. 2022. *GLOBAL Energy Review: CO2 Emissions in 2021*. https://www.iea.org/reports/global-energy-review-co2-emissions-in-2021-2. Accessed 11 November 2022/.

IPPC. 2014. *AR5 Synthesis Report: Climate Change 2014 Summary for Policymakers*. https://www.ipcc.ch/report/ar5/syr/

———. 2021. *Climate Change 2021: The Physical Science Basis Summary for Policymakers*. Accessed 21 November 2022.

Kameyama, Yasuko. 2002. International Initiatives on Global Environmental Issues. In *Iwanami Lecture Environmental Economy and Policy Studies Vol. 6 – Global Environmental Issues and Global Community*, ed. Tsuneyuki Morita and Akihiro Amano. Iwanami Shoten.

Lee, Xiang., and Kobayashi, Masaya. 2021. Chapter 9 Shinkokuka suru kankyo mondai to shokuryo anzen hosho: Kankyo teki kosei to kodo keizai gakuteki apurochi (in Japanese). [The escalating environmental issues and food security: Environmental justice and behavioral economics approach]. *In Kouseishakai no bijon: Gakusaiteki Apurochi niyoru Riron, Shisou, Genjou Bunseki (in Japanese) [Vision for a Fair Society: Theory, Thought and the Analysis of Status Quo through Interdisciplinary Approaches]*, ed. Jiro Mizushima, Chiyo Yonemura, and Masaya Kobayashi. Tokyo: Akashi Shoten.

NHK NEWS. (2021). *COP26 Launching an International Framework for the Phased Abolition of Oil and Natural Gas Production*. https://www3.nhk.or.jp/news/html/20211112/k10013345161000.html. Accessed 13 November 2021.

Thaler, Richard H., and Cass R. Sunstein. 2009. *Nudge: Improving Decisions About Health, Wealth, and Happiness*. Trans. Masami Endo. Nikkei BP.

UNEP. 2020. *Emissions Gap Report 2020*. https://www.unep.org/emissions-gap-report-2020. Accessed 11 November 2022.

UNISDR. 2018. *ECONOMIC LOSSES, POVERTY & DISASTERS 1998–2017*. https://www.undrr.org/publication/economic-losses-poverty-disasters-1998-2017. Accessed 11 November 2022.

4

An Investigation Through Philosophy and Case Studies on Regional Integration, Migrants and Refugees, and the COVID-19 Crisis

Gerald Moshammer, Natanaree Posrithong, and Hikari Ishido

1 Introduction

This chapter looks at philosophically oriented studies on the linkage between regional integration and the COVID-19 pandemic, taking EU and ASEAN as comparative cases.[1] Section 2 discusses what perspectives need to look at regional integration and the COVID-19 pandemic. In

[1] This chapter is re-translated into Japanese based on the discussions of the authors at the online research meeting "Whither Regional Integrations: Comparison of ASEAN and EU from Philosophical and Politico-Economic Perspectives" held on February 8, 2021.

G. Moshammer • N. Posrithong
Mahidol University International College, Nakhon Pathom, Thailand

H. Ishido (✉)
Graduate School of Global and Transdisciplinary Studies, Chiba University, Chiba, Japan
e-mail: ishido@faculty.chiba-u.jp

H. Ishido et al. (eds.), *Social Fairness in a Post-Pandemic World*,
https://doi.org/10.1007/978-981-19-9654-2_4

Section 3, we compare ASEAN and the EU on the premise of this methodology, and discuss regional integration and the concept of "fairness" by taking the case of vulnerable groups such as migrant refugees, and the COVID-19 pandemic. In the final Conclusion, we make a tentative conclusion on the concept of fairness in relation to regional integration.

2 What Integration and Justice for Whom? Methodological Considerations on ASEAN and EU

The recent COVID-19 crisis has put the globe under a stress test. The pandemic has heightened uncertainty, randomness and chaos, hitting a nerve of particularly post-industrialized societies that, through steady progress in science and technology, have become accustomed to at least a basic threshold of social stability, socioeconomic continuity and existential predictability. In light of the threat of mass mortality, the medical sciences were called upon to find remedies in order to restore a sense of manageability of the crisis, leading to measures that have ranged from more direct interventions such as vaccination, mask wearing and enhanced sanitation to more indirect systemic approaches such as social distancing and lockdowns. An extraordinary health crisis like the COVID-19 pandemic poses a challenge not only to science and healthcare providers; it equally demands decisive policy-making, while at the same time offering large-scale business opportunities for the pharmaceutical marketplace. In fighting pandemics, public health policies are mainly concerned with a virus' transmissibility, the severity of the illness it evokes and the excess mortality it ultimately may cause, which links to a rather straightforward moral imperative, given that the antecedent of the following conditional holds: If a particular public health intervention X is safe and necessary in order to reduce the risk of harm to random members of a community, then any member of that community is obligated to accept the repercussions of such intervention.

Such ethical logic is rooted in reciprocity and the Golden Rule, calling on cooperation similar to what common arguments regarding climate change seem to invoke. However, in game-theoretic terms, a deadly virus puts more psychological pressure on cooperation than potential distant harm something like possible climate change may impose on the world, making 'defectors' immediately more suspicious. Furthermore, while climate change challenges current lifestyle choices, what has been presented as the strongest countermeasure against the COVID-19 pandemic, namely mRNA vaccination, has not been equally made available for the world population. Hence, the situation has presented itself as a kind of paradox, as not everyone who has had access to vaccination wanted to sign up for it, while individuals from poorer regions were initially simply left out. Indeed, the narrative of the necessity of cooperation in terms of mass vaccination received initially a predominantly national interpretation, with each country seeking to secure its own vaccine stockpiles. Travel restriction have been signaling a similar strategy of protecting national interests in terms of medical safety, which clearly indicates the predominance of ethical inward orientation in times of existential crises, especially when there is a limited supply of resources that are deemed necessary.

However, whether, for instance, a novel medical intervention like (mRNA) vaccination is actually safe and necessary for every individual constitutes in principle a legitimate scientific question. In addition, doubts have been raised regarding public health strategies such as social distancing and lockdowns, not only regarding their general efficiency and durability, but also as to potential negative economic, psychological and, ultimately, physiological unintended consequences and system effects they create. Subsequently, the threat that a pandemic poses may lead policy-makers and public health officials to overstate the safety and efficacy of emergency policies in order to give credit to the aforementioned moral imperative of cooperation. Yet independent from a particular assessment of how the COVID-19 pandemic has played out so far, what seems undeniable is that the methodology of the medical sciences, being concerned with the human body as a biological system of high complexity, as well as the modeling of social systems, such as the estimation of infection rate functions or systemic repercussions of lockdowns, not only have to deal with partial uncertainties, but also need to take into account possible unknown unknowns.

This is to say that probably at no stage of a pandemic, and certainly not at its beginnings or during the transitioning between virus variants, the nature of the biosciences and the very subject matter of public health add up to a straightforward engineering problem. Alone the changing of vaccination goalposts, from full long-lasting protection to risk reduction regarding illness associated with the virus with the additional requirement of regular booster shots, exemplifies the fluidity of crisis management and the need for recalibration of scientific claims and abilities. Obviously, there exist established models of evidence-based medicine, strict methodological standards such as randomized clinical trials and, after all, real groundbreaking modern medical achievements, not least with general vaccination campaigns. Ultimately, it is rather unsurprising that a complex operation such as a global response to a deadly pandemic ultimately produces data points that give rise to more critical reevaluations. For instance, Malhotra (2022a, b) scrutinizes what he calls misinformation during the rollout of mRNA vaccines by also questioning how the medical profession juxtaposes private and public interests. Indeed, the ongoing retrospective processing of medical repercussions of the mass vaccine rollout has already lead to curious findings.

An increasing number of studies, for instance, address myocarditis as a possible risk factor, especially for younger men receiving mRNA vaccination (see, for instance, Matar et al. 2022 for an overview), which, based on its own study, led Florida to controversially declare that 'the State Surgeon General recommends against males aged 18 to 39 from receiving mRNA COVID-19 vaccines' (floridahealth.gov). Messenger RNA Covid-19 vaccines were found in breast milk (Hanna et al. 2022), which indicates biodistribution of COVID-19 vaccine mRNA, i.e. lipid nanoparticles, to distant mammary cells, seemingly countering initial evaluations of what mRNA vaccinations are supposed to do. On October 11, 2022, Robert Roos, a member of the European Parliament, asked Janine Small, an executive at Pfizer, whether "the vaccine (was) tested on stopping the transmission of the virus before it entered the market," with Small replying, "no, we had to work with the speed of science." Such dismissive and rather incomprehensible statements by leading actors in the crisis, in addition to the emergence of a more balanced and differentiated discussion regarding risk-benefit profiles in relations to vaccination against COVID-19, highlight that during the pandemic authorities around the world have been shaping (medical) information and exerting central power in order to streamline public health operations, possibly at the cost of transparency.

French et al. (1959), see also Raven 1993) suggested a now-seminal typology of forms of authority, differentiating bases of power as coercive, reward, legitimate, referent, expert and informational. Through the lenses of their framework, one can view the COVID pandemic as an ongoing struggle to establish legitimacy, particularly in calling upon experts and scientific facts in the promotion of public health measures. Equally, however, coercive and discriminatory policies have taken place against those who rejected the promoted standard medical procedure, mainly in form of restricting mobility and access to social life of those without or without sufficient vaccination. Such invasion into individual rights in relation to a medical intervention is obviously degrading the medical standard of informed consent, which, in a retrospective assessment of the global COVID-19 management, may well create broader distrust in declarations of medical expertise and the functioning of public health and the pharmaceutical industry as a whole. It is noteworthy that particularly also Western nations, which often are seen as rather individualistic, have resorted to social engineering measures that remind of a possible sociopolitical connection between the occurrence of pathogens and authoritarian tendencies (Murray et al. 2013).

Decision-making in public health has to juxtapose the methodological challenges of medical research, the probabilistic nature of decisive decision-making, the principal tension between individual rights and rights of society at large, the imperative of international distributive justice as well as the business appetite of pharmaceutical players that are enlisted on stock exchanges. Unfortunately, the demarcation lines between these areas have often become blurred in official narratives, public relation initiatives and on dominant social media, with the tendency to reduce the topic of COVID-19 containment to an overly simplified dichotomy between 'fact checking' and 'fake news.' Fairness and justice, however, can only be debated with the goal of compromise and mutual consent if their factual basis itself receives a fair measurement, which, in relation to a pandemic, must from the onset include the admission of limits to medical knowledge, its predictable power and certainty, particularly in light of a new virus and vaccination technique. The cost of violating such modesty is an irreparable loss of trust in authorities, agencies and political institutions.

3 Comparison of EU and ASEAN Under the COIVD-19 Pandemic

Vaccine Supply

It is a straightforward comparison; the supranational jurisdiction law has a prominent role in the EU (EU Charter of Fundamental Rights), but in ASEAN, the ASEAN Charter exists, and the laws and regulations of individual states are at the forefront. The principle of non-interference with domestic affairs has been maintained in the ASEAN Charter. So the centralized function appears to be more prominent in the EU.[2] Therefore, in response to the COIVD-19 pandemic, EU measures to restrict the export of vaccines outside the EU were introduced at the end of January 2021. As the aftermath could lead to the collapse of the international supply chain of vaccines, it has been widely reported.[3]

This means that the centralized EU system will emerge as a "clumsy response" (a measure that is not well received outside the region) in the event of an unexpected COVID-19. Due to the slow supply of vaccines, some citizens (for example, in Hungary) have turned to Russian-made vaccines outside the EU, for example. Thus, there are complaints about regional integration that the centralized process of regional integration is not really being utilized flexibly and fast enough. On the other hand, in ASEAN, there is a sense of expectation that vaccines imported from outside the region such as China and India, and the debate on export restrictions has not grown.

[2] Of course, as in the case of Brexit, there is a strict national or citizen-level idea that we do not want to obey the law that came into effect at the EU headquarters (Brussels).

[3] Online coverage of CNBC, a news agency on February 1, 2021, "Export Controls on Covid Vaccines from Europe could spark collapse in global supply, experts warn".

Discussion and Identity That Slips Through Regional Integration

Regional integrations such as the EU and ASEAN are sometimes very strong, but there are various forms of integration that are also very strong, involving them. It is the result of space-time compression, simply meaning that geographic markets are no longer so important in the age of digital technologies such as the Internet. For example, during the period of waiting at home affected by the coronavirus pandemic, the chess community over the internet has formed its group building with incredible momentum around the world. Like this, there is a connection that slips through regional integration.

While people around the world with the same interests (whether chess or vaccine manufacturing) form groupings including regional integrations, the possibility of collaborating through digital technology is increasing as well, and this digital community sometimes creates common identity. It can be more of a sense of identity than regional integration and, in some cases, equal to or much stronger than a national identity as revealed in regional integrations. It can be pointed out that regional integration may at times be socially below the list of people's identities.

This perspective of identity seems to be a real challenge for regional integration. Basically, because the nation-state still has a strong "national" consciousness, it seems very difficult to convince the national when the nation-state government must give up something for the benefit of other countries (for example, curbing domestic consumption to provide vaccines abroad). The EU is often accused (we will not discuss here whether the accusation is justified). For example, when the Greek financial crisis of 2008 came up, some Nordic countries said that the problem was with the Greeks (should not be a matter of regional integration). The nation-state is even more important, and regional integration is not really in line with the nation-state. That is notable in both the EU and ASEAN.

A "World" That Doesn't Belong to Anyone

According to Roloff (2020), the world of the covid pandemic is "not the world of anyone (private goods)," not just politically, but also economically. With the promotion of cooperation among nations, there is no waiting desired to provide global public goods, after setting an international agenda. For example, no country in the world would come forward to support or provide what we need during this pandemic. So when talking about the COVID-19 pandemic, the depiction of "not in anyone's world" seems to be accurate, both in a good way and in the bad sense of not being able to get cooperation.

Basically, that is exactly what is happening in the EU right now. Of course, many of the EU member states are often referred to as "global influencer countries" because many EU member states are influential in the world, but does the EU contribute to its global role?

One example of this is not the EU action, but an initiative called the Inclusive Vaccine Alliance (IVA) promoted by EU member states France, Germany, Italy, and the Netherlands. In June 2020, IVA jointly secured 400 million vaccines under a contract with a vaccine manufacturing company (AstraZeneca). This will basically be used for the vaccination of residents in the region, but if there is a surplus, will it be provided to foreign countries as well? AstraZeneca said in a related statement, "This new agreement gives all EU member states the option to use the vaccine in a fair manner without any interest in the global pandemic."[4] If the EU could take over the IVA's efforts and expand its offerings to other EU member states (and even countries outside the EU), this would be a "fair" concept. And this seems to be an initiative. However, at this time, it is not supposed to be truly open to the outside of IVA.

Compared to the EU, ASEAN responded differently. Member states appear to be acting according to national priorities rather than regional integration (ASEAN). ASEAN is somewhat prepared to deal with epidemics (or pandemics concerned about spreading more widespread infections) such as SARS and H1N1 types. When COVID-19 has been

[4] Reuters, 14 August 2020 (https://jp.reuters.com/article/health-coronavirus-eu-astrazeneca-idJPKCN25A1WT).

epidemic, as was the case with past responses, each country's policies seem to prevail, and activities that look at the common interests that regional integration should have are secondary.

Comparison Between Singapore and Cambodia

Some examples from ASEAN, the WHO sought to regulate active case tracking and case tracking advice globally, but in certain countries such as Singapore, Malaysia, and Cambodia has been implemented. Let us make a brief comparison between Singapore and Cambodia. Of course, it is well known that Singapore and Cambodia have very different economic and social conditions. When we see the various countermeasures for COVID-19 and consider various reports together, this shows that Cambodia has given complete priority to national interests and wanted to maintain a close relationship with China. Cambodia underestimated the risk of COVID-19 at first and refused to take strict action. This is probably because they wanted to maintain a close relationship with China.

On the other hand, Singapore is not only an ASEAN regional leader but also a global leader. Singapore is far more prudent with regard to pandemics than some ASEAN member countries, such as Cambodia, which has a weak healthcare system. In this way, one vision, identity, and community in ASEAN are a "utopia" (that is, a place that does not exist).

Important Concerns

Table 4.1 shows an essential matter of concern in COVID-19. On the left of Table 4.1, "vaccine nationalism." As mentioned above, when we talk about the production and supply (export) of vaccines in the EU's global role (including member countries) or as a hub for vaccine production (especially the concentration of pharmaceutical companies from overseas), the role of ASEAN is one of the most important considerations. Therefore, for example, it can be expected that the development of vaccines can be promoted by involving companies in the ASEAN

Table 4.1 Concerns things about regional integration of the COVID-19 pandemic after 2021

Global competition for vaccines ⇧ Vaccine nationalism	Pandemic and inequality	Authoritarian incentive to limit civil rights
• The global role of the EU (including member countries) • ASEAN as a vaccine manufacturing hub	• Poverty is an obstacle to the implementation of strict lockdown • Rights of immigrants, refugees, and internally displaced persons • Returning gender issues regarding women (girls)	• Declaration of emergency • Restrictions on freedom of movement

Source: Created by the author

region. The "pandemics and inequality" as the aforementioned poverty, immigrants, refugees, internally displaced persons, and gender issues surrounding women, also need to be addressed as regional integration. It can be pointed out that Europe is also facing a slowdown in growth (especially in Mediterranean countries such as Portugal, Spain, Italy, and Greece), but economic disparities in ASEAN are likely to be even greater than in Europe. Therefore, these issues must be overcome by ASEAN in particular.

In ASEAN as well, the number of migrant workers is on the rise due to the progress of regional integration, but migrant workers, as well as refugees and internally displaced persons, seem to raise another issue of vaccine nationalism. In Thailand, where one of the authors (Natanaree Posrithong) is from, there is already much debate about whether to vaccinate a group of migrant workers, such as Burmese workers, a discussion which marks an example of what is called "vaccine nationalism." It is not only a global issue but also an interstate issue that constitutes regional integration.

It is said that the total number of migrant workers from around ASEAN to the informal sector in the ASEAN region is about 200 million; this means that many workers are not part of the formal labor system. So, they are facing a more difficult situation than formal workers or national in accessing healthcare and vaccines. That issue is also should be focused on in ASEAN (and also in the EU).

It was only in March 2021 that the Thai Ministry of Labour began to discuss the plan about offering free COVID-19 vaccines to migrant workers.[5] In the case of Thailand, non-registered migrant workers were the concerned group. Given the intensified political situation in Myanmar, many more refugees fled their country to Thailand and cause the rising number of unregistered immigrants. With the unclear vaccine management on the Thai side and the growing concern, the number of vaccinated foreigners in July 2021 remained as low as 3.43%, where 42% were Burmese immigrants.[6] The initial procedure first allowed the employers to register their foreign employees for vaccines in February 2021. Nevertheless, the access to vaccination was only reserved for those with work permits and had to be done by Thai employers, not the workers themselves.[7] With the assistance from various international organizations, the Migrant Hot Line and counseling services were the additional help for the unregistered migrant workers. Similar reports were made for Singapore, another ASEAN country that relies heavily on foreign labour. The unsanitary living conditions in crowded dormitories resulted in the high number of COVID-19 cases among the migrant workers. The criticism was raised that the government imposed the hidden lockdowns exclusively on migrant workers when the basic facilities are far from adequate. The main reason for this hidden lockdown, which began in March 2020, dates back to the time when the main clusters were located at the workers' sites. The government claimed the need to quarantine these workers still by September 2021 with the blame on high concentration of cases among the workers that was accounted for 74% of all cases in the country.[8] Although the vaccination access was not problematic in the case of Singapore, the restrictions on the movement of foreign migrants demonstrate the violations of human rights by the Singaporean government.

[5] TDRI, 23 June 2021 (https://tdri.or.th/en/2021/06/migrant-workers-must-get-shots-too/).

[6] TDRI, 28 July 2021 (https://tdri.or.th/en/2021/07/new-tactics-to-help-migrant-workers/).

[7] Covid-19 Information Centre, 8 February (https://www.facebook.com/informationcovid19/posts/265371115081220/).

[8] Financial Times, 6 June 2022 (https://www.ft.com/content/4c63dea0-9ebd-4170-b978-5dce0c5e7f99).

Gender recession is also an issue that is not well addressed when talking about the COVID-19 pandemic, at least in the context of ASEAN. In fact, girls and women were not just in access to the vaccine but were also heavily affected by the pandemic during the blockade. For example, there are already reports of an increasing number of cases of domestic violence. There is also domestic violence, and access to education, especially for girls and women in poor areas. Gender recession must also be overcome as one of the challenges in this global vaccine competition.

Gender barriers, which were created by the patriarchal norms and traditions in ASEAN region, have even deepened during the pandemic. Women, in particular, are directly affected by the mobility restriction due to the required carework, which also resulted in the increased reports of gender-based violence. From early 2020, five countries in ASEAN have declared nationwide lockdowns, including Laos, Malaysia, Thailand, Singapore, and Vietnam.[9] In the case of Thailand, the government has released 19 consecutive emergency decrees since March 2020 with the last one to date ending in September 2022.[10] This means that curfews and ban on public gatherings were strictly imposed during the pandemic. During this period in which schools were shut and there was a loss or reduction in family income, women had to take up more duties and responsibilities within the household. The unpaid carework, which required girls and women to perform for the maintenance of the everyday life inside the households was already as high as 606 million women worldwide prior to the pandemic was expected to be higher during the lockdowns.[11] From cooking, cleaning, taking care of the sick, to monitoring the children's online classes, the burden on unpaid carework caused constraints on both their mobility and economic independence. As a consequence of this, the ASEAN-wide report has shown that the cases of domestic violence has increased significantly. In the early months of lockdown, Malaysia reported 2000 cases or more of domestic violence;

---

[9] OECD, 6 May 2020 (https://www.oecd.org/coronavirus/policy-responses/covid-19-crisis-response-in-asean-member-states-02f828a2/).

[10] TAT, 14 October 2022 (https://www.tatnews.org/2022/09/thailand-ends-covid-19-emergency-decree-on-30-september-2022/).

[11] Kate Power 21 June 2020 (https://www.tandfonline.com/doi/full/10.1080/15487733.2020.1776561).

and similar reports were also seen in the Philippines, where there were 2183 cases of violence against women and 2077 against children in Luzon region alone.[12] The reason for the increase in violence can be related to the anxiety within the households from economic constraints due to the men's loss of income.

In addition, consideration should be given to "Incentives to Suppress Civil Rights by Authoritarianism," that is, to consider how to prevent the issuance of a state of emergency and the restriction of freedom of movement rampant. In particular, it is assumed that national "justice" may differ from true "fairness" at the citizen level, so, even if it is necessary for national security, it is not endorsed by so-called "human security." Effective measures to curb implementation as regional integration is needed.

As shown in Table 4.1, if the action of these three concerns is synergistic, "global competition for vaccines" (in a bad sense) will happen. This aspect has actually been observed in the EU, and in ASEAN, concerns over securing vaccines also have been expressed in the daily reports.

Regional Integration and Creation of New Opportunities

The only way to make regional integration work is to create new opportunities. From economic thinking, scale economies, or social innovation is effective. Of course, when cooperating between nations as regional integration, it is possible that a particular group of people will benefit more than another. Therefore, regional integration with a relatively low centralized function, such as ASEAN, couldn't touch on this issue of "distribution fairness" anyways.

However, as the Kishida Cabinet of Japan argues as "new capitalism," if it involves "growth," that is, the creation of new opportunities, the "pie" itself that should be distributed will expand, and a struggle for the limited vaccination it does not always have and this seems to be how future fair society should be in which nations should cooperate when a

[12] Shebana Alqaseer et al. (https://asia.fes.de/news/covid-women-asia)

certain scale can be secured as regional integration. Of course, the development of vaccines and medicines entails significant business risks. If it is successful, not only makes rules of profit sharing but also requires a detailed design of intellectual property rights. Although this chapter does not strictly define the concept of a fair society, the concerns raised in Table 4.1, as regional integration, the attitude (Mana) of taking risks and resolving is an integral part of the concept of fairness. Even in a diverse and complex global society, humanity (which can be rephrased as manners) is a necessary quality that its members should possess even in an emergency.

4 Conclusion

In this chapter, we have made a philosophical and case study of the COVID-19 pandemic and regional integration. There have been many studies on the economic situation of regional integration (for example, for ASEAN, Urata and Ushiyama 2015; Ing et al. 2020), but what is the vision of a "fair society" (Mizushima et al. 2021)? It seems that there are not many studies centered on normative viewpoints. In this chapter, although it is very elementary, we have discussed the points that as a result of COVID-19 freedom restriction, the support of externality, and a global "manner" was needed.

As a global manner to regional integration, the willingness to create "new opportunities" beyond narrow vaccine nationalism is indispensable in after-corona. And it is not only to the EU and ASEAN but also to the globally observed regional integration (for example, the African Union (AU) and the Gulf Cooperation Council in the Middle East). Also, as mentioned before, the problem of poverty is a permanent problem on a global scale. At the end of 2021, the time of this chapter's writing, every time a new variant of COVID-19 was reported, a strict city blockade was implemented, hindering poverty levels in many parts of ASEAN. Moreover, under this situation, the rights of vulnerable groups such as migrant workers, refugees, and internally displaced persons could be further put aside.

When discussing regional integrations or potential cooperation between multiple regional integrations, not just opportunities, but sharing risks, or securing some kind of "self-sacrificing pool" between community members is also necessary. Specific issues, such as regional integration and immigrants, refugees, internally displaced persons, and gender, do not have a simple solution. But at least within the regional integration and among multiple regional integrations, citizens should have some "manners" that exceed legal regulations, refraining from profit-inducing lobbying activities. Then the "co-creation of new opportunities" (including, for example, international co-development of vaccines and therapeutic agents) is important for sure to realize a futuristic fair society after the COVID-19.

References

French, J.R., B. Raven, and D. Cartwright. 1959. The Bases of Social Power. *Classics of Organization Theory* 7: 311–320.

Hanna, N., A. Heffes-Doon, X. Lin, et al. 2022. Detection of Messenger RNA COVID-19 Vaccines in Human Breast Milk. *JAMA Pediatrics*. https://doi.org/10.1001/jamapediatrics.2022.3581.

Ing, Lili Yan, Martin Richardson, and Shujiro Urata, eds. 2020. *East Asian integration: goods, services and investment*. Keiso: Shobo.

Malhotra, A. 2022a. Curing the Pandemic of Misinformation on COVID-19 mRNA Vaccines Through Real Evidence-Based Medicine-Part 1. *Journal of Insulin Resistance* 5 (1): 8.

———. 2022b. Curing the Pandemic of Misinformation on COVID-19 mRNA Vaccines Through Real Evidence-Based Medicine-Part 2. *Journal of Insulin Resistance* 5 (1): 10.

Matar, R.H., R. Mansour, H. Nakanishi, K. Smayra, J. El Haddad, D.K. Vankayalapati, et al. 2022. Clinical Characteristics of Patients with Myocarditis Following COVID-19 mRNA Vaccination: A Systematic Review and Meta-Analysis. *Journal of Clinical Medicine* 11 (15): 4521.

Mizushima, Jiro, Chiyo Yonemura, and Masaya Kobayashi, eds. 2021. *Vision of Fair Society: Analysis of Theory, Thought, and Current Situation by Interdisciplinary Approach*. Akashi Shoten.

Murray, D.R., M. Schaller, and P. Suedfeld. 2013. Pathogens and Politics: Further Evidence that Parasite Prevalence Predicts Authoritarianism. *PloS One* 8 (5): e62275.

Raven, B.H. 1993. The Bases of Power: Origins and Recent Developments. *Journal of Social Issues* 49 (4): 227–251.

Roloff, Ralf. 2020. COVID-19 and No One's World: What Impact for the European Union? *Connections: The Quarterly Journal* 19 (2): 25–37.

Urata, Shujiro, and Ryuichi Ushiyama. 2015. In *The Realities of ASEAN Economic Integration*, ed. Shigezaburo Kabe. Bunshindo.

5

Challenges and Possibilities for Global Economic Cooperation after COVID-19: Focus on East Asia

Kuihua Han

1 Introduction

In Japan, the third emergency declaration of the year due to novel coronavirus infections (COVID-19) was lifted on October 1, 2021. The lifting of restrictions came after two and a half months, having been extended and re-extended since July 12. According to the Prime Minister's Office, as of November 25, 76% of the population in Japan has been vaccinated against COVID-19.[1] The number of COVID-19 infections has rapidly decreased due to the vaccine's effectiveness, with the number of infections dropping to less than 100 people per day. The government has announced economic support measures, such as the nationwide reopening of GoTo Travel, due to the easing of restrictions. However, even in developed countries, such as the U.S. and Germany, the pandemic is still very severe,

[1] According to "About the COVID-19 Vaccine" on the Prime Minister's Office website. https://www.kantei.go.jp/jp/headline/kansensho/vaccine.html.

K. Han (✉)
Graduate School of Social Sciences, Chiba University, Chiba, Japan

H. Ishido et al. (eds.), *Social Fairness in a Post-Pandemic World*,
https://doi.org/10.1007/978-981-19-9654-2_5

with about 100,000 and 50,000 cases respectively, and no end in sight. In Japan, the economy is currently booming, but there are concerns about a sixth wave of infection.

Besides COVID-19, protectionism, and trade frictions, beginning with the US Trump Administration's announcement of their "America First" policy in 2018, led to the creation of the worrying phrase "the US–China Trade War." As a result, the US implemented additional tariffs on China and other trade deficit partners and regions such as Japan, South Korea, and the EU. For example, the Trump Administration raised tariffs on Chinese high-tech products to 25%. In addition, most of the countries, including China, who were on the receiving end of additional tariffs have responded with retaliatory tariffs against the US (the exception being Japan), and even after several years, the US and China are still in talks. The International Monetary Fund (IMF) predicts that if the US and China implement additional tariffs of 25% on all goods from each other, the US real gross domestic product (GDP) will fall by 0.6%, China's GDP by 1.5%, and global GDP by 0.2%.[2] The first US–China summit between President Biden and President Xi Jinping took place on November 16, 2021. While there is hope that this meeting between the leaders of the US and China will have a positive impact on the trade talks that will take place in the future, the impact of the trade war between the US and China on the global economy goes far beyond the bilateral relationship between the countries. An announcement on July 1 last year, by Japan's Ministry of Economy, Trade and Industry (METI), led to revision of the export control categories for South Korea, and the subsequent restrictions on the export of polyimide fluoride, resist, and hydrogen fluoride from July 4. Thus, Japan, China, and South Korea, which had been affected by the trade friction between the US and China, now faced additional problems.

The pandemic occurred in an atmosphere of trade frictions, and in 2020 and 2021, economic activities have become more uncertain during the pandemic. Growth has declined sharply not only in Japan but across

[2] The Sankei News, "US-China 'Tariff War' Weighs on Global Economy, Increases Burden on US Companies, Cools Consumption," May 10, 2019, https://www.sankei.com/economy/news/190510/ecn1905100031-n1.html.

the whole global economy. There was negative growth in 2020, except for some countries like China.

The future of the global pandemic is not yet clear, and it continues to pose a major problem. Although the economy is gradually recovering from the COVID-19 crisis, the importance and necessity of global economic cooperation for economic growth is increasing after COVID-19.

2 Economy and Trade in East Asia

The countries of East Asia, including Japan, China, and South Korea, account for a high percentage of the world economy's GDP. They made up 5.8%, 16.4%, and 1.9% of the global economy in 2019, respectively, less than the top-ranked U.S. (24.5%), but in terms of global GDP, Japan was in third place, China in second, and South Korea in 11th.

In 2020, the global economy was reduced in size due to the COVID-19 pandemic, and economic growth rates in most countries were negative. Table 5.1 shows the International Monetary Fund's (IMF) outlook for economic growth. The economic growth rate in each country will noticeably decrease in 2020. The global economy is down 3.2%, Japan is down 4.7%, South Korea is down 0.9%, and China is up 2.3%, which is bucking the trend.

Economic growth in the post-COVID-19 period has varied across countries. The IMF predicts that the world economy will rise 6.0% in 2021 and 4.9% in 2022. The 2021 forecast predicts high growth due to the rebound in 2020, but it depends on the state of the future recovery.

Table 5.1 IMF's Economic Growth Rates in Major East Asian Countries (Actual and Projected) Unit: %

	2018	2019	2020	2021 (predicted value)	2022 (predicted value)
Japan	0.3	0.0	△4.7	2.8	3.0
China	6.6	6.0	2.3	8.1	5.7
Korea	2.9	2.2	△0.9	4.3	3.4
USA	2.9	2.2	△3.5	7.0	4.9
World	3.6	2.8	△3.2	6.0	4.9

Source: Compiled by the author from the IMF's "World Economic Outlook" for each year

According to WTO, world trade in 2021 will be US$22.328 trillion in exports and US$22.586 trillion in imports, representing growth of 24.9%, 26.3%, and 26.3% over the previous year, respectively. Japan, China, and Korea's exports are expected to increase by 17.9%, 29.9%, and 25.7% from the previous year, while imports increased by 21.0%, 30.1%, and 31.5% from the previous year, respectively.[3] According to the Ministry of Finance, Japan, from January to September this year, Japanese exports increased 17.9% y/y, while imports increased 41.2% y/y.[4] According to the Ministry of Trade, Industry and Energy, Korea, Korea's exports grew 12.3% y/y and imports 25.1% y/y from January to September of this year.[5] Similarly to Japan, the growth rate of imports exceeded that of exports in South Korea. Meanwhile, according to the General Administration of the Customs People's republic of China (GACC), from January to August this year, China's exports grew 13.5% y/y, while imports grew 4.6% y/y.[6] Export growth outpaced imports. It is expected that China's imports and exports will continue to grow steadily, creating a mutual effect between China, Japan, and Korea, and that the synergistic effect will further stimulate the world economy, including Japan's, and that the day will soon come when the economy will return to pre-corona economic activity.

Next is an observation on trade. Table 5.2 shows the percentage, ranking, and growth rate of each country's imports and exports in world trade between 2018 and 2020. All exports and imports in 2019 and 2020 have negative growth rates, with the exception of China's exports. The growth rate of world trade exports dropped from 7.6% in 2018 to -2.8% in 2019 and -7.4 percent in 2020. Japan contributes to 3.8% of global exports, a figure that will not change significantly, but the growth rate will decrease from 5.7% to -9.1%. Hence, in the ranking of the world's

[3] WTO STATS. https://stats.wto.org. Accessed 20 October 2022.

[4] Ministry of Finance, Japan. https://www.customs.go.jp/toukei/shinbun/trade-st/gaiyo2022_09.pdf. Accessed 21 October 2022.

[5] Ministry of Trade, Industry and Energy, Korea. http://www.motie.go.kr/motie/ne/presse/press2/bbs/bbsView.do?bbs_seq_n=166120&bbs_cd_n=81&currentPage=191&search_key_n=title_v&cate_n=&dept_v=&search_val_v=. Accessed 1 October 2022.

[6] General Administration of Customs People's republic of China. < http://www.customs.gov.cn/customs/302249/zfxxgk/2799825/302274/302275/4556778/index.html> Accessed 11 September 2022.

Table 5.2 Percentage, rank, and growth rates of each country's imports and exports in world trade (2018–2020)

			Japan	China	Korea	USA	World
2018	Export	Ratio (%)	3.8	12.7	3.1	8.5	100.0
		Rank	4	1	6	2	
		Growth rate (%)	5.7	9.9	5.4	7.6	10.2
	Import	Ratio (%)	3.8	10.8	2.7	13.2	100.0
		Rank	4	2	9	1	
		Growth rate (%)	11.4	15.8	11.9	8.5	10.3
2019	Export	Ratio (%)	3.7	13.1	2.9	8.6	100.0
		Rank	5	1	7	2	
		Growth rate (%)	△4.4	0.5	△10.4	△1.3	△2.8
	Import	Ratio (%)	3.7	10.8	2.6	13.3	100.0
		Rank	4	2	9	1	
		Growth rate (%)	△3.7	△2.7	△6.0	△1.8	△2.8
2020	Export	Ratio (%)	3.6	14.7	2.9	8.1	100.0
		Rank	5	1	7	2	
		Growth rate (%)	△9.1	3.6	△5.5	△12.9	△7.4
	Import	Ratio (%)	3.6	11.5	2.6	13.5	100.0
		Rank	4	2	9	1	
		Growth rate (%)	△11.9	△1.0	△7.1	△6.2	△7.6

Source: Compiled from WTO data

exporting countries, Japan's position has also changed from fourth to fifth. The share of China's exports has gradually increased from 12.7% to 14.7% of the world's total, and it continues to hold top rank among the world's exporters. China's export growth rate is positive, but only 0.5% in 2019, recovering to 3.6% in 2020. This recovery in China is because the domestic economy recovered quickly due to lockdowns and other strict COVID-19 measures. The share of South Korea's exports decreased from 3.1% to 2.9%, and its ranking changed from 6th to 7th. Except for a small increase in China's exports in 2019 and 2020, both global and national trade economies have shrunk.

Finally, we will look specifically at the trade of Japan, China, and South Korea, which are the largest economies and major trading partners in East Asia. Table 5.3 shows the top three major trading partners of Japan, China and Korea. Japan's major trading partners are China, the US, and South Korea, while South Korea's major trading partners are China, the US, and Japan, and China's major trading partners are the US, Japan, and

Table 5.3 Trade Value and Percentage of Japan, South Korea, and China by Major Partner Country in 2019 (US$1 million, %)

Japan				Korea				China			
	Trade Value	Ratio	Rank		Trade Value	Ratio	Rank		Trade Value	Ratio	Rank
China	303,892	21.3	1	China	243,431	23.3	1	USA	541,820	11.9	1
USA	221,676	15.5	2	USA	135,704	13.0	2	Japan	314,747	6.9	2
Korea	75,894	5.3	3	Japan	75,999	7.3	3	Korea	284,538	6.2	3
Japan Trade amount	1,426,492	100.0		Korea Trade amount	1,045,435	100.0		China Trade amount	4,567,520	100.0	

Source: Compiled from "World Statistics 2021"

South Korea. Japan, China, and South Korea are in each other's top three major trading partners, and, as neighbors, transportation costs are a favorable part of trade costs. Furthermore, a regional value chain has been formed in Japan, China and South Korea, and there is a lot of intra-industry trade, which means that these countries have a close economic relationship with each other.

Increasing trade, especially exports, is problematic because of rising trade barriers such as protectionism. Amid protectionism and a global pandemic, economic cooperation will be necessary for a shrinking economy and trade. The next section will examine economic cooperation through economic integration, and then we will examine economic cooperation outside of economic integration.

3 Economic Cooperation in East Asia (1): Possibilities and Challenges of Economic Partnership Agreements (EPAs) and Free Trade Agreements (FTAs)

While there are various levels of economic integration, this chapter considers free trade agreements (FTAs). They aim to eliminate tariffs among member countries, but each country gradually eliminates or lowers tariffs based on a tariff concession table. Fair rules are created, and trade barriers are eliminated under those rules to expand trade and revitalize the economy. The effects of FTAs are "static effects, which include trade creation effects, trade conversion effects, and terms of trade effects, in addition to dynamic effects, which include market expansion effects and competition promotion effects" (Abe and Ishido 2008: 92). The elimination of tariffs in an FTA expands the intra-regional trade of member countries (trade creation effect), expands the market, and, if economies of scale work, price reductions become feasible (market expansion effect).

FTAs began in the 2000s, but recently mega-FTAs have become the norm. In Japan, Economic Partnership Agreements (EPAs) are more common. Mega FTAs in East Asia include the Regional Comprehensive Economic Partnership (RCEP), the Trans-Pacific Partnership (TPP), and the Japan-China-Korea (CJK) FTA, for which negotiations are underway.

Table 5.4 Impact of RCEP on China's Trade (Jan.–Aug. 2022, %)

Countries and Regions	Total amount of trade		Exports		Imports	
	Growth rate	Percentage in RCEP	Growth rate	Percentage in RCEP	Growth rate	Percentage in RCEP
ASEAN	13.3	49.1	19.4	56.6	5.8	41.6
Japan	△1.3	18.7	6.6	17.8	△7.5	19.7
Korea	7.2	19.2	16.2	16.9	1.0	21.5
Australia	△3.8	11.6	23.6	7.8	△13.7	15.4
New Zealand	5.0	1.4	15.5	0.9	0.1	1.8
RCEP	6.8	100.0	16.4	100.0	△1.4	100.0
World	9.5	–	13.5	–	4.6	–

Source: General Administration of Customs People's republic of China (2022) Available at: http://www.customs.gov.cn/customs/302249/zfxxgk/2799825/302274/302275/4556778/index.html (Accessed 11 September)

General Administration of Customs People's republic of China (2022) Available at: http://www.customs.gov.cn/customs/302249/zfxxgk/2799825/302274/302275/4556778/index.html (Accessed 11 September)

Regional Comprehensive Economic Partnership (RCEP)

The RCEP declared the launch of negotiations in November 2012, was signed eight years later, on November 15, 2020, and is scheduled to enter into force on January 1, 2022. The 14 member countries are the 10 ASEAN countries, plus Japan, China, South Korea, Australia, and New Zealand. According to the Ministry of Foreign Affairs, it "accounts for about 30% of the world's GDP, total trade, and population, and about 50% of Japan's total trade."[7] India withdrew from the negotiations in November 2019. Tables 5.3 and 5.4 in Sect. 2 confirm the close economic relationship between China, Japan and South Korea, and the conclusion of RCEP will mark the first time that China, Japan and South Korea will conclude an FTA. Note that an FTA between China and South Korea came into effect in December 2015.

[7] Ministry of Foreign Affairs website, "Regional Comprehensive Economic Partnership (RCEP) Agreement," March 2021. https://www.mofa.go.jp/mofaj/files/000231134.pdf.

The Trans-Pacific Partnership (TPP)

The TPP began negotiations at its first meeting in March 2010, and Japan joined the negotiations in July 2013. It was signed in February 2016, and, following the U.S. withdrawal in January 2017, there are 11 member countries. It was signed in March 2018 by 11 member states, Australia, Brunei, Canada, Chile, Japan, Malaysia, Mexico, New Zealand, Peru, Singapore, and Vietnam, and entered into force on December 30, 2018. It is called the Comprehensive and Progressive Agreement on the Trans-Pacific Partnership (TPP11). It accounts for 13% of the world's GDP, 15% of the world's total trade, and about 7% of the world's population.

China–Japan–South Korea Free Trade Agreement (FTA) Negotiations

Negotiations for a China–Japan–South Korea (CJK) FTA were declared open in November 2012 but came to a halt after the 16th negotiation meeting in November 2019, with each country pointing out that progress has been slow. As mentioned in Sect. 2, the GDP of China, Japan and South Korea in 2019 exceeds 24% of the world's GDP, and, furthermore, China and South Korea account for more than 26% of Japan's total trade. The effect of the RCEP, which will come into effect next year, states that "the RCEP will account for about 30% of the world's GDP and total trade, and about 50% of Japan's total trade," indicating that Japan, China and South Korea will contribute 80% of RCEP's GDP. China and South Korea also contribute 50 percent of Japan's total trade in the RCEP. The Ministry of Foreign Affairs says, "the GDP and trade of the three countries account for about 20% of the world's total and about 70% of Asia's total. The inclusion of both countries is also essential for Japan to maintain and enhance its economic growth. The focus will be on how much value can be added beyond the RCEP. Through the strengthening of economic relations between the three countries, China, Japan, and South Korea, this will contribute to the stability of the region and the strengthening of diplomatic relations."[8] China and South Korea have also said many times that they will accelerate negotiations, but the result is that "progress is slow" and negotiations have been stalled for two years. A CJK FTA is about as far along in the negotiations as the EU–Japan Economic Partnership Agreement, which came into effect in February 2019, and the RCEP, which was signed in November 2020.

While India's return to the RCEP and the US return to the TPP are being discussed, on September 16, 2021, China submitted an application to New Zealand, a TPP depositary, to join the FTA. Several Chinese media outlets, citing Australian reports, said that New Zealand Prime Minister Jacinda Ardern said that China should be allowed to join the CPTPP if it meets the requirements. Joining the TPP will require the consent of all member countries. For greater economic growth of China, Japan and South Korea, and especially for the expansion of trade exports, various forms of cooperation, including the negotiation of a CJK FTA, will be necessary.

Impact of RCEP Entry into Force on China's Trade

15 countries signed the Regional Comprehensive Economic Partnership Agreement (RCEP) on November 15, 2020, and it is the largest FTA signed; as of October 23, 2022, it has entered into force in 12 countries, excluding Indonesia, Myanmar, and the Philippines. This chapter will examine the impact of the RCEP, which has already entered into force in 12 countries, on China's trade.

According to the GACC, China's total trade from January to August increased 9.5% y/y to \$4191.4 billion, of which exports increased 13.5% to \$2376.0 billion and imports increased 4.6% to \$1815.4 billion, with a notable increase in exports (Table 5.4). Turning to the countries participating in the RCEP, total trade from January to August increased 6.8% y/y, with exports up 16.4% and imports down 1.4%.

From January to August 2022, total trade increased y/y, led by ASEAN, followed by Korea and New Zealand (in percentage growth terms), while

[8] Ministry of Foreign Affairs website, "China–Japan–South Korea FTA Negotiations," April 2020. https://www.mofa.go.jp/mofaj/files/000264138.pdf.

Japan and Australia decreased: ASEAN grew by 13.3% y/y (exports by 19.4% and imports by 5.8%), Korea by 7.2% y/y (exports by 16.2% and imports by 1.0%), and New Zealand by 5.0% (exports by 15.5% and imports by 0.1%). (exports up 16.2%, imports up 1.0%), and New Zealand was up 5.0% (exports up 15.5%, imports up 0.1%). Japan's trade fell 1.3% y/y (exports up 6.6%, imports down 7.5%), while Australia's trade fell 3.8% y/y (exports up 23.6%, imports down 13.7%). In particular, ASEAN's total trade, exports, and imports both exceeded the aforementioned increases in total trade with China and RCEP.

Although China's overall trade with Japan declined by 1.3%, exports grew by 6.6%, and imports declined by 7.5%, Japan remains China's top three trading partner. China's top three countries and regions in terms of total trade from January to August 2022 are the United States ($515 billion), South Korea ($245.5 billion), and Japan ($239 billion). The top three countries and regions in terms of exports are the United States, Hong Kong, and Japan. The top three countries and regions in terms of imports are Taiwan, South Korea, and Japan.

The RCEP's share of China's trade was 30% of total trade, the RCEP will undoubtedly exert as much influence on China's trade as it has on other countries. In terms of total trade value, the participating countries in RCEP are South Korea (19.2%), Japan (18.7%), Vietnam (11.7%), Australia (11.6%), Malaysia (10.3%), Indonesia (7.5%), Thailand (7.1%), Singapore (5.5%), the Philippines (4.5%), and ASEAN as a whole accounted for 49.1% of the total.

According to the GACC, exports of rare earth, raw aluminum, and cars (including chassis) increased by 76.3%, 62.9%, and 56.2%, respectively, from January to August.[9] Imports of fertilizers rose 83.7%, coal and lignite 53.1%, crude oil 48.7%, and natural gas 44.4%.[10]

In the global recession due to COVID-19, Russia's invasion of Ukraine, and other factors, the dollar-yen (exchange) rate recently rose to as high as 151 yen to 1 dollar, but trade in China appears still to be robust in

[9] General Administration of Customs People's republic of China. http://www.customs.gov.cn/customs/302249/zfxxgk/2799825/302274/302275/4556778/index.html. Accessed 11 September 2022

[10] General Administration of Customs People's republic of China..http://www.customs.gov.cn/customs/302249/zfxxgk/2799825/302274/302275/4556800/index.html Accessed 11 September 2022.

2021. hope the results mentioned above on this basis will be a driving force not only for China but also for the RCEP and the global economy, including Japan.

4 Economic Cooperation in East Asia (2): Possibilities and Challenges Other than Economic Integration

Next is a discussion on economic cooperation other than FTAs that include the Japan-China Trilateral Cooperation Secretariat, the Japan–China High-Level Economic Dialogue,

China's One Belt One Road, "China–Japan–Korea + X" cooperation, The China-Northeast Asia Expo, and the "Greater Tumen Initiative."

Japan–China–Korea Trilateral Cooperation Secretariat

Japan-China-Korea Trilateral Cooperation Secretariat was established on May 17, 2011, to promote peace, stability, and prosperity among the three countries. It holds international forums on trilateral cooperation between Japan, China, and Korea. However, the forums have not been held last year or this year due to COVID-19.

Japan–China High-Level Economic Dialogue

The Japan–China High-Level Economic Dialogue was held in Tokyo on April 16, 2018, for the first time in about eight years. According to the Ministry of Foreign Affairs of Japan, it is "a forum for regular dialogue among economic ministers to discuss from a broad perspective the resolution of problems and the promotion of cooperation in the economic field from the perspective of strategic reciprocity." It was agreed to be established in October 2000 when Prime Minister Shinzo Abe visited China. The first meeting was held in Beijing on December 1, 2007, the second in Tokyo on June 7, 2009, and the third in Beijing on August 28, 2010. The most recent, fifth meeting was held on April 14, 2019, in Beijing.

China's "One Belt One Road"

"One Belt One Road" is the concept of a huge economic zone connecting China and Europe. It includes the overland route, the "Silk Road Economic Belt," (丝绸之路经济带) as the "One Belt," and the sea route, the twenty-first Century Maritime Silk Road ("21世纪海上丝绸之路"), as the "One Road." The goal is to create a huge economic zone in cooperation with other countries. The cooperation in "One Belt One Road" has five main links ("五通"), one of which is "trade facilitation" ("贸易畅通"). In the area of "trade facilitation," China will promote trade and investment facilitation between China and the countries participating in the "One Belt One Road" initiative, and continuously improve the business environment. In addition, the "One Belt One Road" International Cooperation Summit ("一带一路国际合作高峰论坛") was held from May 14 to 15, 2017 in Beijing, China, where representatives from 130 countries and 70 international organizations gathered.

"China–Japan–Korea + X" Cooperation ("Trilateral + X" Cooperation)

Fifty-two memorandums of cooperation were signed between Japanese and Chinese enterprises at the Japan–China Third Party Market Cooperation Forum. It was held for the first time in Beijing on September 25, 2018, and sees the two countries cooperate in the Eastern Economic Corridor, Thailand's economic zone, as a third country for Japan and China. The Japan–China Third Country Market Cooperation is one part of the Japanese government's "infrastructure system export strategy" and part of the Chinese government's "One Belt One Road" initiative. The signing of numerous MOUs by large companies in a short period of time, and the implementation of these projects at the fastest possible pace, is the first such cooperation between China and Japan to date.

During a situation that is far from trade liberalization, such as the trade friction between the US and China that began with US protectionism, the trade friction between Japan and South Korea that began with Japan's exclusion of South Korea from its "whitelist countries," the Japan–China Third Country Market Cooperation in Thailand could be a shift in perspective from inward-looking competition to outward-looking cooperation. First, it is expected that "cooperation" in the corridor (e.g., mutual supply of intermediate goods and services in the region) will develop in a broad sense.

Also, at the ninth Japan–China–South Korea Foreign Ministers' Meeting (August 21, 2018) held after three years, the three countries agreed to cooperate with each other in a "third country," which they described as "three countries + X" cooperation. China's Ministry of Foreign Affairs said in publicity materials from August 19, 2019, "China hopes the meeting of Foreign Ministers of China, Japan and South Korea will create a plan for the future development of trilateral cooperation," looking ahead to the future development of trilateral cooperation and jointly maintaining regional peace and stability. According to an article in Korea's JoongAng Ilbo electronic edition of the same day, "'South Korea–China–Japan + X' Cooperation Agreement: South Korea, China and Japan Join Forces to Expand into Markets of Three Countries," at the 9th South Korea–China–Japan Foreign Ministers' Meeting. It was held at a time when the conflict between South Korea and Japan was becoming more serious, and an agreement was made to create a "South Korea–China–Japan + X" cooperation system for economic cooperation among the three countries. Currently, China and Japan are cooperating to enter the Thai market, which is a third country, but it seems that this cooperative system will be replaced by a cooperative system between South Korea, China, and Japan. The three countries emphasized the importance of unwavering cooperation among themselves.

China–Northeast Asia Expo & "The Greater Tumen Initiative"

I would like to focus not only on economic cooperation at the national level, but also on cooperation with local governments. The 13th China–Northeast Asia Expo will be held in Changchun on September 23, 2021, and the theme will be "join hands with Northeast Asian countries for new development."[11]

---

[11] Northeast Asia is often referred to as "北東アジア" (literally "northeast Asia") in Japan, but in South Korea and China it is also referred to as "東北亜" ("Tohokua"), using a traditional notation.

Ren Hongbin, Vice Minister of Commerce of China, assessed that China and Northeast Asian countries have been cooperating in economy and trade, overcoming the negative impact of the COVID-19 crisis, and showing good development momentum. Vice Minister Ren made the following specific points. First, China and Northeast Asian countries have deepened their development strategies and cooperation, building the "One Belt One Road" initiative together. They've continued to deepen their development strategy cooperation with Northeast Asian countries, such as Russia's "Eurasian Economic Union," South Korea's "New Southern" and "New Northern" policies, and Mongolia's "Steppe Road" initiative. Also, cooperative relations between China and North Korea continue to rise to a new level. The Third Country Market Cooperation between China and Japan has produced fruitful results, cooperation for connectivity in the region has made steady progress, and economic and trade cooperation between the countries continue to expand.

Second is the rapid growth of trade cooperation. China has long been the largest trading partner of the five Northeast Asian countries. In 2020, trade between China and five Northeast Asian countries was about $717.7 billion, accounting for about one-sixth of China's total trade. In the first half of 2021, trade between China and the five Northeast Asian countries totaled about $417.9 billion, up 26% from a year earlier. China–Russia and China–South Korea trade volume is expected to reach another record high this year.

Third, there has been a steady improvement in investment cooperation.

Fourth, regional cooperation continues to deepen. With the official signing of the RCEP, the level of liberalization and facilitation of intra-regional trade and investment will be further improved, the construction of the China–Mongolia–Russia Economic Corridor will be accelerated, and the "Greater Tumen Initiative" cooperation will become increasingly practical.[12] China, Japan and South Korea have made remarkable achievements in cooperation on economic and technological exchanges in the Yellow Sea Rim. The countries involved actively interacted under

[12] Tumen is in China's Jilin Province, and the Tumen River (written as "豆滿江" in Korean) borders North Korea.

multilateral frameworks such as the G20 and Shanghai Cooperation Organization (SCO) and played an important role in promoting an open global economy.

Vice Minister Ren said that the "Greater Tumen Initiative" is also an important sub-WTO plus within the region, in terms of its role in regional cooperation in Northeast Asia, with member countries including China, Mongolia, Russia and South Korea. Meanwhile, Japan mainly participates in the local government cooperation mechanism. The "Greater Tumen Initiative" focuses on strengthening the coordination of the regional development strategies of member countries and promotes cooperation among initiatives such as China's "One Belt One Road" initiative and "Northeast Revitalization Strategy," South Korea's "New Northern" and "New Southern" policies, Russia's "Eurasian Economic Union," and Mongolia's "Steppe Road" to bring synergy to the joint development of the region.

According to the website of the "Greater Tumen Initiative," it was established in 1992 as a framework for intergovernmental cooperation; instead of participating as a whole nation, however, each country designates a major administrative region to participate. Four northeastern provincial districts from China, three eastern provinces from Mongolia, three provinces and three cities from South Korea, and Russia's Primorsky Territory are all participating. North Korea has withdrawn. Japan is represented by Niigata Prefecture. The secretariat is apparently located in Beijing.

Regarding the three countries, Vice Minister Ren said that China, Japan and South Korea are neighbors, with strong economic complementarities, close industrial chains and supply chains. They are important economic and trade partners with each other. He also noted that the pandemic affected China, Japan and South Korea and the regional economy to varying degrees, and brought uncertainty to the mutual industrial chain and supply chain cooperation. However, the economic and trade cooperation between China, Japan and South Korea overcame the impact of the pandemic and grew in the opposite direction due to the joint efforts of all parties involved.

In the first half of 2021, the bilateral trade volume increased by 23.7% and 28.5% respectively, two-way investment was vigorous, showing the resilience and vigorous vitality of economic and trade cooperation among China, Japan and South Korea. The rising and continuing stability of industrial and supply chain cooperation among the three countries is also reflected in the above statements. Of course, this includes the natural reactionary effect from the pandemic, but also indicates that China is expecting to deepen economic ties, including trade, between China, Japan and South Korea and within the region.

5 Conclusion

The global economy and world trade in 2020 will be reduced in scale as mentioned above, which is a concern. Since the GDP and trade of the three countries account for about 20% of the world's total GDP and 70% of Asia's trade, they will continue to be greatly affected by the decline in the world economy and world trade, and vice versa. Japan, China, and South Korea are major trading partners with each other and have formed a close supply chain for industrial products. As the global trade environment changes drastically, close, and risk-responsive cooperation among China, Japan and Korea is still required for parts and final goods that cannot be supplied by a single country. For example, an FTA could support so-called "cross-border sub-contracting," in which small and medium-sized enterprises in Japan, China and South Korea cross national borders on a horizontal basis to order parts from each other. Also, under the rules of the FTA, there could be a beneficial system in which each company brings its own appropriate technologies and jointly develops new products. The RCEP coming into effect will improve the level of liberalization and facilitation of intra-regional trade and investment. It'll further deepen the close relationship between China, Japan and South Korea in the industrial and supply chain in the Asia-Pacific region. It is hoped that this will contribute to the economic and social cooperation among the three countries in the future. Intra-industrial trade among China, Japan and Korea has been formed as a supply chain representing trade in intermediate goods in the industrial sector. Thus, export restrictions on intermediate goods and raw materials may be applied in the short term (especially between Japan and Korea). However, in the long term, expectations for a CJK FTA should be high for all three countries. Along with the entry into force of the RCEP, this is the time when it is most necessary to proceed with negotiations for a CJK FTA that will bring added value, exceeding that of the RCEP.

In addition, the three countries would like to see joint implementation of infrastructure-related projects, even if on a small scale, in the "fourth countries" outside the region (specifically, the ASEAN countries participating in the RCEP negotiations), as soon as possible. It is expected that these multilayered movements for regional integration and economic cooperation among China, Japan and Korea will have a synergistic effect in the medium and long term, and that negotiations for a CJK FTA will progress together with the "three Countries + X" cooperation among China, Japan and Korea.

References

According to 'About the COVID-19 Vaccine' on the Prime Minister's Office website. Accessed 11 September 2022. http://www.customs.gov.cn/customs/302249/zfxxgk/2799825/302274/302275/4556778/index.html.

General Administration of Customs People's republic of China. http://www.customs.gov.cn/customs/302249/zfxxgk/2799825/302274/302275/4556778/index.html. Accessed 11 September 2022. https://www.kantei.go.jp/jp/headline/kansensho/vaccine.html.

Ministry of Finance, Japan. Accessed 21 October 2022. https://www.customs.go.jp/toukei/shinbun/trade-st/gaiyo2022_09.pdf.

Ministry of Foreign Affairs website. 2021. Regional Comprehensive Economic Partnership (RCEP) Agreement, March. https://www.mofa.go.jp/mofaj/files/000231134.pdf

Ministry of Trade, Industry and Energy, Korea. Accessed 1 October 2022. http://www.motie.go.kr/motie/ne/presse/press2/bbs/bbsView.do?bbs_seq_n=166120&bbs_cd_n=81&currentPage=191&search_key_n=title_v&cate_n=&dept_v=&search_val_v=.
The Sankei News. US-China 'Tariff War' Weighs on Global Economy, Increases Burden on US Companies, Cools Consumption. Accessed 10 May 2019. https://www.sankei.com/economy/news/190510/ecn1905100031-n1.html.
WTO STATS. Accessed 20 October 2022. https://stats.wto.org.

Part II

Regional Focus

6

Social Justice and the Response to the COVID-19 Crisis in European Countries

Jiro Mizushima

1 Introduction

"Nous sommes en guerre (We are at war)."

On March 16, 2020, as the novel coronavirus was spreading, French President Emmanuel Macron gave a televised address to the French people. He warned that the country was "at war" against the novel coronavirus and announced that a lockdown would be imposed to contain the spread of the virus. This was followed by a general prohibition of meetings and gatherings and a general ban on going out throughout France. The closure of schools and the ban on the operation of restaurants and cinemas had been already announced (Sakai 2021). As a result, in French cities, there were almost no people on the streets during the day. Police personnel were deployed on the streets to look out for violations. Going out was only allowed for reasons such as hospital visits, shopping, or commuting (for those who could not telework), and violators were fined as

J. Mizushima (✉)
Graduate School of Social Sciences, Chiba University, Chiba, Japan
e-mail: mizushima@msg.biglobe.ne.jp

H. Ishido et al. (eds.), *Social Fairness in a Post-Pandemic World*,
https://doi.org/10.1007/978-981-19-9654-2_6

much as 135 euros. As the situation around infections improved in mid-2020, various restrictions were eased, but infections began spreading again from the end of 2020, and the same lockdown policy was reinstated.

Thus, France and other European countries generally adopted strict measures against COVID-19, including lockdowns. In addition to lockdowns, mandatory mask wearing was widely implemented. In 2021, when the COVID-19 vaccine became increasingly available, some European countries began to promote vaccination through the "COVID Pass," which has been criticized as an indirect imposition of "mandatory" vaccines by the state. In the United States (US), coronavirus responses, especially in metropolitan areas, such as New York City and state, have many aspects in common with European countries, such as lockdowns and mandatory mask wearing.

In European countries and the US, where the concept of "human rights" was cherished and the respect for individual freedom seems to have taken root, it is surprising that lockdowns that strongly restrict people's freedom have been widely implemented, and that mandatory masks and vaccines have been promoted. In these countries, freedom of assembly, freedom to go out, and freedom to conduct business, etc. were restricted across the board, and people's voluntary actions were greatly restricted. In addition, despite the EU's commitment to the "free movement" of EU citizens within the EU, EU member states introduced a full range of border controls that greatly undermined that "freedom" and imposed strong restrictions on the entry of foreigners. It can be said that countries that respect freedom are actively pursuing policies that appear to undermine freedom.

These policies were developed in contrast to Japan's emphasis on "self-restraint." The Japanese government, which is believed to have interventionist bureaucracy, was reluctant to adopt mandatory measures to contain the outbreak. This "unexpected" contrast of policy outcomes between Western countries and Japan is an interesting puzzle.

This chapter looks at the impact of the pandemic on national, political, and social systems from an international comparative perspective, focusing mainly on European countries. Through comparisons and contrasts, this chapter will clarify the ways in which the state and society are organized in countries around the world (including Japan) and contribute to solve the "puzzle" mentioned above.[1]

2 International Comparison of Pandemic Response

The "Two Types of Controls" Perspective

As is well known, the disease caused by the novel coronavirus, named COVID-19, is characterized by its high risk of causing severe illness and death, especially in the elderly and people with underlying diseases, as well as by its unparalleled strength of infectivity, which can cause interpersonal infections even in asymptomatic infected people through droplet infection. If left unchecked, the spread of COVID-19 would have placed a heavy burden on healthcare systems, leading to the collapse of medical care and further increasing the number of victims. To prevent this, infection control measures that extend to the level of citizens' ordinary lives are important, and it is considered essential to bring about so-called behavioral changes among people.

However, the policy measures taken to achieve this prevention of infection in civil society have varied widely around the world (For the various types of measures, see also Greer et al. (2021)) .

Here, let us focus on the fact that there are "two types of controls," "administrative controls" and "social controls," as control means over the lives of citizens for the purpose of infection control.

First, "administrative controls" refers to direct intervention and control using administrative mechanisms, based on laws, ordinances, and other regulations. These include orders banning the operation of restaurants and other businesses, prohibiting people from going out without a valid reason, requiring people to wear masks, and requiring people to present their vaccine certificates when entering restaurants and other

[1] This work was supported by JSPS KAKENHI Grant Number JP21H04386.

establishments after the vaccine has become widely available, with violators being subject to administrative sanctions, including fines.[2]

In contrast, "social controls" refers to controls at the level of civil society, so to speak, based on "social awareness," rather than administrative mechanisms. For example, even if it is not compulsory to wear a mask, if society as a whole shares the awareness that wearing a mask is the norm, and if people feel uncomfortable about those who do not wear a mask and criticize them both covertly or overtly, individuals will feel that they are required to wear a mask whether they like it or not, and will wear a mask in most cases. There are no explicit penalties, so non-wearers will not be fined, but the majority are likely to choose to wear them for fear of being subject to some form of exclusion at the civil society level.

Focusing on the "two types of controls" described above, we can classify them into four patterns on the basis of the presence or absence of these controls as follows (Fig. 6.1). The vertical axis shows the strength of "administrative controls" and the horizontal axis shows the strength of "social controls."

Focusing on the "two types of controls" described above, we can classify them into four patterns on the basis of the presence or absence of these controls as follows (Fig. 6.1). The vertical axis shows the strength of "administrative controls" and the horizontal axis shows the strength of "social controls."

Type 1: Western Type

The first type on the upper left is a pattern of strong "administrative controls" and weak "social controls," typical of Europe and states in the US. This is a pattern of dominance of "administrative control," in which

[2] As for the strictness of measures adopted by the governments, The Oxford Coronavirus Government Response Tracker (OxCGRT) project calculated a Stringency Index, based on nine responses, such as school closures and workplace closures. A higher score indicates a stricter response (i.e. 100 = strictest response). According to this Index, when we look at the first months of the outbreak of the pandemic in the spring of 2020, the contrast is quite clear: the scores of most European countries reached 70 or more, even 93 (in case of Italy in April, 2020), and the maximum score of China was 81.02. In contrast, the maximum score of Sweden was 64.81 during that period and that of Japan was only 47.22. For Stringency Index see the site https://ourworldindata.org/covid-stringency-index (last viewed on November 7, 2022)

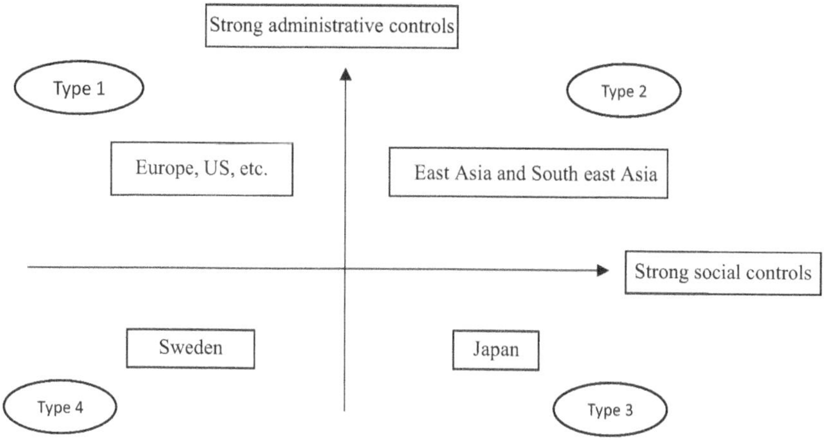

Fig. 6.1 International comparison of COVID-19 responses focusing on "two types of controls"

strong lockdowns, such as business suspensions and curfews, are used to cut off interpersonal contact and force behavioral change in accordance with the law. The specific details of the lockdown in Europe and the US include a ban on going out in principle, a ban on going out at night, a ban on business in principle, mandatory telecommuting, measures to close schools, a ban on large group gatherings, and a ban on long-distance travel (Obayashi 2021). In this pattern, "social control" is rather weak, and administrative controls come to the fore from the viewpoint that voluntary behavioral changes at the citizen level cannot prevent the spread of the disease. In fact, in many European countries, while there is a strong sense of discomfort at the citizen level regarding mask wearing, the wearing of masks has been made compulsory in order to make it more common. However, this pattern, which legitimizes the state's intervention in civil society, is strongly opposed by civil society and has triggered countermovements such as the anti-lockdown movement and the anti-vaccine movement in many countries.

What was characteristic of the EU countries in their COVID-19 response was that the introduction of border controls due to the pandemic was based on the perspective of maintaining security, in response to the "threat to public policy or domestic security" rather than "public health" (Okabe 2021, 7). In other words, border controls were introduced as a result of the pandemic being perceived as a threat to national security, a kind of "fateful crisis" of the country.

(1) type 2: East and Southeast Asian Type

The second type on the upper right is a pattern in which both "administrative controls" and "social controls" are strong, which is often seen in East and Southeast Asia (excluding Japan). China, Taiwan, South Korea and Singapore fall into this type. In these countries and regions, administrative structures (without necessarily adopting a lockdown approach) actively intervened in the lives of citizens, restricting business activities and gatherings, as well as pursuing infected people and those they had been in close contact with by tracking their individual activities, and "administrative controls" were widely implemented. Moreover, in these countries and regions, awareness of the need to prevent infection is shared at the civil society level, and violations of various rules may be subject to condemnation at the citizen level. On the surface at least, the government's firm stance to contain the infection generally received support from citizens. This East Asian pattern of coexistence of "administrative controls" and "social controls" has resulted in the lowest level of deaths per capita internationally.

(2) Type 3: Japanese Type

The third type, shown below right, is a pattern typical of Japan, in which "administrative controls" are weak and "social controls" are strong. As is well known, in Japan, although "state of emergency declarations" were often issued, they were basically only "requests." People were "asked" to refrain from going out or traveling long distances, and there was no ban on such activities. However, "self-restraint" at the citizen level has widespread, and activities such as gatherings, events, and dinners with large groups of people, which are considered to have a high risk of spreading infection, have been drastically reduced. Almost all of the restaurants and large-scale retail stores followed the requests to suspend or shorten the business hours. In Japan, The term "avoidance of the 3Cs"—confined spaces, crowds, and close-contact settings—gained popularity in usage and shared as a slogan.

Although the wearing of masks was not made compulsory, it became an extremely common phenomenon to wear masks when going out. In regions with few infections, a sense of avoidance toward visitors from other prefectures and metropolitan areas even surfaced. It can be said that "social controls" at the level of civil society operated with or beyond the intentions of the government. It is sometimes pointed out that "peer pressure" in Japanese society is behind this. In any case, in Japan, infection prevention measures were developed on the premise that "social controls" would be triggered.

As a background to this somewhat unusual response to COVID-19, in which "social controls" without "administrative controls" came to the fore, we can consider there to be an unusually strong "fear" of COVID-19 in Japanese society.

Figure 6.2 graphically depicts the fear of COVID-19 among people in different countries. The horizontal axis is time, and the vertical axis is the percentage of respondents who answered "very" or "somewhat" scared that they will contract COVID-19. The plots from top to bottom represent Japan, USA, UK, France, and Sweden respectively.

As is apparent at first glance, the number of people in Japan who were afraid of getting infected is remarkably high. To begin with, Japanese people feel a strong threat, despite the fact that the number of both infections and deaths is much lower than in Western countries, in other words, the risk of being infected is clearly lower (Ikeda 2020). Regardless of the government's policy, Japanese people share and "internalize" a sense of caution against the spread of COVID-19 at the social level.

Kenichi Ikeda (2019) detailed the strength of subjective threats in Japanese society, not only related to COVID-19. According to Ikeda, the fear of war, terrorism, and civil war is also extremely strong in Japan. Even though the objective fact is that Japan is not at a higher risk of being involved in war, terrorism, or civil war than other countries, the fear of the same is among the highest in the world. Given these facts, it can be said that Japan is a country where self-control and mutual monitoring through citizens' "fear" and "social controls" have had a certain effect, without the need to invoke strong "administrative controls."

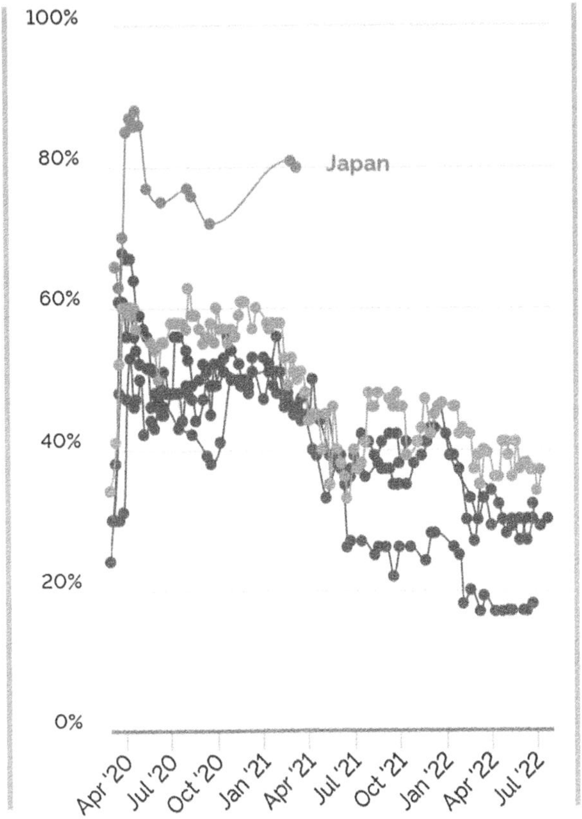

Fig. 6.2 Ratio of fear of COVID-19 (From top to bottom: Japan, USA, UK, France, and Sweden). (Source: YouGov, YouGov COVID-19 tracker: Fear of catching https://yougov.co.uk/topics/international/articles-reports/2020/03/17/fear-catching-covid-19 (last viewed on November 7, 2022))

(3) Type 4: Sweden

The final type is the fourth type on the lower left. This type of pattern is typical of Sweden, where both "administrative controls" and "social controls" are weak. As will be shown later, although measures such as the prohibition of large-scale gatherings were adopted in Sweden, compulsory measures such as curfews, suspension of business, and closure of restaurants and similar places were not basically adopted, and citizens' lives were generally similar to pre-pandemic times. Controls at the civil society level were also weak. For example, as of April 2020, when comparing people's behavioral change in Western countries (Imperial College London 2020a), only 6% of people in Sweden "always/frequently worn a face mask outside my home," which is an extremely low percentage. Thirty-eight percent "avoided working outside the home," and 50% "avoided going to shops," which is also the lowest level compared to other Western countries. The percentage of respondents who expressed fear of COVID-19 infection was also low (Fig. 6.2). As Prime Minister Löfven said, the emphasis in Sweden, which respects civil liberties, was on an "adult response" to control the spread of infection to a certain level through voluntary and autonomous prevention, rather than through coercion or pressure by the state or society. This "autonomous" course, lacking strong control measures, has led to a clearly higher mortality rate than in neighboring countries, but the country's strategy has generally been accepted by the population. Regardless of the merits or demerits of such a policy, Sweden's policy of securing civil liberties without invoking either "administrative controls" or "social controls," while accepting a certain increase in the number of deaths due to infections, can be seen as the result of a policy choice based on a certain value judgment.

(4) Scale of infection in terms of the four types

Next, what can be said about the relationship between the four types described above and the scale of COVID-19 infections? Let us take a look at Fig. 6.3 below. Figure 6.3 compares the cumulative number of deaths caused by COVID-19 per million population in each country/region, and the damage caused by the COVID-19 in each country/region is clearly visible.[3]

[3] It should be noted that given the high degree of comorbidity associated with the COVID virus, it is not easy to confirm the exact number of COVID-19 deaths. It is well known that the number of excess deaths is also useful to understand the impact of COVID-19 and it is estimated by WHO for the years 2020 and 2021. According to the estimate of WHO, the overall trend of the rate of excess deaths per country per capita corresponds to that of confirmed COVID-19 deaths: High rate of excess deaths in continental Europe, followed by Northern European countries and low rate in East and Southeast Asia, including Japan (WHO 2022)

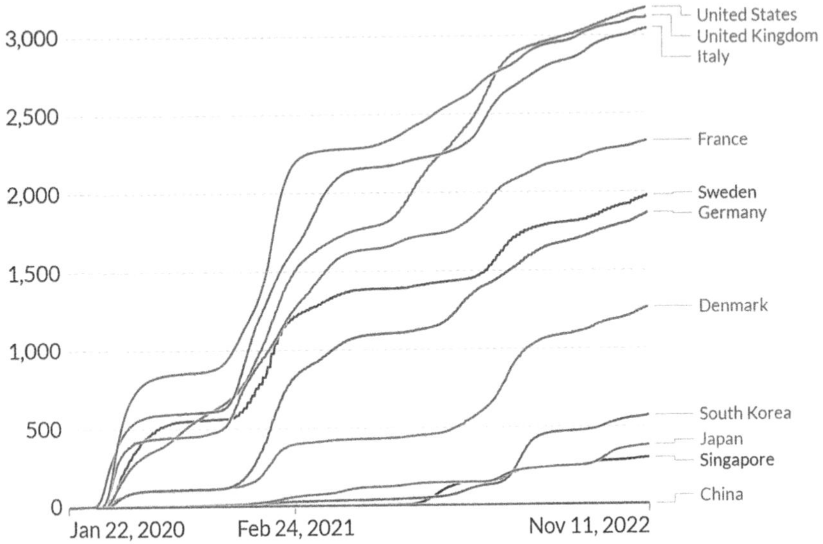

Fig. 6.3 Cumulative confirmed COVID-19 deaths per million people. [From top to bottom: USA, UK, Italy, France, Sweden, Germany, Denmark, South Korea, Japan, Singapore, China]. (Source: Our World in Data, https://ourworldindata.org/covid-deaths Mathieu et al. (2020) (Last viewed on November 11, 2022))

For example, the number of deaths in the second type (East and Southeast Asian countries) and the third type (Japan), where "social controls" are strong, is much lower than the number of deaths in the world as a whole. In fact, East and Southeast Asian countries, including Japan, are known to have generally controlled the number of deaths. Considering that behavioral changes at the citizen level, such as limiting contact with others in daily life and wearing masks, play a major role in preventing the spread of COVID-19, it is somewhat understandable that of the two types of control, in which "social controls" are strong, the damage is relatively lower.

Meanwhile, European countries belonging to the first type are characterized by an extremely high number of deaths per capita. In the case of European countries, which mainly rely on "administrative controls," it can be said that the spread of COVID-19 could not be controlled only by methods such as lockdowns, and this led to an increase in the number of victims.

In addition, it seems surprising that the number of deaths in Sweden, a country in the fourth type where both "administrative controls" and "social controls" are weak, is lower than in European countries belonging to the first type. However, the number of deaths in Sweden is exceptionally high when compared to its geographical neighbors, Norway and Denmark. It may be said that the neighboring Nordic countries, unlike Sweden, invoked "administrative controls" and chose to respond in the same way as the first type, thereby succeeding in significantly curbing the number of deaths compared to Sweden.

3 Developments in European Countries

Responses of Germany, Italy, and the United Kingdom

In the previous section, the responses of various countries to the spread of COVID-19 were compared for the sake of international comparison, focusing on the four types. This section will build on the previous discussion and closely examine the responses of European countries and then consider the issues surrounding state intervention in civil society that characterize the European COVID-19 response.

In Germany, a sense of crisis rapidly grew in mid-March 2020, following the spread of the virus. From mid to late March, Chancellor Angela Merkel and 16 state chancellors held consultations, which led to the closure of schools and daycare centers, a ban on gatherings and mandatory maintenance of social distance, restrictions on going out, a ban on the operation of restaurants, and a ban on the operation of services that involve physical contact. The basis for this was the Infectious Diseases Protection Act, which gives state governments the right to make decrees to prevent the spread of infectious diseases, and also allows them to restrict the constitutional rights of freedom (freedom of movement, freedom of assembly, etc.). The response to the outbreak, however, varied from state to state depending on the extent of infections, with severe curfews imposed in the southern states, where there were many infected people, and slightly less restrictive curfews in the relatively infection-free northern states. In Germany, the wearing of masks on public transport became compulsory in April, and a COVID-19 contact verification app was introduced in June (for the policy development in Germany, see also Yokota (2022)).

In Germany, Chancellor Merkel, who is also a scientist, emphasized her professional and scientific knowledge and responded to COVID-19 through "reading and understanding of information" (Morii 2021: 118), and gave a televised speech to the public in which she spoke of the need for strict infection prevention measures in her own words. For example, in a speech on March 18, 2020, Chancellor Merkel described the situation in March as the most serious national crisis since World War II and sought public understanding by stating that restrictions on individual mobility were necessary to prevent the collapse of healthcare due to the spread of infection. By appealing to both intellect and emotions, Chancellor Merkel succeeded in establishing effective communication with the people and winning their support.

In Italy, where COVID-19 first spread in Europe and the number of infected people increased rapidly, a strict lockdown was implemented in March 2020 (Yasoda 2021). The first cluster is believed to have occurred in the town of Codogno near Milan and the spread of the disease was particularly pronounced in northern Italy, in the regions of Lombardy and Veneto, where commerce and industry are well developed. The lockdown was initially imposed in the northern part of the country and then extended to the rest of the country, and it was decided that curfews would be imposed, schools would be closed for extended periods of time, bars and other food businesses would be shut down, stores (except supermarkets and pharmacies) would be closed, and interstate travel would be banned. The government made extensive use of "legal decrees" or "Prime ministerial decrees," which are timed delegated legislation, to enable emergency responses. Italy, in particular, has a weaker healthcare system than other European countries, and a lack of healthcare infrastructure is believed to be behind the high fatality rate, especially in the early stages of the pandemic. In some respects, the implementation of strict lockdowns may have barely compensated for the fragile healthcare system. In October

2020, the wearing of masks outdoors was made compulsory in view of the renewed spread of COVID-19 that autumn.

Initially, some European countries tried to come to "coexist" with COVID-19 while also suppressing it, keeping restrictions on social life to a certain extent, and yet keeping away from a hard line of lockdown measures and strict border controls, as in France and Italy. Britain and the Netherlands belong to this group. The United Kingdom (UK) initially took the "herd immunity" route, stating that "when 60% of the British population were infected, herd immunity would be achieved" (Ikemoto 2021: 292), but the first wave of infections resulted in a large number of deaths, mainly among elderly people in nursing homes, making the UK the worst-hit in terms of deaths in Europe. In the UK, no quarantine measures were initially taken for people entering the country, and this is also believed to have contributed to the worsening of the infection rate in the country as people who entered the UK from countries where COVID-19 was widespread during the early stages of the pandemic did not have a required quarantine period. In fact, Prime Minister Boris Johnson showed little interest in the issue of COVID-19 and attended few relevant meetings. The idea of concern about the impact of restrictions on economic activity seems to have been strong.

However, even in the UK, the need for a change in policy became apparent, and a nationwide lockdown was implemented in late March. There were subsequent announcements that stores other than those selling daily necessities would be closed, meetings would be banned, restaurants would be closed, and going out would be banned except for once-a-day exercise and the purchase of daily necessities (in the UK, public health policies vary according to region in England, Scotland, Wales, and Northern Ireland).

(5) Sweden's response

In Sweden, COVID-19 spread mainly in Stockholm and other large cities in March 2020 (Yoshitake 2021). From that month onwards, large gatherings were banned and visits to elderly people's homes were banned. In November, additional measures were put in place, including a ban on events and gatherings of more than eight people.

However, Sweden's response was extremely lax compared to that of its neighboring country, Denmark, which had already taken large-scale measures as early as March 11, such as closing schools, placing civil servants on home leave, and closing various public facilities and restaurants. There were few prohibitions in the daily lives of citizens: recommendations were the main focus, and no severe restrictions were imposed. No measures were taken to close elementary and middle schools, and although social distancing in restaurants was encouraged, shops basically remained open, shopping was possible as usual, and bars and restaurants were open. The situation was in stark contrast to Denmark.

In a speech on March 22, Prime Minister Löfven called on people to fulfill their responsibilities and to "behave like adults." As argued by Nobuhiko Yoshitake, a researcher of Nordic politics, it can be said that Sweden's countermeasures aimed to "control infection with moderate measures, avoid medical collapse, and prevent infection based on people's self-responsibility, so that citizens' lives and economic activities could be maintained" (Yoshitake 2021: 167). Wearing masks was not mandatory and was left to voluntary decisions.

Behind this distinctive Swedish path was also the support of the public. There was also a high level of confidence in the Public Health Agency, which is responsible for infection response. The Public Health Agency held a press conference every day at a regular time and provided information based on scientific findings on the daily infection situation, thereby accurately providing information to the public and gaining their trust.

In contrast, the number of deaths from COVID-19 per capita in Sweden was clearly higher than in the neighboring countries of Denmark and Norway. Neighboring countries were wary of the infection situation in Sweden, and even in the summer of 2020, when the infection rate had decreased somewhat and border closures in neighboring countries had begun to be lifted, they took measures to delay the lifting of the closures for Sweden, which had a high number of infected people.

A particular problem was that the deaths were concentrated among the elderly. It is significant that the infection spread to elderly facilities through caregivers. In response to the spread of infections, King Carl XVI Gustaf, aged 74, made a statement at the end of 2020 criticizing the government's COVID-19 response as "a failure." The king's direct criticism of government policy was unusual and drew much attention.

Intervention in the Lives of Citizens

There were also differences between countries in whether citizens wore masks and whether they were mandatory.

According to a survey conducted in May–June 2000 (Imperial College London and YouGov 2020), the percentage of respondents who answered, "Very willing" or "Quite willing" to the question, "How willing or not are you to wear a face mask or covering if international organizations advised it?," was over 80% across the board in East and Southeast Asian countries, including Vietnam, the Philippines, China, Singapore, and Thailand. In contrast, among European countries, Italy and Spain exceeded 80%, while Germany, the US, the UK, and France were only at 60%–70%, and Sweden and Denmark were only in the 40% range (Japan is not included here).

A survey conducted between April and October 2020 on mask wearing also reveals changes that occurred over that six-month period, with particularly interesting results (Imperial College London 2020b). In response to the question, "Thinking about the last 7 days, how often have you worn a mask outside your home?," the percentage of those who answered, "Always" in East and Southeast Asian countries generally reached 70% or more as of April, and the percentage increased slightly through October. (In China, however, the percentage of those who always wear masks has been declining.) In contrast, in many European countries (excluding Northern Europe), "Always," was less than 50% in April, but it has risen significantly throughout 2020, reaching a level comparable to East and Southeast Asian countries as of October. The UK stands out in terms of this change in mask-wearing rates, with the percent of mask-wearing shoppers in grocery stores showing a remarkable increase of 67% between June and October. In contrast, in Sweden and other Nordic countries, the percentage of respondents who answered, "Always," throughout 2020 was only in the single digits (the Netherlands also had a low percentage of "Always," after Nordic countries).

However, the obligation to wear masks have been crucial to the rise in mask-wearing rates in the UK and other European countries over the last six months. In the summer of 2020 in the England, the wearing of masks on public transport, in medical institutions, and in shops, including supermarkets, became compulsory and fines for violators came into effect. The impact of mandatory mask wearing in shops in late July was particularly significant, with the wearing rate in the UK rising by more than 30% over ten days in late July alone. Conversely, this indicates that it would have been extremely difficult to achieve a significant increase in mask wearing rates without a state mandate.

The same is true of the issues surrounding vaccination. The EU Digital COVID Certificate became operational in July 2021. It certifies that the person has been vaccinated or has tested negative. Although the method of use differs from country to country, France, Italy, Spain, the Netherlands, and other countries require that the card be presented when entering restaurants and facilities, and when using public transportation. Although there has been no enforcement of a mandatory vaccine for the general public, there is no doubt that non-vaccinated people find it difficult to go about their daily lives, which provides a strong impetus for vaccination. Some countries also make vaccination compulsory for certain professions, including healthcare workers.

Resistance by Civil Society

However, the strong state interventions in civil society in European countries, such as curfews, compulsory wearing of masks, and "mandatory" vaccinations, has been strongly opposed by society. Counter-movements that are anti-lockdown and against COVID-19 policies have been gaining support in various countries since mid-2020, and not a small number of them have become violent.

The Netherlands, in particular, is known as a country that respects civil liberties, but has implemented relatively strict "administrative controls" to contain the outbreak, resulting in a large gap between the two ideals, and counter-movements against COVID-19 measures have often formed. Those who see the policy measures against COVID-19 as "repression by state power" and "dictatorship through medicine" have often staged protests. "I want to be responsible for my own health...the government is treating us like kindergarten children," said one participant in a demonstration (AD, July 24, 2021).

The Netherlands is characterized by a diverse range of sectors criticizing the government's COVID-19 response and calling for deregulation. In August 2021, for example, the entertainment industry aligned itself and staged a nationwide demonstration with the participation of hundreds of organizations and operational entities. The governing body of the internationally renowned North Sea Jazz Festival also joined in. A total of 70,000 people took part in the demonstrations in Amsterdam, Rotterdam, Utrecht, and other cities.

As a result of widespread vaccination in the country, from September 2021, people in the Netherlands are required to present a "COVID entry pass" when visiting restaurants, cultural facilities, and attending events, but this has also been met with strong opposition. One opposition lawyer lamented that "for the first time since the World War II, first- and second-class citizens have emerged in the Netherlands," and criticized the fact that non-vaccinated people are being targeted. Discourse often compares the harsh measures to curb the spread of COVID-19 in the Netherlands to the repression of the German occupation during World War II, leading to criticism of the "COVID Gestapo" (NRC, September 21, 2021).

4 The Political Transformation Brought About by the Pandemic: The Re-emergence of National Politics

Introduction of Border Controls

As we have seen, countries have stepped up state intervention in response to the spread of COVID-19, but the political transformation caused by the pandemic is not limited to that. This section focuses on the "re-emergence of national politics" and considers it from several perspectives.

First, there is the issue of border control. In the EU, the right to free movement within the EU is recognized as a right of EU citizenship, and many of the member states constitute an intra-regional free movable space known as the Schengen area. However, as a result of the spread of COVID-19, the survival of this right to free movement was threatened and so was the principle of solidarity, which is the joint management of the borders of the EU by the member states (Okabe 2021: 3). In March 2020, the EU banned traffic between the Schengen area and the outside world, while guaranteeing free movement within the area for internal citizens, but many EU countries had already introduced their own national border controls in response to the pandemic. In the EU, regarding the policy on the movement of people, it has been emphasized that EU policy is generally accepted by the member states and is equally enforced in all the member states. However, the principle of "solidarity" was undermined by the imposition of individual border controls in each country that emphasized prompt response. Even Germany, the core country of the EU, decided to introduce border controls immediately. Some countries, such as the Netherlands, have opened their borders to EU citizens and citizens of the Schengen area. Nevertheless, many of the countries that did not introduce border controls were small countries, and the introduction of border controls by each of the influential countries caused a major impediment to the mobility of people within the EU.

Recovery Fund

In the middle of 2020, the internal EU conflict over the European recovery fund also surfaced. It is a common understanding that large-scale fiscal mobilization is required in EU countries to deal with pandemics. Already as of March, the EU had decided to activate the general escape clause of the Stability and Growth Pact, which requires each country to have fiscal discipline, and has allowed the shelving of fiscal discipline for each country (Morii 2021: 120–121). Nevertheless, in the case of Italy and Spain, which were hit particularly hard by COVID-19, the shelving of fiscal discipline alone is unlikely to be sufficient to deal with the economic crisis caused by COVID-19, as these countries were in a difficult fiscal situation to begin with.

In response to this, a European recovery fund was proposed, which would provide support to countries in southern Europe with weak financial foundations and help Europe as a whole to recover. Moreover, on this occasion, Germany, which had been critical of the "profligate budgeting" of southern European countries during the eurozone crisis and had demanded the first draft of austerity measures from southern European countries, changed its stance and tried to actively respond to and support the southern European countries suffering from the spread of COVID-19, which can be said to be an important "policy shift" in Germany (Morii 2021: 121). In May and June 2020, a blueprint for a recovery fund was drawn up around an agreement between France and Germany, and the EU Commission proposed the establishment of a 750 billion euro recovery fund around this blueprint. Of that 750 billion euros, 500 billion would be issued as non-repayable grants and 250 billion would be loans.

However, it was the small countries of the "North" that stood in the way. The four countries of the Netherlands, Sweden, Denmark, and Austria formed a scrum (known as the "frugal four") and opposed the implementation of massive financial support from the standpoint of fiscal discipline. They argued that it should be based on loans rather than grants. The spearhead of the four nations was the Netherlands, led by Prime Minister Rutte. The Netherlands argued that recipient countries of the recovery fund should be required to implement domestic reforms in pensions, taxation, labor, and other areas, to which French President Macron and German Chancellor Merkel both expressed their discomfort. Spanish Prime Minister Sánchez criticized the inappropriateness of combining the recovery fund with a "different set of policies." Italian Prime Minister Conte strongly opposed Rutte, saying, "it is an insult not only to the European Commission, but to all of us" (Yasoda 2021: 102). Furthermore, Hungarian Prime Minister Orbán even described the Dutch stance as the same as the methods of the former communist regime (The Guardian, July 20, 2020).

The Logic of the "Frugal Four"

Behind the hardline stance of the frugal four countries was the thought that if they were to easily approve financial assistance to the "southern" countries, it might invite criticism from within their own countries. In the Netherlands, for example, a "soft" response to the southern countries ahead of the general elections in the spring of 2021 could have led to criticism, especially from right-wing populist parties. In that sense, the opposition by the frugal four nations was in part a "pose" for domestic relations. One EU diplomat commented on this inward-looking approach, saying that "The Dutch have never cared about having a pretty face in these talks," and described it as follows. "They come to Brussels to defend their national interest." "They irritate many because their bluntness can be seen as arrogance." (Financial Times, July 9, 2020) The situation was similar in Sweden. In Sweden, it was not easy to justify the transfer of subsidies to countries in the south while imposing a heavy tax burden on the population and requiring a large budget for the response to COVID-19, and "it was inevitable that the opposition would object to this plan" (Yoshitake 2021: 172). In July 2020, after a long summit meeting, the total amount of the recovery fund was kept at 750 billion euros as originally proposed, but certain concessions were made at the insistence of the frugal four countries: the amount of subsidies was reduced from 500 billion euros to 390 billion euros, and the amount of loans was increased from 250 billion euros to 360 billion euros (Yoshitake 2021: 170–172). In the end, there was unanimous approval to introduce a recovery fund.

Conflicts also arose on a different level over the recovery fund. Sweden and other countries insisted that the payment of the European recovery fund be conditional on the "rule-of-law" in the recipient countries, but this was opposed by Poland and Hungary, which continued to criticize the EU over the "rule-of-law" (Yoshitake 2021: 172). In the end, Poland and Hungary agreed that the decision on the "rule-of-law" would be left to the European Court of Justice.

Vaccine War

The UK government announced in July 2020 that it would not participate in the EU's joint procurement of COVID-19 vaccines. This was due to the fact that vaccine development was already progressing in the UK, and participation in joint procurement meant that it could not negotiate individually with pharmaceutical companies, in addition to the fact that it had no say in the governance of joint procurement (Ikemoto 2021: 298). Having chosen this unique route, the UK was the first country in the world to approve a vaccine co-developed by Pfizer (USA) and BioNTech (Germany) and began vaccinations on December 9, 2020. They also approved vaccines from AstraZeneca (UK) and Moderna (USA) (it should be noted that the early approval of this vaccine is not directly related to the UK's withdrawal from the EU's joint procurement) (Ikemoto 2021: 297).

Meanwhile, in the EU, the problem of delayed vaccine supply emerged in 2021. In late January, it was revealed that mass production at AstraZeneca's plant in the EU would be delayed, and, separately, that production at Pfizer's and BioNTech's plants in Belgium would also be reduced (Ueta 2021b: 77). The EU side criticized AstraZeneca for the delay in supply, and put restrictions on vaccine exports outside the EU, in a desperate attempt to secure the vaccine.

As a result, there was marked contrast in the situation between the EU and the UK, which was well ahead in terms of vaccination. While the conflict of interest between the EU and the UK over vaccines stopped short of becoming an all-out conflict, there was talk that this was immediately before the outbreak of the "Vaccine War."

Pandemics in the Age of Populism

Finally, let us consider the relationship between the pandemic and populism, which has been gaining momentum in many countries in recent years. Right-wing populist forces are strengthening their presence with their radical criticism of immigrants and refugees and their "home country first" policies. How has this populism, which symbolizes national politics so to speak, developed with the spread of COVID-19?

On the one hand, there were populist forces who saw the pandemic as an opportunity to gain further support. In France, for example, where the death toll was high and the government's response to COVID-19 was viewed as problematic, Marine Le Pen of the National Rally, a populist critic of the government, succeeded to some extent in gaining support. In the presidential elections and general elections in 2022, Marine Le Pen and the National Rally were quite successful in gaining more support than the previous elections. In Italy, the government led by Prime Minister Draghi was supported by a large coalition of left and right powers, but his increasingly technocratic government has issued a series of COVID-19 responses by government ordinances, which normally would not be the case, and under these circumstances, the right-wing populist opposition, Brothers of Italy, has expanded its support base. In the general elections in September 2022, Brothers of Italy became the largest party in parliament and in October the party's leader, Giorgia Meloni, was sworn in as the prime minister.

On the other hand, populist leaders who have succeeded in gaining support and rising to power by appealing to popular sentiment and criticizing the established elite tend to disregard scientific knowledge and adhere to a political style in which they speak face-to-face with people. As is well known, US President Trump has repeatedly made statements downplaying the threat of COVID-19 and he was indecisive about preventing infection. This passive stance on the part of the federal government has been criticized by many quarters for contributing to the explosive spread of COVID-19 infections in the US, which leads the world in total deaths, and was subsequently said to have contributed to Trump's defeat in the presidential election in the fall of 2020. A similar case is the defeat of Bolsonaro in the presidential election in Brazil in the fall of 2022, after his refusal to recognize the threat of COVID-19 and his preference for going out to speak with his supporters without wearing a mask.

In this way, even if there is a "re-emergence" of national politics, it is not clear whether this will immediately lead to the political expansion of populist forces.

5 Conclusion

In this chapter, four types of COVID-19 responses have been presented from the perspective of international comparison and examined with an emphasis on Europe. What, then, does the discussion in this chapter suggest about the nature of "fairness"?

The first type (European countries) and the third type (Japan), which are located at opposite ends of the spectrum with respect to COVID-19 response, differ in the way in which the issues surrounding "fairness" and "unfairness" appear. First of all, in Japan, where the request for "self-restraint" became the core of infection control measures without a clear obligation, if people had a sense of "unfairness," it was because of the "unfairness" of the situation in relation to others, such as "someone is behaving without complying with the request for self-restraint" or "everyone is wearing a mask, but this person isn't." In contrast, in Europe, if there was an object to be criticized as "unfair," it was above all state power that forcibly restricted people's freedom, and governments that exercised power unilaterally without regard to the will of their citizens. It can be said that the framework for considering "unfairness" under the pandemic differed depending on the type. The result is mutual surveillance in Japan based on nonverbal understanding, and clashes in Europe between obvious state power and citizens.

In view of the fact that more unusual events, whether they are pandemics or disasters, are likely to occur in the future, it may be necessary for Japan to ensure a sense of "fairness" by clarifying relevant rules, and for Europe to restore a sense of "fairness" through careful communication based on dialogue and mutual understanding between state and various actors in civil society. COVID-19 poses a serious challenge in terms of "fairness" and "unfairness."

References

AD, July 24, 2021. Duizenden mensen demonstreren tegen coronamaatregelen. https://www.ad.nl/binnenland/duizenden-mensen-demonstreren-tegen-coronamaatregelen~ac9c6081/?referrer=https%3A%2F%2Fwww.google.com%2F. Accessed 4 Nov 2022.

Financial Times. July 9, 2020. Dutch Resistance Stands in Way of Deal on EU Recovery Fund. https://www.ft.com/content/13c622ad-9b1b-44ca-8054-206841c77a18. Accessed 12 November 2022.

Greer, Scott, et al., eds. 2021. *Coronavirus Politics: The Comparative Politics and Policy of COVID-19*. Ann Arbor: University of Michigan Press.

Ikeda, Kenichi. 2019. *Uncertainty of Governance and Reality of Japanese Politics: Undercurrents and International Comparative Contexts Before and After the Change of Government*. Bokutaku-sha.

———. 2020. *Virtual Empathy Overcomes 'Uncertainty of Governance'*. PHP Research Institute, https://thinktank.php.co.jp/voice/6429/. Accessed 1 November 2022.

Ikemoto, Daisuke. 2021. The UK: The COVID-19 Crisis that Accelerated Change. In *The COVID-19 Crisis and Europe: The EU, Its Ten Member States, and the UK's Response*, ed. Takako Ueta, 286–304. Bunshindo.

Imperial College London. 2020a. *Covid-19 and Behaviours in Sweden*.

———. 2020b. *Covid-19: Global Behaviours around Face Mask Use*.

Imperial College London and YouGov. 2020. *Covid 19: Insights on Face Mask Use Global Review*.

Mathieu, Edouard, Hannah Ritchie, Lucas Rodés-Guirao, Cameron Appel, Charlie Giattino, Joe Hasell, Bobbie Macdonald, Saloni Dattani, Diana Beltekian, Esteban Ortiz-Ospina, and Max Roser. 2020. *Coronavirus Pandemic (COVID-19)*. Published online at OurWorldInData.org. https://ourworldindata.org/coronavirus [Online Resource].

Morii, Yuichi. 2021. Germany: The Importance of Its Role in the EU. In *The COVID-19 Crisis and Europe*, ed. Ueta, 112–131.

NRC. September, 2021. Een hele zwik aan grondrechten wordt voor ongevaccineerden bij het grofvuil gezet. https://www.nrc.nl/nieuws/2021/09/23/een-hele-zwik-aan-grondrechten-wordt-voor-ongevaccineerden-bij-het-grofvuil-gezet-a4059530. Accessed 10 November 2021.

Obayashi, Keigo. 2021. Memorandum on the Constitutional Problems of the COVID-19: Focusing on Lockdown and Vaccine. *Chiba University Law Review* 36 (2): 59–94.

Okabe, Midori. 2021. The COVID-19 Crisis and the Synchronization of EU Border Controls: Focusing on the Future of EU Citizenship and Solidarity. In *The COVID-19 Crisis and Europe*, ed. Ueta, 3–21.

Sakai, Kazunari. 2021. France: The Macron Regime on Trial and the Quest for EU Solidarity. In *The COVID-19 Crisis and Europe*, ed. Ueta, 132–153.

The Guardian. July 20, 2020. EU Leaders in Bitter Clash Over Covid-19 Recovery Package. https://www.theguardian.com/world/2020/jul/19/eu-leaders-extra-time-tempers-fray-coronavirus-recovery-summit-angela-merkel-emmanuel-macron. Accessed 7 November 2022.

Ueta, Takako, ed. 2021a. *The COVID-19 Crisis and Europe: The EU, Its Ten Member States, and the UK's Response*. Bunshindo.

———. 2021b. The COVID-19 Crisis and EU Integration: The Development of Strengthening Integration through Trials. In *The COVID-19 Crisis and Europe*, ed. Ueta, 45–85.

World Health Organization. 2022. Global Excess Deaths Associated with COVID-19, January 2020–December 2021 https://www.who.int/data/stories/global-excess-deaths-associated-with-covid-19-january-2020-december-2021. Accessed 4 November 2022.

Yasoda, Hiroto. 2021. Italy: Focus on the Response After the Recognition of the Situation. In *The COVID-19 Crisis and Europe*, ed. Ueta, 89–111.

Yokota, Akemi. 2022. *The COVID-19 Crisis, Lawmaking and Administration: The Multistage Revision of the Infectious Diseases Protection Act*. Kobundo.

Yoshitake, Nobuhiko. 2021. Sweden: Between an Independent Path and EU Cooperation. In *The COVID-19 Crisis and Europe*, ed. Ueta, 154–176.

7

Well-being and Fairness in the COVID-19 Crisis in Japan: Insights from Positive Political Psychology

Masaya Kobayashi

1 Positive Political Psychology

This chapter is one of the products of studies that attempt to bridge the gap between political/public philosophy and positive psychology. Positive psychology is an empirical and scientific branch that focuses on studying positive human psychological states. This research has led to the proposal of an empirical political psychology called "positive political psychology."[1]

[1] Masaya Kobayashi "Political Philosophies and Positive Political Psychology: Inter-Disciplinary Framework for the Common Good," *Frontiers in Psychology*, no. 12, 2021; M. Kobayashi, "Psychological Examination of Political Philosophies: Interrelationship Among Citizenship, Justice, and Well-Being in Japan," *Frontiers in Psychology*, no. 12, 2022.

M. Kobayashi (✉)
Graduate School of Social Sciences, Chiba University, Chiba, Japan
e-mail: masaya_kobayashi@nifty.com

H. Ishido et al. (eds.), *Social Fairness in a Post-Pandemic World*,
https://doi.org/10.1007/978-981-19-9654-2_7

So then, this chapter will discuss "Well-being and Fairness in the COVID-19 Crisis" from this perspective.[2]

Our research team has recently conducted three empirical studies (2020–2021) that observed happiness or well-being, and since the world is amid the COVID-19 pandemic, these measured its impact. Since happiness has multiple meanings, the concept of well-being is often used in scientific research. The following is a brief overview of the results.

Martin Seligman, the founder of positive psychology, proposed a multi-dimensional theory of well-being in *Flourish: A Visionary New Understanding of Happiness and Well-being* (2011), and it has become one of the standard theories. His PERMA model measures human well-being in five dimensions: P for positive emotion, E for engagement, R for relationships, M for meaning, and A for accomplishments.[3]

2 The Decline of Well-being during the COVId-19 Crisis

I first present an analysis of the results from Survey 1 conducted by Mitsubishi Research Institute with my collaboration in June 2020. This was a survey of 5000 people (Table 7.1) and was done at the initial stage when the issue of COVID-19 first became severe; therefore, we examined the changes in individuals' perceived subjective well-being.

The second and third surveys were conducted in March 2021 and at the end of October 2021 as part of our research project on fairness, and common questions were incorporated into the survey questions so that there would be continuity with the 2000 survey. These included 6885 and 2658 respondents, respectively (Table 7.1). Then, we examined how

[2] A related paper concerning COVID-19 is: Masaya Kobayashi, Hikari Ishido, Jiro Mizushima and Hirotaka Ishikawa, "Multi-Dimensional Dynamics of Psychological Health Disparities under the COVID-19 in Japan: Fairness/Justice in Socio-Economic and Ethico-Political Factors," *International Journal of Environmental Research and Public Health*, 2022. This paper (Sect. 4.1) briefly explains the concrete situation of development of COVID-19 crisis in Japan.

[3] Martin E.P.Seligman, Flourish: A Visionary New Understanding of Happiness *and Well-being*, New York, Free Press, 2011, especially, Ch.1.

Table 7.1 Attribution (Survey1.2.3)

	Survey 1 (%)	Survey 2 (%)	Survey 3 (%)
N	5000	6885	2658
Number of questions	383	401	174
Residence			
prefecture with big cities*	3780 (75.6)	2435 (35.4)	1181 (44.4)
prefecture without big cities	1220 (24.4)	4450 (64.6)	1477 (55.6)
Sex			
Male	2500 (50.0)	4427 (64.3)	1759 (66.2)
Female	2500 (50.0)	2458 (35.7)	899 (33.8)
Age			
10s	833 (16.6)	37 (0.5)	7 (0.3)
20s	833 (16.6)	460 (6.7)	132 (5.0)
30s	833 (16.6)	1043 (15.1)	374 (14.1)
40s	833 (16.6)	1738 (25.1)	665 (25.0)
50s	833 (16.6)	1750 (25.4)	681 (25.6)
60s	833 (16.6)	1238 (18.0)	506 (19.0)
70's and above		619 (9.0)	293 (1.0)
Marriage			
Married	2294 (45.9)	4091 (59.4)	1505 (56.6)
Unmarried	2469 (49.4)	2254 (32.7)	923 (34.7)
Parting bereavement	237 (4.7)	540 (7.9)**	230 (8.6)***
Occupation			
Executive, executive of association	46 (0.9)	124 (11.8)	57 (2.1)
Office worker, staff of association	1513 (30.3)	2097 (30.5)	782 (29.4)
Part-time employee, contract employee, dispatched labor	248 (5.0)	410 (6.0)	172 (6.5)
Part-time worker, part-time job, home-based workers without an employment contract	586 (11.7)	806 (11.7)	306 (11.5)

(continued)

Table 7.1 (continued)

	Survey 1 (%)	Survey 2 (%)	Survey 3 (%)
Civil servants	153 (3.1)	257 (3.7)	73 (2.7)
Self-employed, family employee, free lance	302 (6.0)	822 (11.9)	322 (12.1)
Faculty member		123 (1.8)	42 (1.6)
Student	837 (16.7)	96 (1.4)	28 (1.1)
Homemaker	718 (14.4)	767 (11.1)	305 (11.5)
Pensioner	151 (3.0)	603 (8.8)	277 (10.4)
None	393 (7.9)	693 (10.1)	273 (10.3)
Other	53 (1.1)	87 (1.3)	21 (0.8)
Education			
While in high school	373 (7.5)	43 (0.6)	7 (0.3)
Currently enrolled in a vocational or special training school	80 (1.6)	84 (1.2)	28 (1.1)
Currently enrolled in a junior college or technical high school	49 (1.0)	47 (0.7)	9 (0.3)
Currently enrolled in a preparatory school	15 (0.3)	4 (0.7)	0 (0.0)
Currently enrolled in a four-year college or university	381 (7.6)	89 (1.3)	39 (1.5)
Enrolled in a master's or doctoral program at a graduate school	25 (0.5)	19 (0.3)	3 (0.1)
Junior high school graduate or old elementary school graduate	73 (1.5)	175 (2.5)	54 (2.0)
High school graduate/old junior high school graduate	1069 (21.4)	2164 (31.4)	724 (27.2)
Vocational college, Specialized Training College graduated	389 (7.8)	644 (9.4)	264 (9.9)
Junior college/technical college graduate	418 (8.4)	598 (8.7)	231 (8.7)
4-year university graduate	1912 (38.2)	2669 (38.8)	1152 (43.3)
Completed master's/doctoral course or withdrew with credits	216 (4.3)	349 (5.1)	147 (5.5)

Notes: *The ordinance-designated cities in Japan (concerning surveys in this study) were Sapporo, Sendai, Saitama, Yokohama, special wards, Niigata, Nagoya, Osaka, **divorce 418 (6.1)/death 121 (1.8). ***divorce 161 (6.5)/death 47 (1.9)

well-being and other factors had changed at these points compared to the first study.

First, the three shaded bars in Fig. 7.2A show the results of the PERMA profiler form[4] (three questions for each) in Survey 1 and the Fairness Research Survey (Surveys 2 and 3). This comparison shows that there is no significant difference between Survey 1 and Survey 2, but there is a slight decrease in the average of PERMA and general well-being (the overall measure of well-being) and a slight increase in positive emotion and engagement, but a decrease in the other "relationship, meaning, achievement, and health" items.

Survey 2 does not ask about the situation related to COVID-19 itself; rather, it focuses on well-being in general. So, it is understandable that there is little general change compared to the previous year. However, compared to the well-being of a year earlier, we can see that it has fallen slightly. Moreover, when we collate the results of Survey 1 (Fig. 7.1), which asked about the mental state during the COVID-19 crisis, it (after, in Fig. 7.1) is the lowest of the three. In other words, it can be confirmed that the COVID-19 problem has worsened people's well-being and other psychological conditions (Figs. 7.2A and 7.2B).

Furthermore, the rightmost bar in Survey 3 (Fig. 7.2B) shows that PERMA average, general well-being, and each of the other items have all decreased, and that the degree of decrease from Survey 2 is considerably greater than in 'Survey 1→Survey 2'. In other words, the decreasing trend of well-being has continued, and it has become larger over a more extended period of time.

Next, the following graph shows the results of the three surveys regarding the I COPPE scale, devised by Isaac Prilleltensky (University of Miami).[5] This scale is a questionnaire that examines multi-dimensional well-being in various domains of life. Each of the items in the graph in Fig. 7.3 represents overall well-being (OVE: overall), inter-personal well-being (INT: inter-personal), community well-being (COM: community),

---

[4] Butler, J., and Kern, M. L. (2016). The PERMA-profiler: a brief multi-dimensional measure of flourishing. *International Journal of Wellbeing* 6, 1–48.

[5] Prilleltensky, I., Dietz, S., Prilleltensky, O., Myers, N.D., Rubenstein, C.L. Jin, Y., and McMahon, A (2015). Assessing Multidimensional Well-being: Development and Validation of the I COPPE Scale, *Journal of Community Psychology*, 43, n. 2, 199–226.

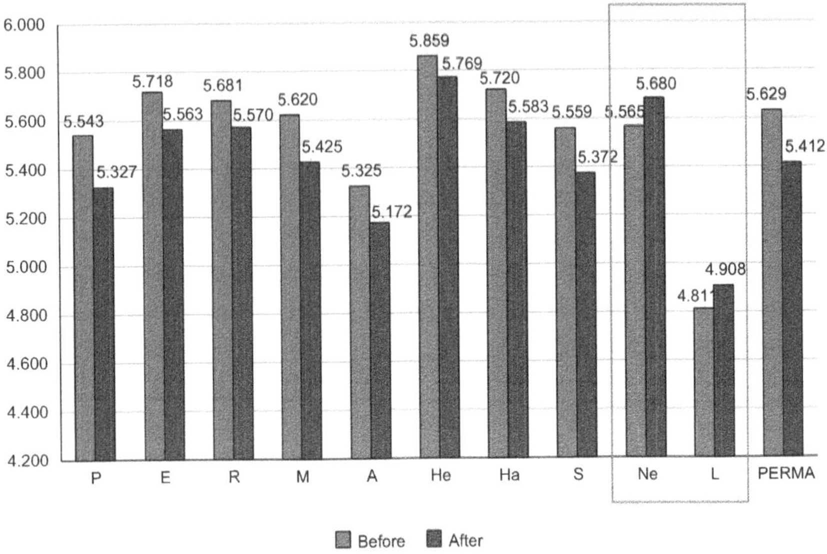

Note: P(positive emotion), E(engagement), R(positive relationship), M(meaning), A(achievement), He(health), Ha(happiness), S(satisfaction), Ne(negative emotion), L(loneliness). The rectanglular box indicates that conditions 'after' are worse that 'before' because high values concerning negative emotion and loneliness indicate undesirable situations. PERMA signifies the average of (P+E+R+M+A).

Fig. 7.1 Subjective Well-being changes before and after COVID-19 (Survey1: May 2020)

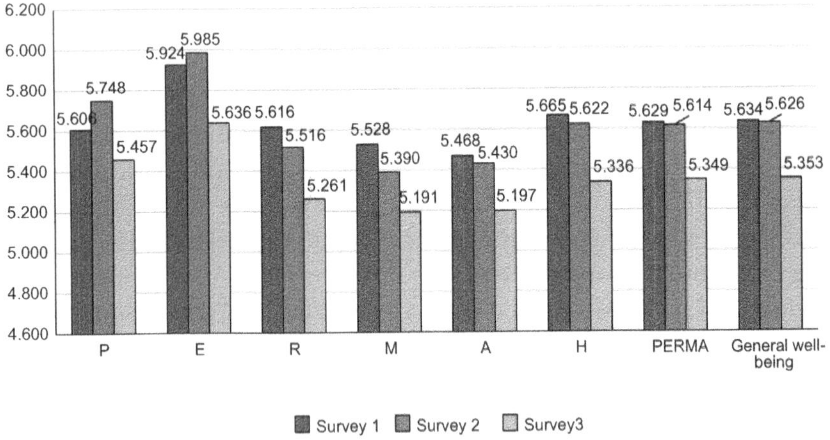

Note: General well-being was calculated as the average of (P+E+R+M+A+Hap). See note of Figure 7.1.

Fig. 7.2A Comparison of three surveys (PERMA indicator)

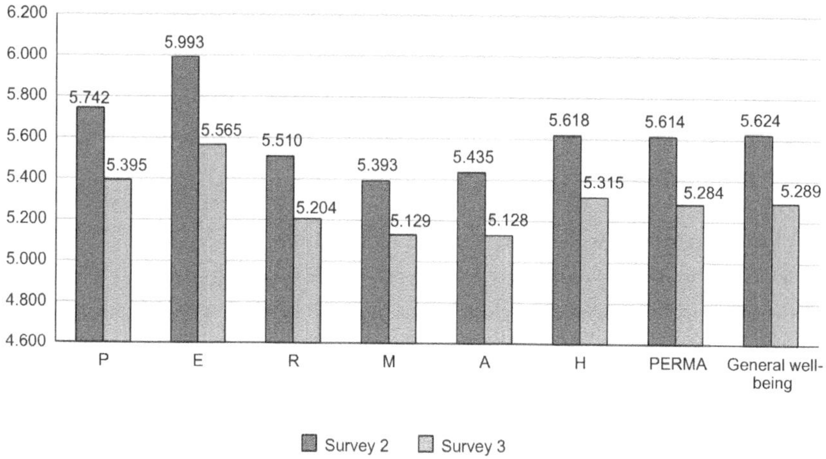

Note: See the note of Fig. 7.2.

Fig. 7.2B Comparison of means (PERMA index) for the same respondents (N1738) in Surveys 2 and 3

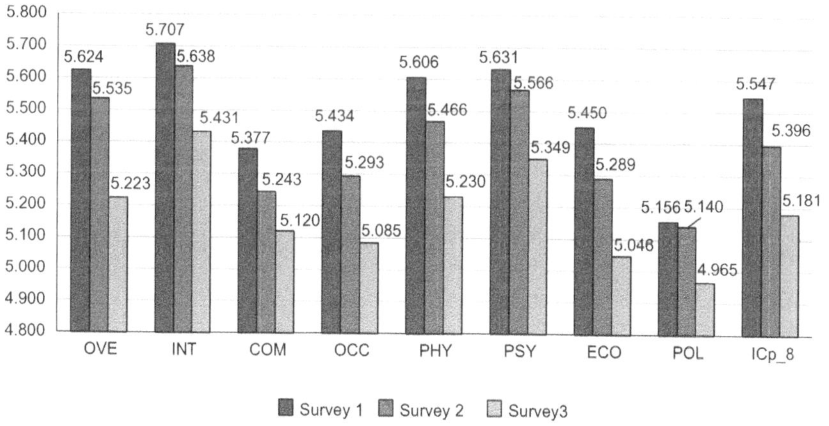

Fig. 7.3 Comparison of multi-dimensional WB in the three surveys (I COPPE index)

occupational well-being (OCC: occupational), physical well-being (PHY: physical), psychological well-being (PSY: psychological) and economic well-being (ECO: economic). In addition, political well-being (POL: political) is a new item that this study added from the perspective of positive political psychology, as mentioned above. Finally, "ICP 8" indicates the average of all of these.[6]

Here, Survey 2 (middle) is lower than Survey 1 (left), and Survey 3 (right) is lower than Survey 2 for all items. Although the populations of these three surveys are different, the results are from the same questions and response styles. Accordingly, this can also be interpreted as a general decline in people's well-being during this period.

Furthermore, the results of a subjective well-being questionnaire called the Life Satisfaction Scale developed by Ed Diener are the same. This questionnaire is the most widely utilized in happiness research and positive psychology. Its result also demonstrates that the WB has steadily and continuously declined during this period.[7]

The following graph (Fig. 7.4) illustrates the extent of eudaimonic well-being (EUD) and hedonic well-being (HED) orientation by using the

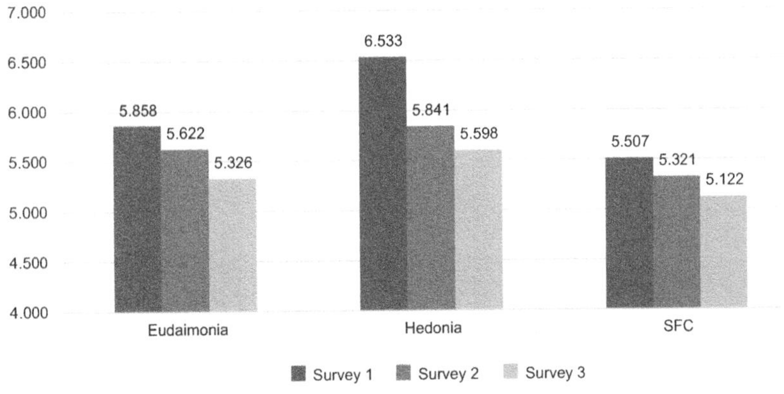

Fig. 7.4 Comparison of Hedonia and Eudaimonia orientations in Survey 3

[6] Prilleltensky, I., Dietz, S., Prilleltensky, O., Myers, N.D., Rubenstein, C.L. Jin, Y., and McMahon, A (2015). Assessing Multidimensional Well-being: Development and Validation of the I COPPE Scale, *Journal of Community Psychology*, 43, n. 2, 199–226.

[7] See Masaya Kobayashi , Hikari Ishido, Jiro Mizushima and Hirotaka Ishikawa, 'Multi-Dimensional Dynamics of Psychological Health Disparities under the COVID-19 in Japan: Fairness/Justice in Socio-Economic and Ethico-Political Factors', *International Journal of Environmental Research and Public Health*, 2022, Fig. 7.2.

questionnaire called HEMA-RX (Veronica Huta[8]). Hedonic well-being represents happiness based on pleasure. Eudaimonic well-being, derived from Aristotle's concept of eudaimonia, is an indicator that measures medium- to long-term well-being with a focus on authenticity, excellence, growth, and meaning with an added ethical perspective. Regarding both measures, the values for all items have fallen in the first, second, and third surveys in turn. The item of satisfaction(SFC) indicates the same finding.

The following graph (Figs. 7.5A and 7.5B) shows the results of various other survey items. These surveys comprehensively investigate society or

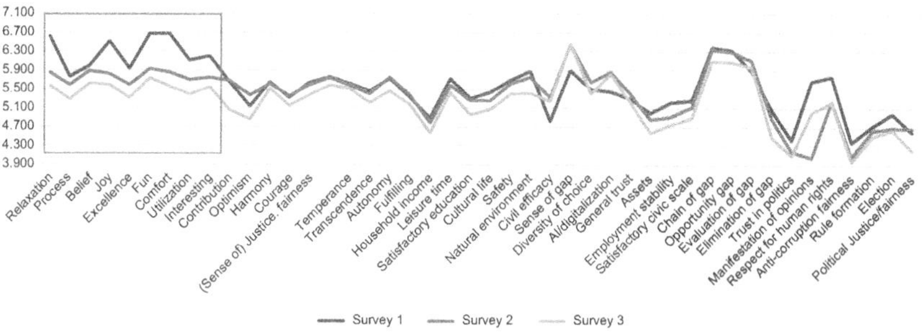

Note: The rectanglular box indicates the orientations concerning eudaimonia and hedonia.

Fig. 7.5A Comparison of other indicators (average values) in the three surveys

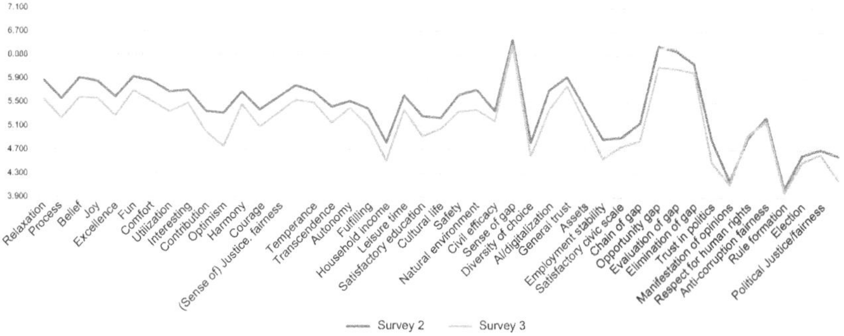

Fig. 7.5B Comparison of other indicators (average values) in the Surveys 2 and 3 (same respondents)

[8] Huta, V. (2016). Eudaimonic and hedonic orientations: Theoretical considerations and research findings. In J. Vittersø (Ed.), *Handbook of Eudaimonic Well-being*. Springer.

community, economy, culture, and politics. Interestingly, a comparison limited to the same respondents in Surveys 2 and 3 shows that the values of many items declined and no items rose (Fig. 7.5B). Among these items, the disparity-related items (disparity perception, disparity chain, opportunity disparity, disparity evaluation, etc.) do not necessarily indicate a worsening situation since a decline in value indicates a narrowing disparity. However, the other items indicate a worsening of the situation.

Thus, well-being and various related indicators clearly indicate the differences during these two years, with well-being and other psychological conditions deteriorating continuously in almost every category. At the same time, deterioration is also evident in many social, community, economic, cultural, and political items.

Therefore, the conclusion is that the COVID-19 crisis has harmed people's well-being and society, including their sense of happiness. This result is in tune with various other research worldwide, including Japan.[9]

[9] Serafini, G., Parmigiani, B., Amerio, A., Aguglia, A., Sher, L. and Amore, M., "The psychological impact of COVID-19 on the mental health in the general population," QJM: monthly journal of the Association of Physicians, vol. 113, no. 8, pp. 531–537, 2020; Gloster, A.T., Lamnisos, D., Lubenko, J., Presti, G., Squatrito, V. and Constantinou, M., et al., "Impact of COVID-19 pandemic on mental health: An international study," 31 December 2020. [Online]. Available: https://journals.plos.org/plosone/article?id=10.1371/journal.pone.0244809; C.-1. M. D. Collaborators, "Global prevalence and burden of depressive and anxiety disorders in 204 countries and territories in 2020 due to the COVID-19 pandemic COVID-19 Mental Disorders Collaborators," THE LANCET, 8 October 2021; Kikuchi, H., Machida, M., Nakamura, I., Saito, R., Odagiri, Y., Kojima, T., Watanabe, H., Fukui, K. and Inoue, S., "Changes in Psychological Distress During the COVID-19 Pandemic in Japan: A Longitudinal Study," Journal of Epidemiology, vol. 30, no. 11, pp. 522–528, 2020; Ueda, M., Nordström, R. and Matsubayashi, T., "Suicide and mental health during the COVID-19 pandemic in Japan," Journal of Public Health, vol. 44, no. 3, pp. 541–548, 2022; Yamamoto, T., Uchiumi, C., Suzuki, N., Yoshimoto, J. and Murillo-Rodriguez, E., "The Psychological Impact of 'Mild Lockdown' in Japan during the COVID-19 Pandemic: A Nationwide Survey under a Declared State of Emergency," International Journal of Environmental Research and Public Health, vol. 17, no. 24, p. 9382, 2020.

3 Polarization in Physical and Mental Well-Being and Change in Values

Survey 1 included as many items as possible to measure the impact of COVID-19; however, as Survey 2 focused on fairness and justice, it reduced the number of COVID-related items; Survey 3 again included COVID-19-related items, although not as many as in the first survey. So then, the results of our analysis focusing on the first and third surveys will be explained.

Figure 7.6 summarizes the results of Survey 1, which asked respondents about their situation before and at the time of COVID-19. As mentioned earlier, well-being declined (Fig. 7.1), and values also fall in other economic and life-related aspects such as satisfaction, assets, income, cost of living burden, housing, and job security in the post-COVID-19 period in terms of individuals' subjective perceptions. Only the remote work implementation and online environments increased: the reason is apparent. The pre-and post-differences for the individual items are not quantitatively large, but the difference is clear.

The following graph (Fig. 7.7A) shows the satisfaction, hope, happiness, and anxiety level in Survey 1. In general, there are more positive people than negative people regarding satisfaction and hope in life, and the same trend appears in this survey (rectangular boxes). However, there

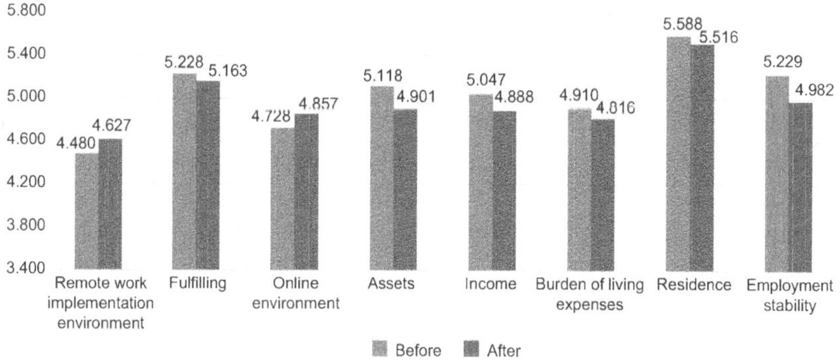

Fig. 7.6 Comparison of WB before and after COVID-19 (Survey 1)

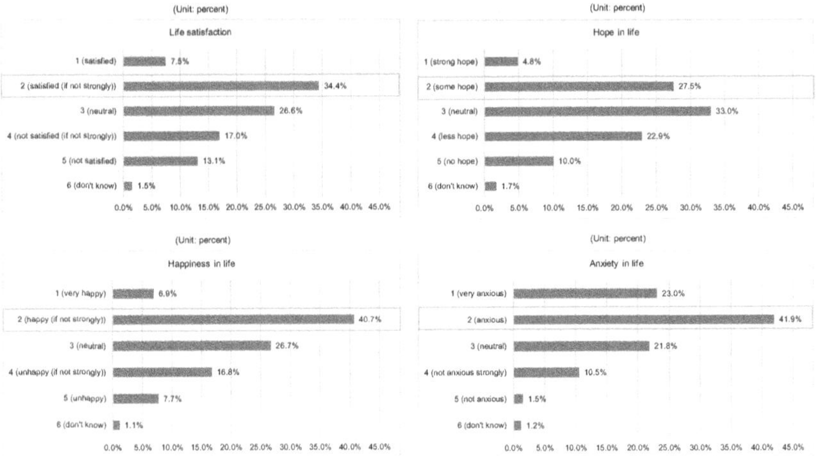

Fig. 7.7A Life satisfaction/ hope/ happiness/ anxiety (Unit: percent)

is a clear negative direction in life anxiety (rectangular boxe), which could be considered an outcome or indicator of the COVID-19 pandemic.

Survey 3 asked about the changes in satisfaction with life and hopes for life (Fig. 7.7B). More than 40% of the respondents were slightly worse off (Scale 5, rectangular box), and overall, there were more changes for the worse than for the better. In comparison with Fig. 7.7A, more people are generally positive in terms of satisfaction and hope, but there is more change in the negative direction. Moreover, concerning both satisfaction and hope, the poles of those who have worsened (scale 1–3) are significantly larger than the opposite polar people who have improved (scale 8–10) (rectangular boxes). A trend toward worsening is discernible from this comparison.

Figure 7.7C shows the survey results for the question, "What are you worried about?" in Survey 1. Naturally, there is a concern about infectious diseases such as COVID-19, which is surrounded by a rectangle (second one from the bottom). However, the following concerns are more than this: about having enough living expenses and getting sick. The other areas enclosed by the rectangle are general anxieties, increasing due to the COVID-19 crisis. In other words, the COVID-19 pandemic seemed to amplify not only anxiety about infectious diseases but also

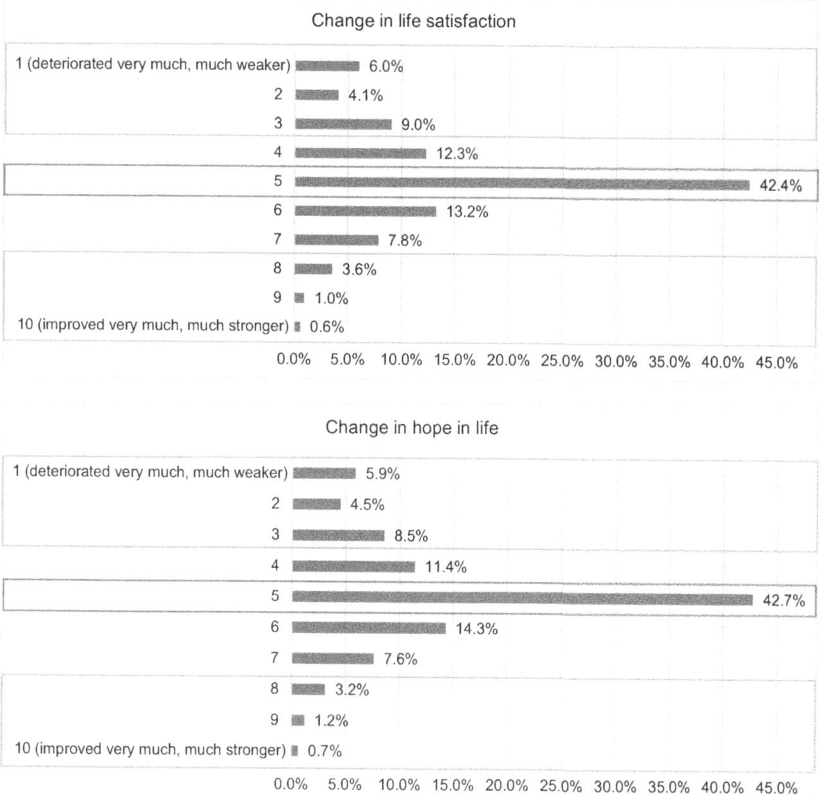

Fig. 7.7B Change of satisfaction and hope in life (Survey 3) (Unit: percent)

anxiety about various aspects of life, and as a result, anxiety, in general, is increasing.

Figure 7.8 shows the results of the three surveys which asked about changes in mental status. In Surveys 1 and 2, there were many people who reported deteriorating mental health, replying "dark feeling, anxiety, and depression." These increased in March 2021 (Survey 2) compared to June 2020 (Survey 1).

The results so far are mainly that many people deteriorated psychologically, including their well-being, due to the COVID-19 pandemic. These

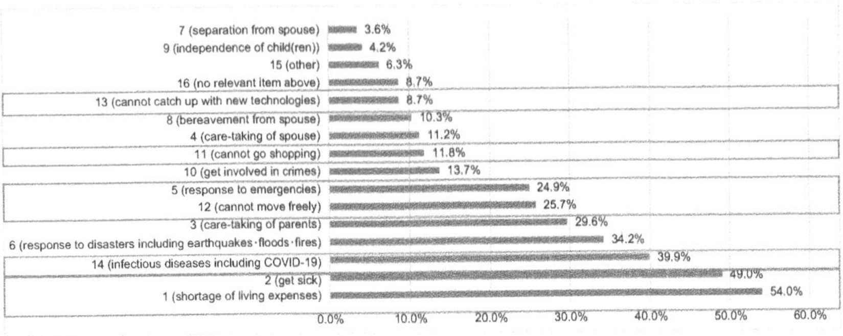

Note: Multiple answeres.

Fig. 7.7C Anxiety items (Survey 1) (Unit: percent). (Note: Multiple answers)

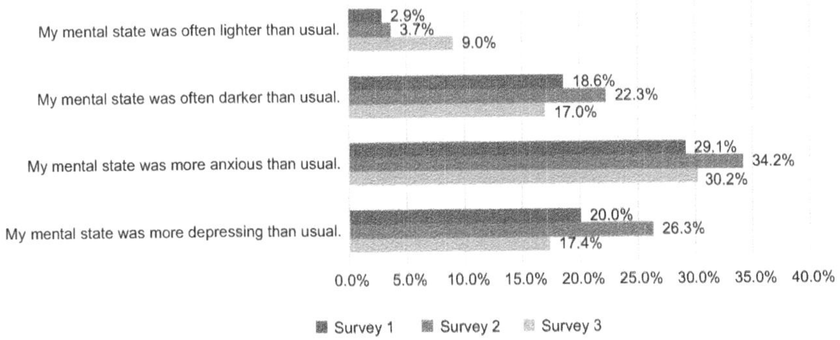

Fig. 7.8 Deterioration of mental state and polarization (Surveys 1–3) (Unit: percent)

results were in line with the supposition before the survey. However, the following results were different from the suppositions before the survey.

When changes in mental state (Fig. 7.8) were examined, in Surveys 1 and 2, of course, more people said that they "felt dark more often than usual," but there were also a small number of people (3–4%) who said that they "felt light more often than usual." Moreover, this percentage increased in Survey 2 compared to Survey 1. In other words, while there were changes in the negative direction as imagined, some people changed psychologically for the better. In this respect, there is bipolar decomposition occurring here. Moreover, this trend became more evident in the second year, in Survey 2. This point was a surprising result.

Furthermore, in Survey 3, "feeling dark, anxious, or depressed" decreased and improved from Survey 2, and "feeling dark or depressed" even improved from Survey 1. As mentioned earlier, well-being has also declined in this survey: however, at this point, the number of infected persons had declined sharply after the peak of the fifth wave in August 2021, so feelings may have turned around. The "feeling light" sentiment rose significantly to 9%.

Secondly, Fig. 7.9A shows the results of Surveys 1 and 2, which asked about physical and mental health changes, employment status, and income (adjusted for the different response scales in each survey). In each of these categories, many respondents selected "not much change," but apart from that, a large number of respondents (10–20%) still selected "somewhat worse." In particular, more respondents chose "somewhat worse" for "mental change" and "income change" than for the other two alternatives (see rectangles below). In all of these areas, respondents who said their situation "has gotten much worse" was two to four times higher in Survey 3 than in Survey 1. On the other hand, 12–13% of respondents said they were (somewhat or very) better off than usual in both Surveys 1

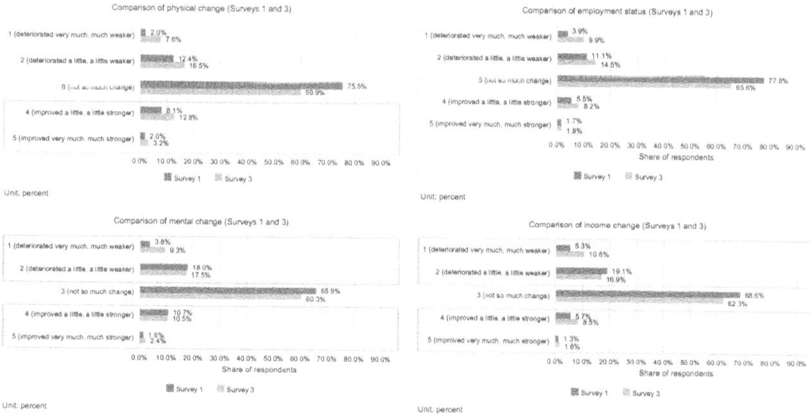

Fig. 7.9A Change in physical/mental/employment/income status(Surveys 1 and 3) (Unit: percent)

and 3 (bottom rectangular box). In other words, there are changes in the negative direction as one would expect, but on the other hand, just over 10% people changed psychologically for the better. In this respect, a bipolar decomposition is taking place here as well. Furthermore, this trend was similar for physical change, change in employment status, and change in income, with Survey 3 showing an improvement of about 15% in physical change (rectangular box).

In a trial analysis of Survey 1, an increase in light feelings in Fig. 7.8 was negatively correlated with physical and mental deterioration in Fig. 7.9A, and an increase in darkness, anxiety, and depression in Fig. 7.8 positively correlated with deterioration in all items in Fig. 7.9A.

The often-mentioned issue of relationships was also examined (Fig. 7.9B), and Survey 1 found that slightly more people said that relationships between family and friends had become "somewhat better" or "somewhat stronger" (about 15%, 10%) than those who said they had become "somewhat worse" (about 4%, 6%). Analysis reveals that this result is also related to the darkness and depression in Fig. 7.8, from which it is possible to see that human relationships are related to the increase and decrease in darkness. Moreover, in Survey 3, in Fig. 7.9B, both those who got better and those who got worse increased, again indicating polarization with prolonged duration. On the worse side, both family and friend ties increased four to five times in the "very much worse" group and more than twice in the "somewhat worse" group, surpassing the better group with friend ties in both groups.

Looking at the findings for mood in the first survey (Fig. 7.10), a majority of people reported having a negative mood and that worry and stress, as mentioned earlier, were found to be common (about 50%, in the lower rectangular box). In contrast, although it is a small number, some people felt joy, love, and hope during the COVID-19 pandemic (about 5–10%, upper rectangular box). Analysis shows that this positive mood is positively correlated with "increased lightness" in Fig. 7.8. Conversely, the negative mood positively correlated with "increased darkness, anxiety, and depression." Depression and stress were negatively correlated with an "increase in lightness," and affection was positively correlated with an "increase in depression."

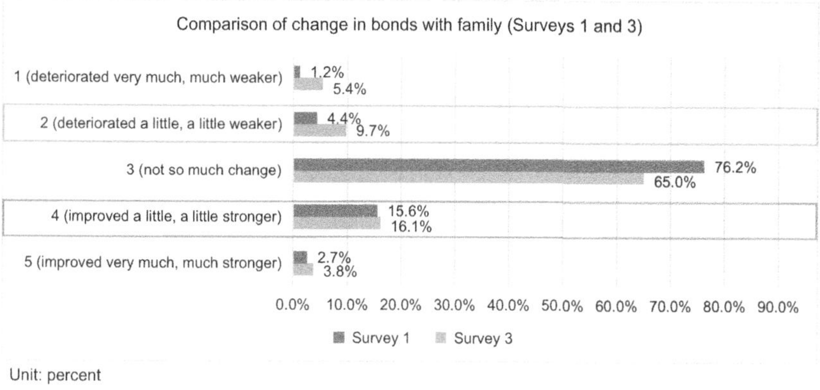

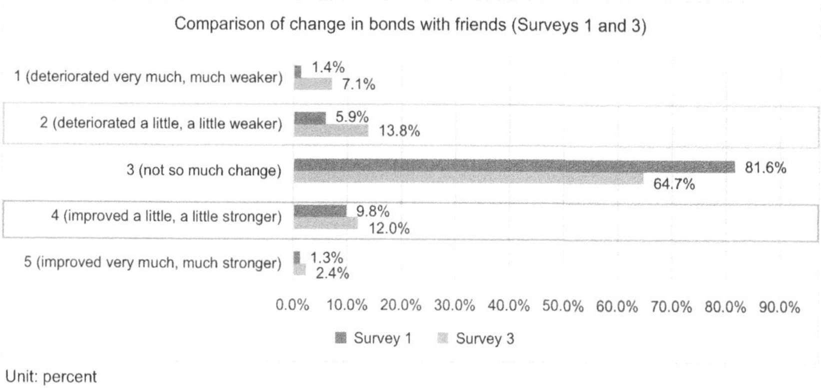

Fig. 7.9B Change in bonds with family and friends (Surveys 1 and 3) (Unit: percent)

Furthermore, "how values and worldviews changed during the COVID-19 crisis" were examined in Surveys 1 and 3, keeping Maslow's hierarchy of needs in mind (Fig. 7.11). At the top of the graph is an item for income insecurity (rectangular box above). In Survey 1, about 30% felt anxious, and analysis shows that this correlates with the "increased darkness, anxiety, and depression" in Fig. 7.8. In Survey 3, these have slightly decreased and turned around.

Concerning values, "I feel like rethinking my way of thinking and living" and "My values and worldview have changed" were selected by about 20% and 15%, respectively, in Survey 1, and increased by 2–3%,

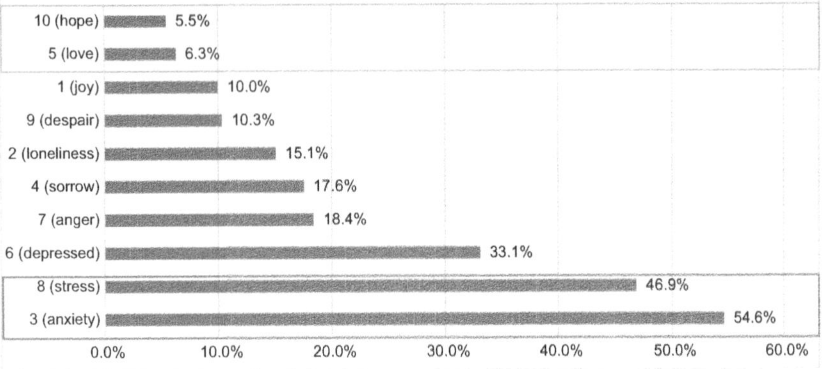

Unit: percent

Fig. 7.10 Mood under the COVID-19 pandemic (Survey 1) (Unit: percent)

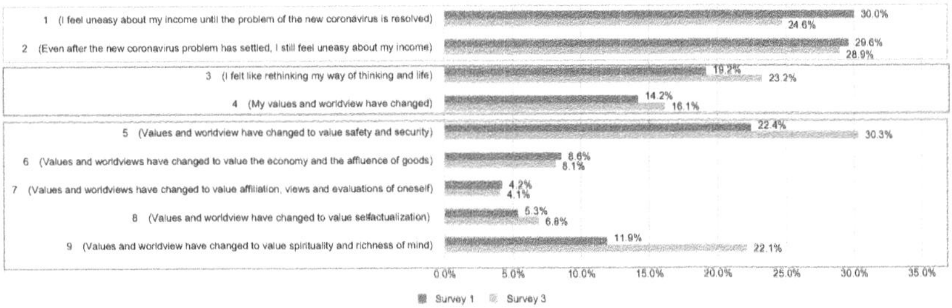

Unit: percent

Fig. 7.11 Comparison of values (Surveys 1 and 3)

respectively, in Survey 3 (see the rectangular box in the middle). The COVID-19 disaster has brought about a change in the way of life and outlook on life for some people. In Survey 1, concerning the relationship between the reassessment of one's way of life/other changes in values and the "increase in light feelings, dark feelings, anxiety, and depression" in Fig. 7.8, the former positively correlated with both "increase in light feelings" and "increase in darkness, anxiety, and depression." That is to say, changes of feelings in both directions correlate with changes in values and reassessment of one's way of life. This finding is also worth noting.

Then, regarding the question, "in what direction are values changing?" the results can be seen in the rectangular box (red) in Fig. 7.11. In

Maslow's hierarchy of needs, there is the need for safety and survival at the foundation, followed by the need for belonging, evaluation, self-actualization, and self-transcendence. In Ronald Inglehart's discussion of materialistic/post-materialistic values (see Addendum) the need for safety and survival is related to economic or materialistic values. The number of people who have changed to value safety and security is 22% and 30% in Surveys 1 and 3, respectively; the economy and material abundance is about 8–9% in these surveys. On the other hand, those who have changed to value self-realization are 5% and 7% in each survey: to value spirituality or spiritual richness are 12% and 22%, respectively. Both correspond to post-materialistic values.

Thus, values at both poles have increased in Maslow's hierarchy of needs: safety and survival at the foundation; self-transcendence at the summit. The need for belonging and self-realization has also increased in some people, but it is not as pronounced as the two poles.

There was a psychological need for safety and security, perhaps because of the unease caused by the COVID-19 crisis. Nevertheless, while living a life of pleasure and enjoyment has become difficult because of the difficulty in being physically close to other people, a certain number of people reevaluated their lives and turned their thoughts inward. This finding was a fascinating result.

Furthermore, comparing Surveys 1 and 3, those who value safety and security increased from 22% to 30%, while those who value spirituality and spiritual richness increased from 12% to 22%, a large increase compared to the others. In other words, here, too, polarization was progressing.

4 Well-being and Factors of Change: Relationship of Three Systems

Next is a brief analysis of "what factors are related to these changes in well-being and mental status," keeping in mind the relationship with fairness. The next Table lists the factors significantly correlating with the respective increases in the negative and positive directions in Survey 1 (Table 7.2A).

Table 7.2A Correlation in Survey 1:WB, Economy, Politics, Societal Community

Increase in Positivity and Negativity (※)	Positive emotion (before and after COVID-19), loneliness, less of depression, each of PERMA, satisfaction, happiness, virtue, eudaimonia, hedonia, extrinsic, life satisfaction, hope in life, fulfillingness (before/after COVID-19), worthiness in life, asset. income (present before COVID-19), sense of burden of living expenses (present before COVID-19), sufficient income, residential environment employment stability (present > before COVID-19), work you hope for, re-employment potential, intention for a side job, freelance, satisfaction with stratification, work engagement, work satisfaction, fulfilling leisure, fulfilling education, fulfilling cultural life, sense of security, natural environment, civil efficacy, respect for human rights, chain of gap, widening gap in opportunities, diversity of choice, digitalization (speed/skill/social bond/ acceleration), resilience, medical environment, exercise/foods, ties with neighbors, general trust, trust in relatives and neighbors, service and donation, crimes/disasters/personal information/COVID-related safety, good family ties, greeting neighbors, place for relaxation, someone to rely on, attachment to local community, area of activeness, social resilience
Increase in Negativity (only)	Negative emotion, hedonia, anxiety about life, sense of burden of living expenses (present > before COVID-19), anti-corruptive fairness in politics, recognition of gap, economic gap, gap elimination, COVID-related gap widening, trust in national politics, trust in politics, trust in friends

※ Coefficients concerning negativity are generally larger than coefficients concerning positivity

Note: An increase in Positivity means the presence of a significant correlation (5%) between lightness and the positive direction; an Increase in Negativity means the presence of a significant correlation between the negative emotions (darkness, anxiety, depression) and the positive direction

These items relate to well-being, economic, political, and societal community systems. The coefficients for negativity are generally more prominent than those for positivity. There are many items where the positive direction correlated with increased lightness, and the negative direction correlated with increased darkness, anxiety, and depression. For some items, there was only a correlation between the negative direction and the increase in darkness, anxiety, and depression: no correlation between the positive direction and the increase in lightness. The list includes these as well.

Table 7.2B 7.3 Correlation in Survey 2: WB, Economy, Politics, Societal Community

Increase in Positivity and Negativity (※)	positive emotion, negative emotion, loneliness, less of depression, each of PRMA, satisfaction, happiness, virtue, extrinsic, hope in life, worthiness in life, worthiness in work, assets, sense of burden of living expenses, sufficient income, residential environment, employment stability, work you hope for, satisfaction with stratification, work engagement, work satisfaction, fulfilling leisure, fulfilling education, fulfilling cultural life, sense of security, natural environment, anti-corruptive fairness in politics, fairness/justice, civil efficacy, respect for human rights, gap elimination, diversity of choice, trust in national politics, trust in politics, resilience, medical environment, necessities of life, trust/interaction, trust in friends, general trust, trust in relatives and neighbors, service and donation, greeting neighbors, place for relaxation, social resilience
Increase in Negativity (only)	recognition of gap, chain of gap, opportunity gap

※ Coefficients concerning negativity are generally larger than coefficients concerning positivity

Note: An increase in Positivity means the presence of a significant correlation (5%) between lightness and the positive direction; an Increase in Negativity means the presence of a significant correlation between the negative emotions (darkness, anxiety, depression) and the positive direction

Survey 2 was similarly examined, and Table 7.2B shows the results. Again, there are considerable similarities with the results of Survey 1.

In order to clarify the results of this analysis, we next conducted a logistic regression analysis (forced-entry method) on the three surveys to examine the relationship between "changes in lightness, darkness, anxiety, and depression" and the following factors in sub-systems in society. The extracted factors are the human system's general well-being (PERMA index), fairness and justice in the political system, income in the economic system, general trust in the societal community, and cultural life enrichment in the cultural system. Since these items were asked with and without, logistic regression analysis (forced entry method) was conducted for the three surveys.

The logistic regression analysis results in Tables 7.3A, 7.3B, and 7.3C show that the original level of well-being is related to this change in

Table 7.3A Factors of lightness/darkness change: logistic regression based on systems theory (Survey 1)

	Lightness increase	Darkness increase	Anxiety increase	Depression increase
WB (general WB)	0.167	-0.114		-0.144
Politics (fairness/justice)		-0.100	-0.138	-0.168
Economy (income)	0.086	-0.076	-0.104	-0.079
Community (general trust)		-0.040		
Culture (richness of cultural life)	0.109		0.061	

Table 7.3B Factors of lightness/darkness change: logistic regression based on systems theory (Survey 2)

	Lightness increase	Darkness increase	Anxiety increase	Depression increase
WB (general WB)	0.275	-0.068	0.039	-0.172
Politics (fairness/justice)		-0.092	-0.110	-0.072
Economy (income)		-0.104	-0.132	-0.071
Community (general trust)		0.055		
Culture (richness of cultural life)	0.121			

Table 7.3C Factors of lightness/darkness change: logistic regression based on systems theory (Survey 3)

	Lightness increase	Darkness increase	Anxiety increase	Depression increase
WB (general WB)	0.375	-0.134	-0.063	-0.239
Politics (fairness/justice)		-0.122	-0.140	-0.083
Economy (income)		-0.066	-0.088	
Community (general trust)			0.095	
Culture (richness of cultural life)	0.143	0.093		

lightness and darkness. At the same time, in all surveys, we found that politics and economics negatively correlated with darkening (change in a negative direction). In other words, a state of less fairness in politics, or a state of falling income in the economy, is associated with an increase in darkness, anxiety, and depression.

Mental change in Fig. 7.9A is asked only in Surveys 1 and 3, and Tables 7.6A and 7.6B indicate the results (β) of multiple regression analysis (stepwise method). In Survey 1, fairness/justice and income, as well as well-being, have a positive impact on mental change; in Survey 3, in addition to these, cultural life also has a positive impact. In both cases, the impact of fairness and justice is second only to well-being, and the impact of the political system is conspicuous.

Figure 7.12 shows the results of the investigation of the changes before and after COVID-19 in the first survey, using the I COPPE questionnaire developed by Prilleltensky and others mentioned previously. As expected, this reveals that economic well-being, political well-being, community well-being, and occupational well-being have decreased slightly.

Therefore, the relationship between this multi-dimensional measure of well-being (overall, physical, psychological, interpersonal, occupational, community, economic, and political well-being) and the changes in lightness and darkness was examined by logistic regression analysis: Tables 7.4A, 7.4B and 7.4C indicate the results (β). Since cultural well-being

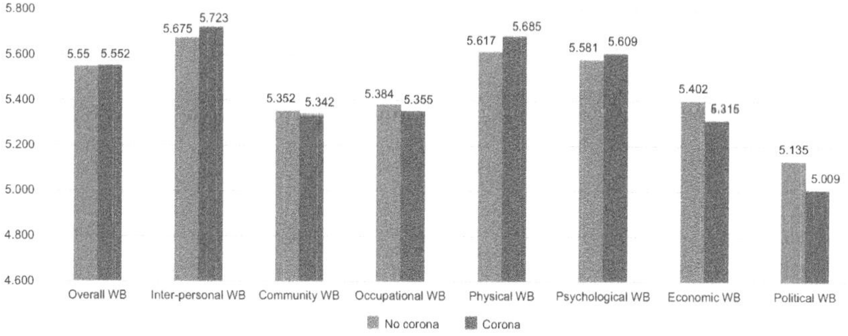

Fig. 7.12 Multi-dimensional WB (Comparison of I COPPE values before and after corona, Survey 1)

Table 7.4A Factors of lightness/darkness change: logistic regression based on systems theory (Survey 1)

	Lightness increase	Darkness increase	Anxiety increase	Depression increase
Overall WB				
Physical WB	0.266		-0.069	-0.080
Psychological WB		-0.174	-0.094	-0.183
Inter-personal WB		0.116	0.181	0.175
Occupational WB				
Community WB		-0.079	-0.056	-0.086
Economic WB				
Political WB		-0.156	-0.149	-0.194

Table 7.4B Factors of lightness/darkness change: logistic regression of multi-dimensional WB (I COPPE, Survey 2)

	Lightness increase	Darkness increase	Anxiety increase	Depression increase
Overall WB	0.128 (0.129)	-0.058		-0.116 (-0.115)
Physical WB	0.120 (0.120)		-0.073 (-0.078)	
Psychological WB		-0.186 (-0.200)	-0.062 (-0.078)	-0.209 (-0.217)
Inter-personal WB		0.147 (0.136)	0.186 (0.176)	0.120 (0.115)
Occupational WB				
Community WB				
Economic WB		(-0.055)	-0.085 (-0.099)	
Political WB		(-0.086)	-0.079 (-0.136)	-0.101 (-0.129)
(Cultural WB)		(0.126)	(0.131)	-0.064

Note: In cases where "Cultural WB" is Included in the regression, the results are shown in parentheses

was examined only in Surveys 2 and 3, parentheses in the respective tables show the results of the analysis concerning it.

The same trend is observed in the three cases. In a sense, it is natural that mental and physical well-being affects mental changes. It is interesting that interpersonal, political, economic, community, and cultural well-being influence the changes in lightness and darkness. Interpersonal

Table 7.4C Factors of lightness/darkness change: logistic regression of multi-dimensional WB (Survey 3)

	Lightness increase	Darkness increase	Anxiety increase	Depression increase
Overall WB	0.173 (0.171)			
Physical WB				
Psychological WB	0.361 (0.387)	-0.174 (-0.250)	-0.238 (-0.131)	-0.351 (-0.361)
Inter-personal WB		0.116	0.093 (0.128)	0.091
Occupational WB				
Community WB		-0.079		
Economic WB		(-0.176)	-0.165	
Political WB	(0.181)	-0.156 (-0.180)	-0.111 (-0.189)	-0.173 (-0.253)
(Cultural WB)	(-0.162)		(0.182)	(0.174)

and cultural well-being is positively related to darkening (increased darkness, anxiety, and depression). Those with high interpersonal and cultural well-being may have become mentally dark by COVID-19, which made communication and cultural activities more difficult.

On the other hand, political, economic, and community well-being negatively relate to darkening. In other words, darkening is suppressed in people with high levels concerning these kinds of well-being. In particular, looking at the three surveys as a whole, political well-being is the most closely related except for mental and physical well-being, followed by economic well-being.

Furthermore, Tables 7.6C and 7.6D (following Fig.7.13) indicate the results of multiple regression analyses concerning the factor of mental changes asked in surveys 1 and 3: the influences of political and psychological well-being are conspicuous. Thus, the two kinds of well-being positively reduce negative mental changes.

In addition, in order to extensively examine the factors contributing to mental change (the objective variable), multiple regression analysis was conducted for Surveys 1 and 3 with the social factors shown in Fig. 7.5 and well-being (PERMA average and SWLS), hedonia-eudaimonia orientation, and attributes (age and gender) as independent variables. Table 7.5 shows the results: The extracted factors common to these two surveys are rule formation ('I think rule formation and change by people

Table 7.5 Multiple regression of factors in mental changes (Surveys 1 and 3)

	β (Survey 1)	β (Survey 3)
R2 (adjusted)	0.068 (0.066)	0.395 (0.383)
SWLS	0.104	
Hedonia orientation	-0.083	
Rule formation	0.063	0.096
Health	0.074	0.105
Negativity	-0.064	
Age	-0.034	
SEX (Male 0: Female 1)	-0.046	
Political WB	0.065	0.075
Virtue	-0.073	
Leisure enrichment	0.054	0.055
Digitalization (advancement)	-0.032	
Anti-corruptive justice	0.038	
Safety		0.088
Employment stability		0.098
Psychological WB		0.116
Positive emotion		0.196
Trust in national politics		0.096
Satisfaction		0.118

Note: There is a difference in the construction of variables: for instance, Satisfaction in Survey 1 is one item, whereas in Survey 3, it is the average of aggregate values

is functioning in society'), health, political well-being, and leisure enrichment (in bold). It is striking that as rule formation is related to citizenship, two items, namely, it and political well-being are political. Moreover, other factors related to politics (underlined), such as anti-corruption fairness in Survey 1 and trust in the national government in Survey 3, confirm that political factors influence mental change. In addition, the R-squared (coefficient of determination) is small in all of these regressions (Table 7.3A onward), and the explanatory power of the objective variable is limited, but since β is 0.395 for Survey 3 in Table 7.5, the above trend can be regarded as existent overall.[10]

[10] Furthermore, in Survey 1, after conducting factor analysis on the survey items, multiple regression analysis was conducted on the relationship between the factors and the light/dark change. We found that "community relations" and "civic publicness" had a very large impact, along with and even more than household income. In other words, political factors such as civic publicness had an impact on light and dark changes. For Survey 2, the analysis method changed and a multiple regression analysis focusing on the aggregate values was conducted, but basically the same trends as in Survey 1 emerged.

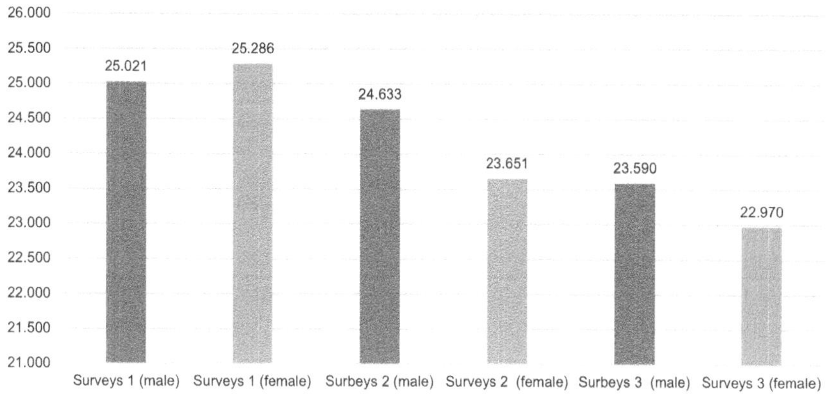

Fig. 7.13 Changes in SWLS in male and female (Surveys 1 to 3)

Table 7.6A Factors of mental change: multiple regression based on systems theory (Survey1)

	Mental change
R2	0.031
WB (general WB)	0.086
Politics (fairness justice)	0.077
Economy (income)	0.054
Community (general trust)	
Culture (richness of cultural life)	

Notes: Italic figures mean 5% significance; Non-italic figures: 10% significance (same below). Score of 5 for the response "significantly improved", and 1 for "significantly worsened." Forced input method is used to indicate statistically significant items (same below)

With regard to attributes, in Survey 1, the mental change was worse for older people and women. This point is a trend also observed in Surveys 2 and 3. Finally, regarding gender, as shown in Fig. 7.13, the SWLS values show a more considerable decrease in well-being for women than for men in the first through third surveys. As a result, well-being was higher for women in Survey 1, whereas it was lower for women in Surveys 2 and 3.

Table 7.6B Factors of mental change: multiple regression based on systems theory (Survey1)

	Mental change (β)
R2	0.348 (0.347)
WB (general WB)	0.356
Politics (fairness justice)	0.191
Economy (income)	0.080
Community (general trust)	
Culture (richness of cultural life)	0.081

Notes: Italic mean 5% significance; Non-italic figures: 10% significance. Score of 5 for the response "significantly improved", and 1 for "significantly worsened"

Table 7.6C Factors of mental change: multiple regression of multi-dimensional WB (Survey 1) (Stepwise method)

	Mental change (β)
R2	0.034
Political WB	0.112
Psychological WB	0.088
Overall WB	
Physical WB	
Inter-personal WB	
Occupational WB	
Community WB	
Economic WB	

Note: Score is adjusted to 5 for the response "Improved significantly", and to 1 for "Deteriorated significantly"

Table 7.6D Factors of mental change: multiple regression of multi-dimensional WB (Survey 3) (Stepwise method)

	Mental change (β)	
R2 (adjusted)	0.321	(0.320)
Political WB	*0.191*	*(0.191)*
Psychological WB	*0.215*	*(0.215)*
Overall WB		
Physical WB		*(-0.064)*
Inter-personal WB		
Occupational WB		
Community WB	*0.094*	*(0.094)*
Economic WB		*(0.072)*
(Cultural WB)		

Note: In cases where "Cultural WB" is Included in the regression, the results are shown in parentheses. Score is adjusted to 5 for the response "Improved significantly," and to 1 for "Deteriorated significantly"

5 Justice/Fairness and Well-being

For the relationship between justice/citizenship and subjective well-being, covariance structure analyses were conducted for Surveys 1 and 2 by constituting theoretical models. Although only the presentation of the results is possible here, it was found that the model that "justice/fairness and citizenship have a positive influence on well-being" fits the data well (Fig. 7.14).

In addition, the correlations between light/dark changes in mood and justice/fairness or citizenship were examined for the three surveys. Figure 7.15A shows the correlations between justice/fairness or political freedom (freedom to express opinions) and light/dark changes. Figure 7.15B shows the results of an exploratory factor analysis (maximum likelihood method, Promax rotation) of the socio-political items (15 items) to extract the factors of justice/fairness and citizenship: next, their correlations with light/dark change. In both cases, justice/fairness and citizenship positively correlated with increases in lightness and

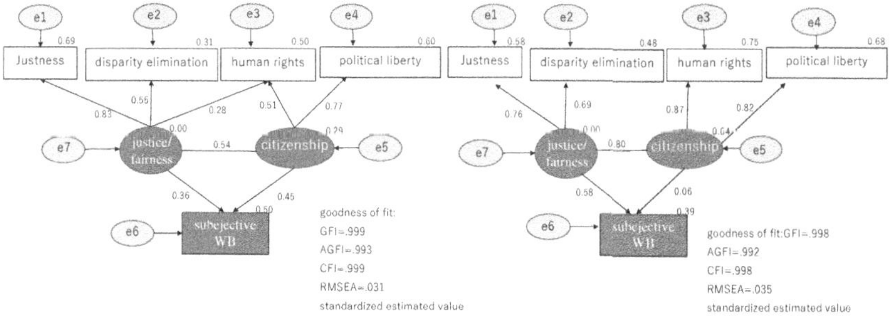

Fig. 7.14 Structural Equation Modeling

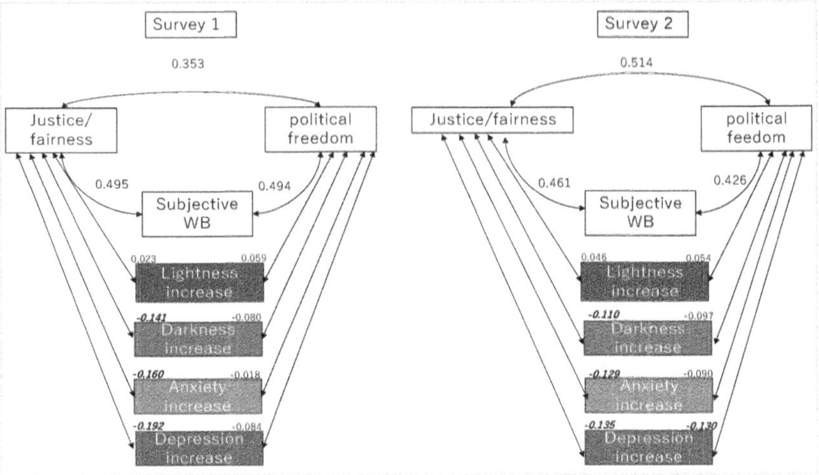

Fig. 7.15A Correlation with justice/fairness, citizenship, and change of mood (change of lightness/darkness)

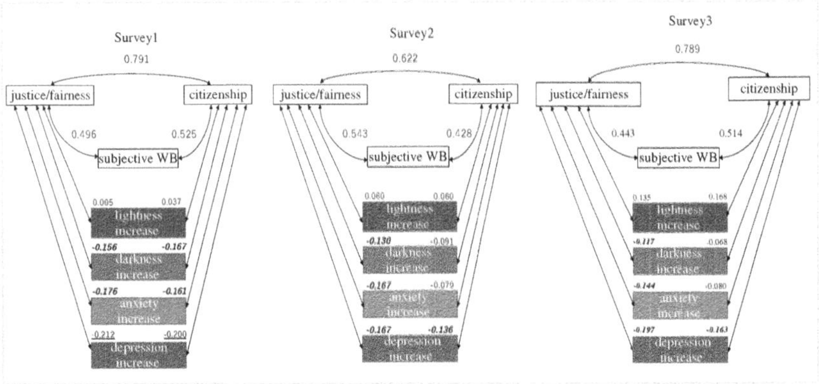

Fig. 7.15B Correlation with justice/fairness, citizenship, and change of mood (change of lightness/darkness)

negatively correlated with negative changes (increases in darkness, anxiety, and depression). In other words, they increase lightness and suppress darkness.

Therefore, combining the results of these analyses, there can be the following inference: justice/fairness and citizenship are related to well-being and changes for lightness and darkness. In other words, justice/fairness or citizenship positively correlated with well-being. They also correlated with changes in lightness and darkness in the COVID-19 crisis, especially for the suppression of darkening or negativization.

Logically, people who are cheerful by nature may also be optimistic about citizenship and fairness and believe that these things are sufficiently present in society to make them feel cheerful even in the face of a global pandemic. However, given that the same results appeared in the multiple regression analysis, it can be presumed that justice/fairness or citizenship are related to changes in lightness and darkness, even when the analysis excludes the original well-being factor.

Interpreting these results, it is conceivable that the sense that "the government does not do enough" or "justice and fairness do not exist in politics and society" during the COVID-19 crisis is causally related to a greater sense of despair and loss of hope in this crisis, which, in turn, is related to lower well-being and increased darkness, anxiety and depression. Of course, this kind of study analyzes correlations, and the causal relationship must be discussed separately. Nevertheless, as mentioned above, the "justice/fairness or citizenship leads to increased well-being" model seems to align well with the available data.

Ideologically, this model is closer to the supposition underpinning communitarianism and republicanism since the models are constructed based on these philosophies. Therefore, the above analysis results can be interpreted to mean that the empirical analysis concerning the COVID-19 pandemic has increased the plausibility of these political philosophies.

6 Conclusion: Declining Well-being, Its Polarization, and the Polarization of Values

In summary, this analysis would conclude that there has been a decline of well-being and the polarization of it and values in the COVID-19 crisis. As might be expected, there is a general increase in anxiety and a decline in well-being despite those whose well-being is improving, and there is a polarization of values into materialistic and post-materialistic/spiritual values. In addition, while there was an unfortunate trend of income insecurity and change, there are also a significant number of people whose relationships between family and friends have changed for the better. This phenomenon is also related to the polarization of values, and these are results that deserve attention. In addition, in terms of attribution, in Survey 1, there was a slight increase in the negative direction for women and older people compared to men and younger people, and the trend concerning women was consistent across the three surveys.

Moreover, justice/fairness or the citizenship were influential for the change for lightness or darkness. Well-being regarding politics, economy, and community is related to mood changes and mental changes. The influence of the political system (in perceptions), including fairness and justice, is particularly significant. Justice and fairness, along with citizenship, are associated with increased well-being, and there is a trend and effect during the COVID-19 crisis to reduce negativity.

Therefore, the issue of fairness is regarded as extremely important. When fairness is achieved, of course, it will help improve people's actual lives and increase their well-being. Furthermore, at the same time, it also suppresses the darker side of the COVID-19 crisis, such as the darkening of feelings and increasing anxiety and depression, and promotes some positive psychological changes in the corona disaster. Therefore, it can be concluded that realizing a just and fair society generally increases people's happiness and, in the case of a global pandemic disaster, increases positive psychological changes and inhibits negative psychological changes.

Addendum: Supplementary Theoretical Arguments

This chapter focuses on our empirical analysis. Nevertheless, the following points can provide supplementary theoretical or philosophical arguments.

1. Philosophical Thought and Empirical Analysis: The background of the empirical analysis is the political philosophy of communitarianism. While libertarianism and liberalism are individualistic in their central conceptions of human rights, the communitarian political philosophy also emphasizes communal elements embodied by the concept of the common good as the purpose of politics. Accordingly, this political philosophy is both individualistic and communal, as this is also called liberal communitarianism.[11]

Communitarianism derives from the classical political philosophies represented by Aristotle: it embraces the original virtue ethics such as his *Nicomachean Ethics*. This point enables us to bridge philosophical insights and empirical science.

There has been a split between normative philosophy or thought and empirical science in modern times. Nevertheless, positive psychology, by way of empirical science, often leads to conclusions that have much in common with Aristotelian classical philosophy and virtue ethics. Based on this foundation, the concept of positive political psychology was proposed, using the concepts of "philosophical science" (science suggested by philosophy) or "scientific philosophy" (philosophy suggested by science), and it aims to cross-link and bridge the two.[12]

2. Relationship between Political Philosophy and COVID-19: In my view, the impact of COVID-19 is tremendous, both ideologically and

---

[11] Michael Sandel, *Justice: What's the Right Thing to Do?* 2009, New York, NY: Farrar, Straus and Giroux; Kobayashi, "Political Philosophies and Positive Political Psychology,"op.cit., section 'The Debate Between Liberalism and Communitarianism: Justice and the Good Life.'

[12] Kobayashi, op.cit., section' Multi-Disciplinary Development for Common Good as Collective Well-Being.'

practically, not only during the COVID-19 crisis but afterward, it will continue for the world and Japan.

The philosophy of utilitarianism, which has played a significant role in the world and Japan up to now, has had a significant impact on economics and policy research and corresponds to the market economy principle, which puts profits first. Accordingly, applying this way of thinking to the COVID-19 situation tends to lean toward policies that balance infectious disease control with considerations for economic growth. Unfortunately, the Japanese government's policies also fall into this category. However, as of the summer of 2020, international comparisons have already shown that countries that took thorough measures to combat the infectious disease are recovering more quickly in economic terms.[13] This result will compel us to reconsider and reflect on utilitarianism.

In addition, libertarianism, the idea of prioritizing the market economy, has swept the world since the 1980s and has had an enormous impact on Japan. This political philosophy corresponds to neo-liberalism in economics, in which the profit-first market economy principle is even more vital than utilitarianism, and theorists oppose government intervention, including welfare, as a principle and try to respect people's freedom to the maximum extent possible. Therefore, advocates of this ideology tend to be reluctant toward strong government measures against COVID-19 and oppose restrictions on behavior such as wearing masks and lockdowns because these restrictions are seen as infringing upon freedom. The Trump administration and its supporters in the US at the initial stage of COVID-19 represent this kind of thought: there have been widespread demonstrations against lockdowns.

[13] Sarun Charumilind, Ezra Greenberg, Jessica Lamb, and Shubham Singhal,'COVID-19: Saving thousands of lives and trillions in livelihoods'(Ending lockdowns alone won't restore confidence or growth. Only when the novel coronavirus is under control will economic growth resume), August 2020, MaKinsey & Company; Economic decline in the second quarter of 2020 vs total confirmed COVID-19 deaths (as of August 30, 2020), Our World in Data; FT Visual & Data Journalism team FT Visual & Data Journalism team, 'Covid-19: The global crisis—in data'(Charts and maps show paradoxes of a pandemic that has claimed a million lives),October,18 2020, Financial Time, especially, figure 'Countries that were unable to control their outbreaks have tended to suffer the most economic pain.'

However, in the US, the UK, Brazil, and other countries, including Japan(especially in 2022), as a result of such policies, the number of infected people and deaths has increased, causing severe damage. Then this policy failure may be one of the reasons why the Trump administration was defeated in the 2020 presidential election. Therefore, in the medium to long term, the experience of the COVID-19 crisis will seem to affect political philosophy, and libertarianism will decline.

Liberalism advocates the dignity of life, the reduction of disparities through welfare, and the protection of the vulnerable, based on the theory of rights. Therefore, it is likely that they will insist on prioritizing countermeasures against infectious diseases and economic measures through benefits and aid: in these respects, they will be able to respond more appropriately than utilitarianism and libertarianism. However, with so much emphasis on respect for freedom, it is not clear from the philosophical standpoint how far we can be sufficiently proactive in fighting infectious diseases through exercising public authority, such as emergency declarations and lockdowns.

In contrast, exercising power for the common good is the goal of politics for communitarianism. Protecting life and health against infectious diseases is nothing less than a public good. Therefore, communitarianism tends to prioritize the public good and argue for more active infection control measures than utilitarianism, libertarianism, and even liberalism.

Among the two dimensions in Mizushima's chapter (Chap. 6), social controls and administrative controls correspond to moral norms and exercising power for the public good in communitarianism. Therefore, from this philosophical perspective, both are important.

In many Western countries, the seriousness of the infection situation has necessitated administrative controls. In Japan, the number of infected people per capita at the initial stage was thought to be relatively low compared to Western countries because of self-restraint and self-regulation, with many people observing the practice of wearing masks. However, due to the government's reluctance to take substantial measures against the spread of COVID-19, the fifth wave in August 2021 caused severe damage due to the collapse of the healthcare system in some areas, such as the Tokyo metropolitan area. The lack of administrative controls for the

Tokyo Olympics and Paralympics can be regarded as a significant reason for this policy's failure.

Thus, from a communitarian perspective, moral norms functioned fairly well in Japan, but the exercise of power for the public good was insufficient: Japan's failure can be attributed to a lack of administrative controls.

Although the empirical analysis in this paper is not directly related to political philosophy, there are two intersecting points to be noted. First, as explained in the text, the "tendency that justice/fairness and citizenship increase well-being" is based on a communitarian hypothesis and has affinities with the ideas of communitarianism.

Second, in terms of changing values, the increase in the number of people who place importance on post-materialistic or spiritual values and relationships with family and friends is in line with the communitarian ideal.

3. Change in Values: The question about values in this survey is designed with the theory of the hierarchy of needs created by Abraham Maslow, one of the founders of humanistic psychology, in mind. Maslow first used the term "positive psychology": today's positive psychology has scientifically and empirically developed the insights provided by Maslow and others in humanistic psychology.

In addition, Ronald Inglehart (d. 2021) investigated the change in values based on Maslow's theory and proposed that a shift was underway "from materialistic values to post-materialistic values" in *The Silent Revolution* (1977) and other books. The generation (A) that grew up during and immediately after the world war experienced economic scarcity and hardships caused by the war, and thus materialistic values (corresponding to safety and survival needs) prevailed. In contrast, the generation (B) that grew up during the subsequent period of benign economic growth saw an increase in post-materialistic values (corresponding to the need for self-actualization), which led to the rise in counter-cultural movements and political participation challenging the elite from the late 1960s.

Later, due to economic stagnation such as stagflation, some argued that this trend had changed and materialistic values had increased again, and there have been debates and changes or developments in Inglehart's argument. Nevertheless, the surveys in this chapter were conducted, taking account of Inglehart's original thesis. The findings show an increasing polar trend concerning values corresponding to either materialistic or post-materialistic values in the COVID-19 crisis.

The increase in materialistic values is similar to the generation affected by World War II at a young age. Therefore, the inference can be that significant crises such as wars and pandemics increased the orientation toward security and economic stability, leading to an increase in materialistic values.

In contrast, the growth of post-materialistic values for self-transcendence or spirituality in these surveys is different from the post-World War II generation and instead has something in common with the "silent revolution" that manifested itself in the late 1960s. This emergence in the surveys can be a result of the fact that under the COVID-19 crisis, it became physically difficult to live a life of everyday pleasures and material desires. Accordingly, people cannot help refraining from going out and staying indoors, which led to an increase in the number of people who paid more attention to internal and mental matters and recognized the value of one's private sphere, including family and spirituality.

The trend toward an increase in both materialistic and post-materialistic values is different from both of the above generations (A and B): it is worth noting for that reason. In positive political psychology, it would be helpful to conduct a survey based on Maslow and Inglehart's arguments to measure changes in values for considering future trends in the world.

This analysis has raised findings worthy of attention in this regard. In addition, it is also interesting to ask, "how large will such a change in values be in the COVID-19 crisis, and what will it be like in the post-COVID period?" Although speculation is the best we can do at this point, it would be valuable to continue the investigation and pay close attention to the impact of COVID-19 on politics and society.

4. Post-COVID Society and Civilization: There is a question: "while the COVID-19 crisis has had a negative effect, there are also positive

changes. But when the COVID-19 crisis eases, and we return to normal life, will this emerging light of hope disappear, and will we return to our original state?" It is true that the idea of "returning to our old way of life, the way the world used to be" is popular, but, in the medium to long term, this experience may have a great impact and cause social and civilizational changes.

Table 7.6 summarizes this trend and potential from the perspective of a civilizational theory of positive social systems.[14] These changes can lead to a society where people have a high level of well-being. Using Seligman's concept of flourishing,[15] such a society can be called a "flourishing society."

Civilizational change is facilitated by internal and cultural factors as well as external and technological factors. This chapter has already mentioned the principles, political philosophy, and way of life/values in Table 7.6 regarding internal and cultural factors. These correspond to economic, political, and cultural systems. For example, regarding the principles of (political) economy, as mentioned above, utilitarianism and libertarianism tend to lean toward the principle of a market economy that prioritizes the pursuit of profit; in contrast, communitarianism affirms intervention from the perspective of the public good to a certain extent and revitalizes the idea of introducing a moral and normative perspective into the economy (moral economy).

As an external and technological factor in Table 7.6, the COVID-19 crisis has led to rapid progress in activities moving online. Digitalization and AI in science and technology are causing changes in society, which used to center on heavy industry: the COVID-19 crisis will undoubtedly accelerate this process. This move will lead to changes in organizations and relationships. Traditional vertical and uniform organizations and relationships will likely change in the direction of horizontal and diverse structures.

At the same time, societies and communities may change into "decentralized, trans (or loosely) bounded societies." For example, the

---

[14] This theory was developed in the author's Japanese writings.

[15] Seligman, *Flourish*, op.cit.

Table 7.6 New Fair Society after Post-Corona Age (Flourishing Society)

	Principle (economic system)	Science and technology	Organization(relationship)	Way of life and values (culturale system)	Political philosophy (political system)	Societal community
Past	prioritizing interests in market economy	smokestack industry	verticality/uniformity	pleasure, Hedonia (hedonic well-being)	utilitarianism, libertarianism, libertarianism etc.	closed, repressive
future	prioritizing life, health, and the natural environment; moral economy	digital (Internet/ AI)	horizontality/diversity	spirituality, Eudaimonia (eudaimonic well-being)	communitarianism	trans(Loosening) boundaries, autonomy and cooperation

COVID-19 crisis has led to an increase in telework and working online. This phenomenon has led to a change in work patterns: residences and offices moved from the city center to the suburbs. These transitions may change the concentration trend in large cities and allow dispersion to the suburbs and rural areas. At the same time, the boundaries between various organizations may become looser than before, allowing people to move between them.

From the perspective of positive social systems theory, each system—political, economic, and cultural—became more differentiated and institutionalized as civilization developed. In this context, anthropology and history have paid attention to 'existence and time outside the institutionalized framework, periphery, and beyond the boundaries. For example, regarding pre-modern civilizations, there is various research: in anthropology, nomads, tricksters, clowns, and extraordinary times of celebration(in contrast to the ordinary everyday); in Japanese history, non-agricultural people (craftsmen and entertainers) in free places that are not under the private control of secular power, such as muen (no relationships) and kugai (a public world); in sociology, marginal man, marginal person, or peripheral person (a person who is influenced by multiple cultures and groups but cannot belong to one). Whereas sedentary societies are static, those who exist on the boundaries have given society a dynamic vitality and have also been a source of creativity and innovation.

However, in a sedentary society, most people live within the boundaries of a community, and since Japan was an agrarian society, people were more likely to belong to a village community. Even after modernization, industrialization, and urbanization, most people have a sense of belonging to, for example, a company as a community. Accordingly, a collectivist culture has persisted and influenced labor.

In contrast, in recent years, individualism and autonomy have been advancing along with the generations. Moreover, unprecedented significant changes and trends have developed due to the COVID-19 crisis. As mentioned above, the shift toward going online and telework, for example, is forcing people to live and work in ways that are not bound or limited by the boundaries of a single community or organization.

There is also a tendency to move to the suburbs, as well as a tendency to shift to a decentralized society, reversing the modern tendency toward a large city center and a monopolar orientation. In other words, situations and behaviors with trans or loose boundaries are no longer limited to a few people, places, and times as in the past but are spreading to many people, places, and times.

If this trend of trans (loosely) bounded societies persists post-COVID, there is a possibility that social changes will occur in the medium to long term that will bring about a civilizational change. However, rather than becoming a completely borderless and fluid society like the concept of the nomadic society in postmodern philosophy, it is probable that we are moving toward an era in which conventional organizations and their boundaries will continue to exist to a certain extent; nevertheless, the barriers will be relaxed, and many people will live and work beyond boundaries on a daily basis, while also belonging to organizations.

This alteration may reduce the constraints of organizations and the oppressive tendencies of controlled societies. This change can result in increased autonomy. Conversely, communities and organizations will not disappear, so the need for cooperation and community under them will persist. Therefore, it may become necessary and possible to balance independence and autonomy with cooperation and collaboration, or in other words, liberty and communality.

This requirement corresponds to the vision of liberal communitarianism. At the same time, from the perspective of positive psychology, closed communities and controlled and repressive organizations may undermine people's autonomy and creativity, resulting in decreased well-being. In contrast, trans or loosened boundaries in communities and organizations may increase people's well-being. This transformation may lead to a flourishing society. Just as those who existed on the boundaries in the past were creative and innovative, trans (or loosening) boundaries are expected to increase dynamic creativity and innovation, leading to economic vitality and prosperity.

The results of this analysis will help consider trends not only in Japan but also across the world. The decline in well-being due to the COVID-19 crisis is probably a global trend, not just in Japan. Humankind is experiencing a great deal of suffering. However, by overcoming these challenges, positive changes in polarization of well-being and values will hopefully continue to develop, and the changes mentioned above in values, political philosophy, and society will be sustained, paving the way for a flourishing society. This vision is only a philosophical and theoretical hope at this stage, but future empirical research may verify the prospect.

Acknowledgments Hirotaka Ishikawa (Ph.D. student, Graduate School of Humanities and Studies on Public Affairs, Chiba University) assisted in organizing and charting the data in this report. I cordially would like to thank him.

References

Butler, J., and M.L. Kern. 2016. The PERMA-profiler: a brief multi-dimensional measure of flourishing. *International Journal of Wellbeing* 6: 1–48.

C.-1. M. D. Collaborators. Global Prevalence and Burden of Depressive and Anxiety Disorders in 204 Countries and Territories in 2020 Due to the COVID-19 Pandemic COVID-19 Mental Disorders Collaborators. *The Lancet*. Accessed 8 October 2021.

Gloster, A.T., D. Lamnisos, J. Lubenko, G. Presti, V. Squatrito, and M. Constantinou, et al. Impact of COVID-19 Pandemic on Mental Health: An International Study. Accessed 31 December 2020. [Online]. https://journals.plos.org/plosone/article?id=10.1371/journal.pone.0244809.

Huta, V. 2016. Eudaimonic and Hedonic Orientations: Theoretical Considerations and research findings. In *Handbook of Eudaimonic Well-being*, ed. J. Vittersø. Springer.

Kikuchi, H., M. Machida, I. Nakamura, R. Saito, Y. Odagiri, T. Kojima, H. Watanabe, K. Fukui, and S. Inoue. 2020. Changes in Psychological Distress During the COVID-19 Pandemic in Japan: A Longitudinal Study. *Journal of Epidemiology* 30 (11): 522–528.

Kobayashi, Masaya. 2021. Political Philosophies and Positive Political Psychology: Inter-Disciplinary Framework for the Common Good. *Frontiers in Psychology* 12. https://doi.org/10.3389/fpsyg.2021.727818.

———. 2022. Psychological Examination of Political Philosophies: Interrelationship Among Citizenship, Justice, and Well-Being in Japan. *Frontiers in Psychology* 12.

Kobayashi, Masaya, Hikari Ishido, Jiro Mizushima, and Hirotaka Ishikawa. 2022. Multi-Dimensional Dynamics of Psychological Health Disparities under the COVID-19 in Japan: Fairness/Justice in Socio-Economic and Ethico-Political Factors. *International Journal of Environmental Research and Public Health.*

Prilleltensky, I., S. Dietz, O. Prilleltensky, N.D. Myers, C.L. Rubenstein, Y. Jin, and A. McMahon. 2015. Assessing Multidimensional Well-being: Development and Validation of the I COPPE Scale. *Journal of Community Psychology* 43 (2): 199–226.

Sandel, Michael. 2009. *Justice: What's the Right Thing to Do?* New York, NY: Farrar, Straus and Giroux.

Sarun, Charumilind, Ezra Greenberg, Jessica Lamb, and Shubham Singhal. 2020. COVID-19: Saving Thousands of Lives and Trillions in Livelihoods'(Ending Lockdowns Alone Won't Restore Confidence or Growth. Only When the Novel Coronavirus Is Under Control Will Economic Growth Resume), August.

Seligman, Martin E.P. 2011. *Flourish: A Visionary New Understanding of Happiness and Well-being.* New York, Free Press, especially, Ch. 1.

Serafini, G., B. Parmigiani, A. Amerio, A. Aguglia, L. Sher, and M. Amore. 2020. The psychological impact of COVID-19 on the mental health in the general population. *QJM: Monthly Journal of the Association of Physicians* 113 (8): 531–537.

Ueda, M., R. Nordström, and T. Matsubayashi. 2022. Suicide and mental health during the COVID-19 pandemic in Japan. *Journal of Public Health* 44 (3): 541–548.

Yamamoto, T., C. Uchiumi, N. Suzuki, J. Yoshimoto, and E. Murillo-Rodriguez. 2020. The Psychological Impact of 'Mild Lockdown' in Japan during the COVID-19 Pandemic: A Nationwide Survey under a Declared State of Emergency. *International Journal of Environmental Research and Public Health* 17 (24): 9382.

8

Coping with COVID-19: Policy Responses and Citizens' Well-Being in Australia

Lindsay G. Oades

This chapter is a personal experience case-study of living in Melbourne, Australia during the COVID19 pandemic period of 2020–2022. Through this personal experience case-study I describe my lived experience in Melbourne during "lockdown," informed by my expertise in psychology and wellbeing, and my interest in political philosophy, to examine social justice issues during the pandemics. I will highlight how the long rivalry between the Australian cities of Sydney and Melbourne played out once again, this time in terms of the politics during the pandemic, illustrating well-known concepts of political philosophy, including positive and negative liberty (Berlin 1969) and Etzioni's (2015) notion of balancing individual rights with responsibilities to the community. The armory of tools from governments, health services and the law, including lockdowns ("stay at home" restrictions, including schools), domestic and national border restrictions, mandatory masks, testing, contract tracing, isolation, quarantine vaccinations with cohort staggered availability, social distancing and designation of essential workers,

L. G. Oades (✉)
The University of Melbourne, Parkville, VIC, Australia
e-mail: lindsay.oades@unimelb.edu.au

H. Ishido et al. (eds.), *Social Fairness in a Post-Pandemic World*,
https://doi.org/10.1007/978-981-19-9654-2_8

sanitization, ventilation and deep cleaning, were all used and conversely criticized depending on political orientations of governments and media.

To understand the psycho-political nature of my experience of the pandemic it is necessary to understand the structure of Australian government. Australia is a federation of multiple states and Australia's population was 25,978,935 people at 30 June 2022. Australia's national federal government during the majority of the COVID-19 pandemic has been the Liberal-National Coalition (i.e. conservative or centre/right parties). They were defeated at the election on 21 May 2022, with the Australian Labor Party forming government (i.e. progressive or centre/left party). The Australian federation of states is made up by six states and two mainland territories. The states make up the federation for the federal government. Consistent with the reflexive nature of a sound lived experience case study (Frechette et al. 2020), it is important to note that I have lived in three Australian states, South Australia, New South Wales and now Melbourne Victoria, all of which are relevant to this piece. Moreover, it is relevant that I am also more on the progressive side of the political spectrum.

Important to understanding the Australian experience, is that almost 8.1 million people, almost 32% of the country's population live in New South Wales; of these, approximately 5.5 million live in Sydney (2021 figures). During the pandemic years of 2020–2022 the state had a Liberal National Party (i.e. conservative) government, the same as the Federal government. This contrasts with Victoria, where I experienced the six lockdowns, and in which can be found the world's longest lockdown (Withers 2021), in Melbourne Victoria is home to 26% of Australia's population, meaning that between them these two states account for some 57% of the country's population. At the time, one state had a conservative government and the other had a progressive government. This set the scene for a major political and ideological battle within Australia, dividing states in ways that I had not seen in my lifetime. Table 8.1 illustrates some of the key events within the respective states representing different sides of the political spectrum.

On the left-hand side of Table 8.1, the economically liberal view and socially conservative view is represented by the Liberal National Party, which is a coalition in Australia. They were the incumbent government at

Table 8.1 Comparison of Liberal National Party and Australian Labor Party responses related to Sydney (NSW) and Melbourne (Victoria) during the COVID-19 pandemic

Liberal/Conversative View (LNP)	Progressive Labor View (ALP)
Federal Government and most populous state NSW	Second most populous state Vic with strong ALP Leader
Prioritising freedom and economy	Prioritising public health interventions and support
2020 low number of COVID infections except for *Ruby Princess* cruise ship in Sydney	2020 highest number of infections due to hotel quarantine breach. Extended lockdown in Melbourne
2021 high number of COVID infections under the Delta Variant	2021 Second extended lockdown (6 in total)
Australia behind on vaccination uptake, due to lack of supply on the part of the Federal government	Conservative media (Rupert Murdoch) give heavy criticism of "totalitarian" lock downs
Federal government prioritized NSW when greater vaccine supply became available	Western Australia and Queensland (Labor) closed borders within the country as they were low infections

a Federal level (until May, 2022); in addition, however, they ran the government in New South Wales, the most populous state. Compare this to the position of the progressive Australian Labor Party; they were not in federal government through 2020–2021, but they are in power in government in the second most populous state of Victoria, under its leader Premier Dan Andrews, who became known as "Dictator Dan" in the popular/conservative media due to the role he played in the six lockdowns in Melbourne (Flower 2022).

The premiers of each of the Australian states have Chief Health Officers, who advise the premiers with regard to public health matters. During the pandemic the state premiers and their chief health officers had unprecedented power and were constantly in the public eye. The federal prime minister formed a national cabinet, which included the federal government, and all the state premiers, making joint decisions, which is quite an unusual structure. Thus, the policy and politics around COVID-19 created new developments in Australia's own democracy.

In 2020, most of New South Wales and indeed the majority of Australia had low infections, with the exception of a couple of outbreaks due to one cruise ship in Sydney. By contrast, the situation in Victoria, the progressive state, was very bad and it experienced an extended lockdown. Again, on the left-hand side of Table 8.1, the other major debate is that the federal government is responsible for vaccinations, and the Australian vaccination uptake for a wealthy nation such as Australia was comparatively slow. In essence, it appeared that the federal government simply did not order enough vaccinations in the first instance. So, while these negative things were happening in Victoria, the conservative voice of Rupert Murdoch, who controls much of the Australian media, criticised the progressive government's policy of locking down the city of Melbourne and the wider state of Victoria. This was echoed across much of the rest of the nation's conservative media which is launching a very heavy attack on the Victorian Government for being totalitarian, intervening too much, and not caring about the economy or individual liberties and rights. Hence the coining of the term "Dictator Dan."

In the second half of 2021, with the rise of the wave of infections due to the Delta virus, Sydney, New South Wales started to experience high levels of infection The received view is that NSW were given priority to the vaccines when they became available. However, on Table 8.1 right side, the Victorian progressive state also got a Delta variant, and, again, went into lockdown, falling behind Sydney in terms of vaccinations.

A further part of one's experience of living in Melbourne, was the knowledge that some states, such as Western Australia, had zero COVID cases for the majority of these two years. However, other states, such as Queensland, have experienced outbreaks. By and large, it is the case that large parts of Australia have experienced little or no COVID-19 infections. So, in essence, what's happening in Sydney and Melbourne has driven most of the political debates around COVID. Western Australia, and to some extent Queensland, were also involved in terms of how the state borders were closed to other states.

Locking down has involved not allowing people to go to work or to school in Sydney and Melbourne, having a travel restriction set as five kilometers from one's home, and not being allowed to visit other people's homes. In particular in Melbourne, which experienced 262 days of restrictions over two years, across six lockdowns, people began to become increasingly frustrated. Many looked for someone to blame, be it a state government or a federal government. Thus, most of the arguments are focused on two key points: (i) whose fault was it for the delays in the vaccination rates?; and (ii) why did people need to be locked down for so long? One of the other big tools is border closures, obviously internationally, but within the country itself with certain states closing the borders to other people from other states, which has separated the country in an unprecedented manner.

One key debate was around the vaccination requirements on people to go back to work. And one of the issues was: should the state or the government mandate the vaccinations, or rather should this a condition of work set by each individual employer? As vaccination rates grew, this debate fell away, as did the number of cases. Recently, there has been some discussion about the rise of some potential treatments for people who have contracted COVID-19.

According to Figure 8.1, Australia now has relatively high vaccination rates. However, the low rates until the steep trajectory in August 2021 is noteworthy. Compare the different shaped curve to that of the United

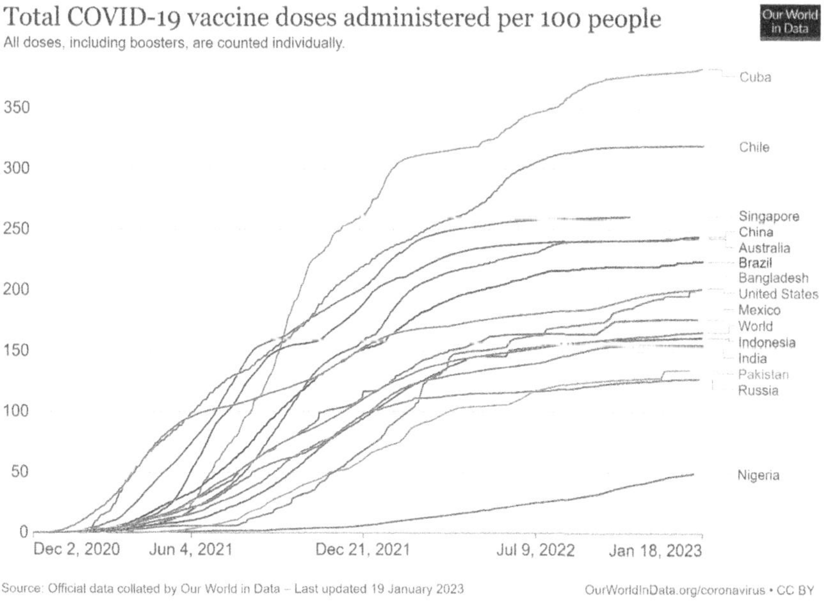

Fig. 8.1 COVID-19 vaccine rollout trajectories

States of America. Whilst both nations have high GDP per capita, the US vaccination rates were comparatively high in 2020 but then flattened in comparison with those of other nations. The Australian case was the converse. For a wealthy nation like Australia, many Australians expected that they would get vaccinated and that it would happen reasonably quickly, similar to the experience of those living in the United Kingdom or Canada. Many believe the conservative federal government simply did not order enough vaccines early enough, and that they then used the attacks on Melbourne and the progressive government as a distraction. Hence, as a direct experience, many Victorians felt either angry that they were being locked down by the state government, or angry at the Federal government for not ordering sufficient vaccines. Because of the slow vaccinations due to the delay in the vaccination supply, the state governments have relied heavily on restrictions and lockdowns. Moreover, there was a significant debate about the individual rights to vaccinations, and there remains a small but active anti-vaccination group, which is influenced in part by Libertarian movements in the USA.

The debates around lockdowns, vaccinations and mask wearing afford have a high degree of relevance to Berlin's (1969) notions of positive and negative liberty, and also to Etzioni's responsive communitarianism (2015), with their aim of balancing individual rights with responsibilities to the community. The lived experience of Melbourne during the pandemic made these vivid real-world debates, rather than simply theoretical concepts of political philosophy.

Positive liberty can be viewed as possession of the power and resources to act, in the context of the limitations e.g. structural, of the broader society which impacts a person's ability to act. This is also often referred to as "freedom to." It is seen as a form of moral prescription, having positive moral content. It may also be conceived as not being subject to any internal restraints, such as lust, ignorance or greed. For example, an animal is not free if they are a slave to their own internal drives.

Conversely, negative liberty, which is freedom from external restraint on one's actions is often referred to as "freedom from." It is seen as empty (or negative) of moral content. Aspects of libertarianism are closely associated with negative liberty.

In this way, concerns about lockdowns ("stay at home" restrictions), mandatory mask wearing and vaccinations (mandated) may be easily viewed through the lens of negative liberty. I need to be free of government constraint. Conversely, the notion of choosing to "do the right thing" so you do not infect others, either by wearing a mask or getting vaccinated, could be construed as a form of positive liberty. Ironically, for some periods within Australia, it may have been simply the slow vaccine supply and uptake which led to longer periods of lockdown. That is, one act to maintain negative liberty was traded for another. Personally I grew very tired of lockdowns, and certainly the impact they had on my family, particularly my children. I also still do not like mask wearing. However, I have been able to see them as part of the set of actions to manage a pandemic, even if not always managed perfectly. I have always been pro-vaccination and have never regarded them as an impact on my liberty; in fact, I construed them as giving me more freedom. This issues are what I refer to as the psycho-politics of the pandemic.

Etzioni's (2015) responsive communitarianism seeks to balance individual rights with responsibilities to the community. To me, this illustrated very closely aspects of decisions having to being taken during the pandemic in Melbourne. Whilst people disagreed with the actions, there were multiple efforts to respond to individual needs while being responsible to the larger community in terms of public health. Indeed, during this period there were losses to negative liberty. Waters et al. (2022) describes many of the psychological responses that people may have or could have used to improve positive liberties within the overall difficult external constraints. That is, whilst some complained vehemently about their individual rights being violated by the government (negative liberty), others accepted the restrictions and focused on managing their internal contracts (positive liberty) through different social and psychological methods as a way of managing 262 days of lockdown. Indeed, some experienced post-traumatic growth. Hence, there are a range of different psychological and political lenses through which people coped.

References

Berlin, I. 1969. Two Concepts of Liberty. In *Four Essays on Liberty*, ed. I. Berlin, 118–172. London: Oxford University Press. New ed. in Berlin 2002: 166–217.

Etzioni, Amitai. 2015. *The New Normal: Finding a Balance Between Individual Rights and the Common Good*. New Brunswick, NJ: Transaction Publishers.

Flower, W. 2022, August 14. *Loved-Up Selfies and Mourning the Death of His CAT: The Cringeworthy Steps Dan Andrews Is Taking to Shed The 'Dictator' Tag He Earned Turning Victoria Into a Global Embarrassment by Locking Its Citizens Up for 262 Days*. Melbourne Correspondent. https://www.dailymail.co.uk/news/melbourne/article-11098071/How-Dictator-Dan-Andrews-trying-erase-Covid-lockdown-tag.html.

Frechette, J., V. Bitzas, M. Aubry, K. Kilpatrick, and M. Lavoie-Tremblay. 2020. Capturing Lived Experience: Methodological Considerations for Interpretive Phenomenological Inquiry. *International Journal of Qualitative Methods* 19: 1–12. https://doi.org/10.1177/1609406920907254.

Waters, Lea, S. Kim Cameron, Katherine Nelson-Coffey, Damien L. Crone, Margaret L. Kern, Tim Lomas, Lindsay Oades, Rhea L. Owens, James O. Pawelski, Tayyab Rashid, Meg A. Warren, Mathew A. White, and Paige Williams. 2022. Collective Wellbeing and Posttraumatic Growth During COVID-19: How Positive Psychology Can Help Families, Schools, Workplaces and Marginalized Communities. *The Journal of Positive Psychology* 17 (6): 761–789. https://doi.org/10.1080/17439760.2021.1940251.

Withers, R.. 2021. A Tale of Two Lockdowns. *The Politics*. July 27. https://www.themonthly.com.au/today/rachel-withers/2021/27/2021/1627365366/tale-two-lockdowns.

9

Mexico Facing the COVID-19 Pandemic: Ineffective Societal and Governmental Responses in a Country with a High Level of Socioeconomic Inequality and a Precarious Health System

Alfonso Torrero Russo

1 Introduction: Important Factors That Hindered COVID-19 Pandemic Appropriate Control

Mexico had an important advantage to prevent a big impact of the COVID-19 epidemic. Since mid-February 2020, two months before a considerable number of cases were reported in the country, in all national and international media of easy access in Mexico, there were stories about important outbreaks of the virus in Asian and European countries. For example, it was shown the tragic and exponential COVID-19 outbreak in Italy during March and April 2020. Even recognizing this and other similar situations, the national government did not take preventive

A. Torrero Russo (✉)
Universidad Autónoma Metropolitana, Mexico City, Mexico
e-mail: alfonsotorusso@xanum.uam.mx

H. Ishido et al. (eds.), *Social Fairness in a Post-Pandemic World*,
https://doi.org/10.1007/978-981-19-9654-2_9

actions to stop the coronavirus outbreak, even when they recognized that sooner or later COVID-19 was going to arrive in the country.

It would be a mistake to say that the government's delayed reaction was the only factor that affected massive coronavirus outbreaks in several Mexican states. A complex combination of factors hindered COVID-19 pandemic appropriate control. Some of the most important ones include the lack of social pressure to attain health and hygiene measures, the lack of penalties for not attaining mandatory governmental regulations, the ineffective healthcare system, the lack of border control, and the misinformation by the government and the populist president discourses. Throughout the chapter, these factors will be described, and consideration given to their specific contextual reality. In the final section, some reflections about Mexico at the present time are shown; that is, the post-COVID-19 scenario in the country.

2 A New Crisis in a Country Characterized by Socioeconomic Unfairness

According to Instituto Mexicano de la Competitividad A.C. (*Mexican Institute of Competitiveness CSO*) (Moy 2022), the last report about poverty in the country showed that in 2020, 43.9% of the population (55.7 million people) lived in multidimensional poverty and 8.5% (10.9 million people) lived in multidimensional extreme poverty. A person is considered to be in multidimensional poverty if his/her income is insufficient to acquire the goods or services to satisfy his/her needs, and lives with at least one of these social deprivations: lack of social security, health security, education, food, housing or basic housing services. If a person has more than three social deprivations, they are considered to be in extreme multidimensional poverty (Moy 2022). This statistic is linked to another one which emphasizes the socioeconomic unfairness that is experienced in Mexico, where more than 60% of families live on US$5 dollars a day or less. The prices of things in Mexico are relatively high, meaning that this daily amount of money does not permit a comfortable way of life, far less being sufficient to maintain a family. Poverty is exacerbated by the economic gap in the country, with the *World Inequality Report 2022* showed that, in Mexico, 10% of the wealthiest people have 30 times more income than 50% of the poorest population (Torres 2021).

There is also a problem related to Mexicans working in the informal sector. 55.8% of the working population are involved in this sector, which means that they do not have social and housing security (INEGI 2021). Many of these informal workers live from hand to mouth, making it very difficult for them to stop working.

However, between the beginning of the COVID-19 pandemic in March 2020 and the end of 2021 some 2.1 million people lost their jobs (Rodríguez 2022). Most of the lost jobs were part of the formal commercial sector: salesmen who had to pay rent, personnel salaries, perishables, etc. In contrast to the actions of the US government, that in Mexico did not support the formal or informal commercial sector with funds, e.g., by providing funds to people who had lost their jobs and could not pay rent. Accordingly, a variety of non-essential businesses, in particular from the formal sector, quickly went bankrupt. Hualde (2020) outlined how the Mexican government took two measures to help citizen during the pandemic. First, it tried to prevent the loss of formal jobs, by asking organizations not to fire their employees; it also made money credits available to small businesses. However, these measures were not promoted in the media, and were also criticized for placing citizens in debt (Hualde 2020).

3 Healthcare Crisis: Inadequate Hospitals Infrastructure and an Insufficiency of Medical Resources

One critical element in controlling a COVID-19 severe infection is the country's healthcare system. Mexico spends relatively on its own healthcare system. For example, the World Health Organization (WHO) recommends that countries invest a minimum of 7% of their GDP in health-related sectors; in the latest figures available, Mexico invested 4.2%, which is a relatively low figure (Instituto de Salud para el Bienestar 2022). The results of this underinvestment are a lack of adequate infrastructure, facilities, tools, health materials and medicines in public hospitals (Badillo 2020).

In consequence, from the start of the pandemic's first wave, in May 2020, small-scale strikes from healthcare workers took place, e.g., Mexican doctors and nurses went on a strike in a Mexico State Hospital asking for adequate materials to work, because they did not have the needed protection against COVID-19 (AFP México 2021).

The scarcity of resources and inadequate infrastructure in public hospitals also affected patients, which suffered from a lack of hospital beds, oxygen tanks and medicines to treat their infections. Patients receiving public health services are less than half of the working force. Normally, workers in the formal economic sector are the ones that pay to receive public health services. The Mexican Law specifies that all workers, from the public or the private sector, are compelled to become affiliated to one of the two main health systems in Mexico: the Instituto Mexicano del Seguro Social (IMSS) (*Mexican Institute of Social Security*) and the Instituto de Seguridad y Servicio Social para los trabajadores del Estado (ISSSTE) (*Institute of Security and Social Services for the State workers*). However, as mentioned before, more than half of the total workers are a part of the informal sector, which commonly means that they do not have free access to health services. Informal workers may buy their affiliation to be part of the IMSS or, in some cases, they may become affiliated to a third public health system that is free, named Secretaría de Salud (*Health Secretariat*). Statistically, the inaccessibility of healthcare services is a serious problem, since 28.2% of citizens do not have access to it, meaning that 35.7 million people have to pay private healthcare services when needed (CONEVAL 2021).

4 Governmental Decisions to Control the COVID-19 Pandemic

In this complex context, the Mexican government took some decisions to reduce the seriousness of the situation that was taking place. From April 2020 to January 2022, their strategy consisted in the mandatory use of masks in enclosed places and intermittent lockdowns of non-essential services e.g., entertainment stores, cinemas, and bars. The common health measures included not having reunions or congregations of more than 50 people, sneezing by following the respiratory etiquette, greeting without hugging or kissing, maintaining a minimum of 1.5 meter distance when interacting with other people, and hand sanitizing at the gates of public and essential places, e.g., convenience stores, food retail stores and drugstores (Gobierno de México 2020). The main advertising strategies, which accompanied the health measures, were two: the repetition of the hashtag #quédateencasa (*#stayathome*) in different governmental acts, commercials and media spots, and the media promotion of a character called Susana Distancia, a word game that includes the name of a woman "Susana" and the word "Distancia" (*Distance*). These two words can be divided in a different form as "Su sana distancia", which means *"your healthy distance,"* a reference to the 1.5 meter measure that people should maintain in social interactions (Secretaría de Salud 2020). Both of these advertising phrases were catchy and memorable, but this did not guarantee that citizens followed its suggestions.

In addition to those two strategies, the Mexican government sent mixed messages related to COVID-19 dangerousness. One common program in the country is the morning conferences given by the president, which are transmitted on public TV and radio shows. During the first semester of 2020, the president gave some of the morning conferences without using a mask. Badillo (2020) wrote an article quoting presidential public declarations related to COVID-19, from January 22 to March 18, 2020. By the end of February, the president was declaring that the coronavirus was not that bad, and that it was not even comparable to influenza. On March 4, the president said that people should hug each other and that nothing wrong was going to happen. Later on in the same month he said that some politicians from opposing parties were given fake news related to the fatality of the coronavirus. Finally, the president remarked that two religious saints' stamps were his protection against COVID-19 (Mendez 2020).

On a different note, the Mexican government proposed and passed a law to cut funds given to non-governmental organizations (NGOs) (Camarena 2021); and, in 2021, a new law was passed to limit the amount of funds that a civil society organization could get from citizens and corporations (Arista 2021). The idea or justification behind these political decisions was that NGOs have led to corrupt activities, including money laundering, in which enterprises gave a big amount of corrupted money to NGOs. This justification was incorrect because there were just two or three cases in which that happened, and the president decided to generalize those situations. Those changes contributed to the diminishing of fairness during the COVID-19 pandemic. The main reason is that Mexican social and health institutions, as mentioned in the socioeconomic unfairness section, do not have the capacity to cover citizens' basic needs, guaranteeing their housing, health and food security, so civil society organizations play an important role in diminishing those social inequalities.

There were some cases in which civil society organizations work together and helped during the pandemic. One action that government did not do but which two NGOs did was the gathering of basic food baskets: the Centro de Acopio Barrio 28 project gave food baskets to workers from the tourism sector that lost their jobs or had a dramatic decrease in their profit (Leon 2020); and the FondoDespensaMX gave food baskets to families in which their parents or economic providers lost their jobs (CEMEFI 2021). Another example was the effort from Fundacion Nemi A.C. (Foundation Nemi CSO), an NGO that donated masks and other healthy materials to three hospitals that needed them. But, in general, there were very low civil society interventions to help during the pandemic (Leon 2020).

5 Lack of Social Pressure and Sanctions for Not Attaining Mandatory Governmental Regulations

Ineffective governmental decisions, an inadequate healthcare system and the high levels of poverty were not the only problems that worsened the impact of the pandemic. Many people, particularly informal workers, did not follow all the supposedly compulsory safety measures established by the Mexican government. It is difficult to criticize their actions because many of them were in the next dilemma "I'm afraid of catching the coronavirus, but I'm more afraid of not getting money to buy food." Probably, most of the population understood this dilemma and preferred not to criticize people that continued working in conditions of close proximity; in addition, policemen did not apply any penalty against people that did not follow government "mandatory" regulations against COVID-19. One article from Noticias ONU (*UN News*) describes this dilemma, which was frequent in countries with a high level of informal jobs and a lack of governmental aid during the pandemic (Noticias ONU 2020). Ureste (2020), a journalist from a critical Mexican magazine called *Animal Político* (*Political Animal*), presented different testimonies of citizens that worked in the informal sector and that decided to continue working even in the context of a high risk of contagion. There were also anti-vax groups which made some small protests that, even if they were not on a large scale as occurred in the US, still misinformed many people (Carrió 2021).

In addition, citizens from Latin American countries, including Mexico, tend to have a closer proximity in their social interactions, when compared to the situation in European and Asian countries. This characteristic could have added another difficulty during the COVID-19 pandemic. In a deeper reflection about social interaction in Mexico, a close proximity while interacting could be perceived as a demonstration of being interested in the person you are talking to. In this case, been close to a person could be seen as an attitude that promotes social fairness.

6 Soft Tourism Regulations with Almost No Restrictions Due to the COVID-19 Pandemic

The Mexican government adopted a very soft position related to tourism control during the COVID-19 pandemic. González (2021) explained the very controversial position of Mexico related to the almost non-regulated entry by air into the country during the pandemic. At no point did Mexico close its airports, and neither did it demand that foreign visitors to take COVID- 19 tests to enter the country, or establish quarantines or other regulations.

Some of the justifications for the lax control were given by the Mexican Subsecretary of Health, Arturo López-Gatell. He mentioned that international travelers were not a risk for Mexicans because it was well documented that, in general, travelers were people of low contagion risk; he also mentioned that people did not travel when they were sick. On the other hand, López-Gatell explained that Mexican tourism was benefiting from governmental politics. Some citizens questioned the Subsecretary discourse, comparing him with a politician and not an epidemiologist. In contrast with the discourse of López-Gatell, La Organization Panamericana de la Salud (*Panamerican Health Organization*) alerted that, in February 2021, a higher number of coronavirus cases and deaths were reported in the tourist states in Mexico (González 2021).

7 Vaccination as the Main Factor to Decrease the Number of Deaths Related to COVID-19

Generally speaking, a substantial decrease in the number of coronavirus cases was achieved when most of the adult population got vaccinated. The next two figures show statistics about deaths related to COVID-19 and the percentage of vaccinated citizens. The first (Fig. 9.1) shows the daily number of deaths from the pandemic peak, January 2021 to October 2022. The second (Fig. 9.2) shows the percentage of citizens vaccinated, with one or more shots, from January 2021 to May 2022. Both figures can be compared and related to the vaccination strategy implemented by the Mexican Healthcare system.

As shown in Fig. 9.1, the pandemic peak occurred in January 2021, reaching a peak of 1458 deaths per day. The number of deaths experienced a substantial decrease in June 2021. This is consistent with the first vaccination stage in which all legal adults, aged 18 and above, could get a first COVID-19 vaccine shot (Capital 21 Web 2020). In September

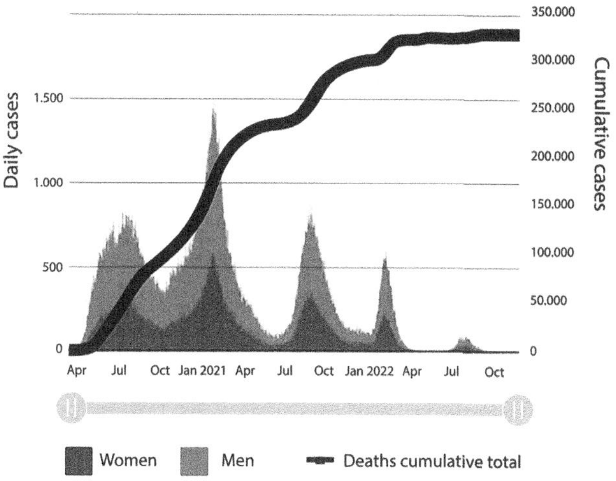

Fig. 9.1 Number of daily cases related to COVID-19 (Gobierno de México 2022)

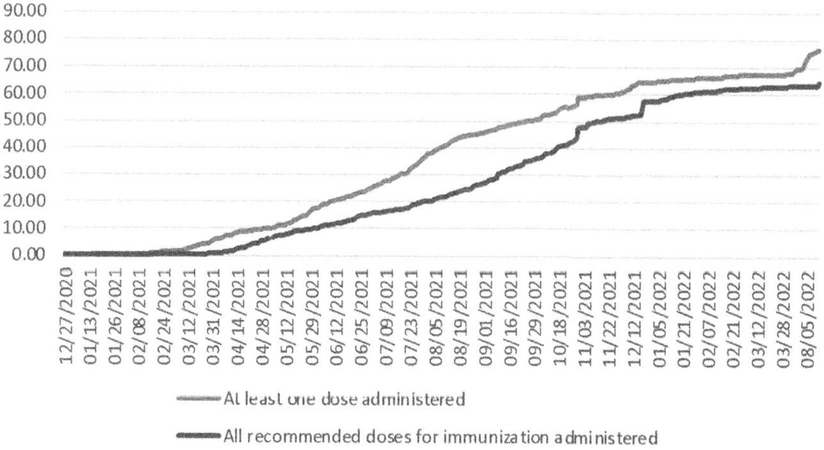

Fig. 9.2 Percentage of the Mexican population vaccinated against COVID-19 (Statista 2022). (Source: Statista HP: https://www.statista.com/statistics/1104529/population-vaccinated-against-covid-19-mexico/ (Accessed October 7)

2021, a new increase in cases was reported, but not even half of the deaths in January 2021 were reported; it was suspected that most of the deaths were of people who had not been vaccinated. In January 2022, there was another increase in the death rate, which was related to the new omicron variant. Before the national vaccination strategy was carried out, the number of deaths was not naturally decreasing. Because of this and the figures data, there seems to be a clear negative correlation between the number of deaths and the population vaccination percentage; a higher vaccination rate led to a lower death rate (Gobierno de México 2022; Statista 2022).

8 The Post-COVID Scenario in México

The post-COVID scenario in Mexico was the result of gradual changes but, officially, mask usage was established as not mandatory in close places on April 26, 2022 (Redacción El Financiero 2022b). On the same day, the Mexican Health Subsecretary expressed that COVID-19 was now endemic in the country; in other words, the coronavirus was a common circulating virus with a high contagion rate, but was not regarded as being of severe concern (Redacción El Financiero 2022a).

On another note, the government continues to limit the possible actions and decisions of NGOs. Social decisions seem to be taken centrally, by a single actor, the government; the president and governmental institutions are the ones that take decisions related to social or other types of welfare. The president still says that NGOs and the private sector are corrupt, useless, and excessively privileged. This attitude is expressed to justify that governmental institutions should be the only ones to create, invest and manage welfare programs and policies, and should take political decisions.

Currently, slow changes in the economic growth are observed in Mexico. All the non-essential services given before the pandemic are allowed to be offered now. However, many organizations and small businesses, which closed during the pandemic, are not able to or do not have the resources to reopen. Neither the government nor civil society have done anything to help bankrupt businesses to open again. But let us not forget that the latter do not have the number of resources of the former. The government cannot solve every social problem it speaks about in its discourses, and hindering civil society simply make the problems worse.

Furthermore, there is a diversity of groups that do not feel supported, or even heard, by the actual government.

In this post-COVID-19 context, civil society should get together with different organizations and social actors, helping each other to strengthen their representativity and decision-making. In the case of a new pandemic or social crisis, other social actors should be better prepared to counterbalance negligent decisions taken by government or other powerful organizations.

References

AFP México. 2021. Las enfermeras denunciaban en 2020 falta de material y de diagnóstico de pacientes con COVID-19. *AFP Factual*. Accessed November 2022. https://factual.afp.com/las-enfermeras-denunciaban-en-2020-falta-de-material-y-de-diagnostico-de-pacientes-con-covid-19.

Arista, L. 2021. De la crítica a la asfixia: la 4T apunta contra las ONGs. Expansión *Política*. Accessed May 2012. https://politica.expansion.mx/mexico/2021/10/31/de-la-critica-a-la-asfixia-la-4t-apunta-contra-las-ongs.

Badillo, D. 2020. Falta de material y medicamentos, explica alta mortalidad por COVID-19: Miguel Ángel Toscano. El Economista. Accessed May 2022. https://www.eleconomista.com.mx/politica/Falta-de-material-y-medicamentos-explica-alta-mortalidad-por-Covid-19-Miguel-Angel-Toscano-20200912-0023.html.

Camarena, S. 2021. La Sociedad Civil en tiempos de AMLO. *El País*. Accessed May 2022. https://elpais.com/opinion/2021-10-23/la-sociedad-civil-en-tiempos-de-amlo.html.

Capital 21 Web. 2020. Etapas de vacunación contra el COVID-19 en México; iniciará este diciembre. *Capital 21*. Accessed November 2022. https://www.capital21.cdmx.gob.mx/noticias/?p=6270.

Carrió, O. 2021. ¿Qué dicen los enemigos de las vacunas anticovid? *Primera Plana MX*. Accessed May 2022. https://primeraplana.mx/archivos/787626.

CEMEFI. 2021. Fondo Despensa MX. *CEMEFI*. Accessed November 2022. https://despensamx.cemefi.org/.

CONEVAL. 2021. Nota técnica sobre la carencia por acceso a los servicios de salud, 2018–2020. Accessed November 2022. https://www.coneval.org.mx/Medicion/MP/Documents/MMP_2018_2020/Notas_pobreza_2020/

Nota_tecnica_sobre_la_carencia_por_acceso_a_los_servicios_de_salud_2018_2020.pdf.

Gobierno de México. 2020. Medidas de seguridad sanitaria. Gobierno de México. Retrieved November 2020. https://coronavirus.gob.mx/medidas-de-seguridad-sanitaria/#:~:text=Acciones&text=Estornudar%20o%20toser%20aplicando%20la,la%20Secretar%C3%ADa%20de%20Salud%20Federal.

———. 2022. Información General: COVID-19. Accessed May 2022. https://datos.covid-19.conacyt.mx/.

González, M. 2021. Coronavirus en México: cómo el país se convirtió en un oasis para turistas internacionales en medio de la pandemia (hasta para los que tienen que pasar cuarentenas). *BBC News Mundo*. Accessed November 2022. https://www.bbc.com/mundo/noticias-america-latina-56035746.

Hualde, A. 2020. La pandemia y el mercado de trabajo en México: efectos graves, perspectivas inciertas. COMECSO. Retrieved November 2020. https://www.comecso.com/wp-content/uploads/2020/08/Covid-06-Hualde.pdf.

INEGI. 2021. Actualización de la medición de la Economía Informal 2003–2020 Preliminar. https://www.inegi.org.mx/contenidos/saladeprensa/boletines/2021/pibmed/pibmed2020.pdf.

Instituto de Salud para el Bienestar. 2022. En México se invierte en el sector salud: Insabi. Gobierno de México. Retrieved November 2022. https://www.gob.mx/insabi/prensa/041-en-mexico-se-invierte-en-el-sector-salud-insabi-300377?idiom=es#:~:text=En%202021%20se%20registr%C3%B3%20un,con%20respecto%20al%20a%C3%B1o%202020.

Leon, A. 2020. Redes de Cooperación y Solidaridad ante la contingencia ocasionada por el COVID-19. En México ante el COVID-19: acciones y retos. Cámara de Diputados; Consejo Editorial H. Cámara de Diputados; y Universidad Autónoma Metropolitana, México, 17–25.

Méndez, J. 2020. El presidente de México utiliza amuletos y estampitas contra el coronavirus. El Periódico. Accessed May 2022. https://www.elperiodico.com/es/internacional/20200319/amuletos-estampitas-lopez-obrador-luchar-coronavirus-7896098.

Moy, V. 2022. Las cifras más recientes de pobreza. IMCO Centro de Investigación en Política Pública. Accessed November 2022. https://imco.org.mx/las-cifras-mas-recientes-de-pobreza/.

Noticias ONU. 2020. Contagiarse o morir de hambre: el dilema de muchos trabajadores durante la pandemia de coronavirus. Naciones Unidas. Accessed November 2020. https://news.un.org/es/story/2020/05/1473962.

Redacción El Financiero. 2022a. López- Gatell dijo que México está transitando a una endemia de COVID-19: ¿Qué quiere decir? El financiero. Accessed November 2022. https://www.elfinanciero.com.mx/salud/2022/04/26/lopez-gatell-dijo-que-mexico-esta-transitando-a-una-endemia-de-covid-19-que-quiere-decir/.

———. 2022b. COVID en México: uso de cubrebocas no es imprescindible, dice López-Gatell. El Financiero. Accessed November 2022. https://www.elfinanciero.com.mx/nacional/2022/04/26/covid-en-mexico-uso-de-cubrebocas-no-es-imprescindible-dice-lopez-gatell/.

Rodríguez, D. 2022. El desempleo no cede: México registra 2,1 millones de desocupados al cierre de 2021. El País. Retrieved November 2020. https://elpais.com/mexico/economia/2022-01-20/el-desempleo-no-cede-mexico-registra-21-millones-de-desocupados-al-cierre-de-2021.html.

Secretaría de Salud. 2020. #Quédateencasa y sigue las recomendaciones de Susana Distancia. Facebook. Accessed November 2022. https://www.facebook.com/SecretariadeSaludMX/photos/a.394407287274637/2916629711719036/?type=3.

Statista. 2022. Share of the Population Partially or Fully Vaccinated Against COVID-19 in Mexico from December 24, 2020 to October 7, 2022. Statista. Accessed November 2022. https://www.statista.com/statistics/1104529/population-vaccinated-against-covid-19-mexico/.

Torres, O. 2021. El 10% más rico de México tiene 30 veces más ingresos que el 50% más pobre. Expansión. Accessed November 2022. https://expansion.mx/economia/2021/12/07/desigualdad-en-mexico-ricos-30-veces-mas-ingresos-mas-pobres#:~:text=El%2010%25%20m%C3%A1s%20rico%20de,Laboratorio%20de%20las%20Desigualdades%20Mundiales.

Ureste, M. 2020. Me da miedo el coronavirus, pero me da más miedo morirme de hambre si no trabajo. Animal Político MX. Accessed November 2022. https://www.animalpolitico.com/2020/03/coronavirus-miedo-cerrar-negocios-trabajo-cdmx/.

10

APEC's Response to the COVID-19 Crisis and Social Justice

Hikari Ishido

1 Introduction

This chapter builds on Mizushima et al. (2021), a sister volume to this book and an earlier study on social justice, to examine global social justice regarding the COVID-19 crisis and APEC, an intergovernmental forum. I aim to develop discussions while focusing on international economics (my main field of study) and interweaving philosophy and ideological beliefs (my minor fields of study). This chapter is organized as follows. In Sect. 2, the concept of "open regionalism" maintained by APEC is introduced and examined. Section 3 is an overview of APEC's response to the COVID-19 crisis, focusing on the facts of the case. Next, Sect. 4, continues the discussion on APEC and global social justice, and the "Conclusion" looks ahead to the role of APEC and the global community in realizing a global and just society.

H. Ishido (✉)
Graduate School of Global and Transdisciplinary Studies, Chiba University, Chiba, Japan
e-mail: ishido@faculty.chiba-u.jp

H. Ishido et al. (eds.), *Social Fairness in a Post-Pandemic World*,
https://doi.org/10.1007/978-981-19-9654-2_10

2 "Open Regionalism" of APEC

APEC's Potential for "Openness" and "Regionalism" ("Two Focal Points")

The Asia Pacific Economic Cooperation (APEC), an international organization established in 1989, is a forum for intergovernmental discussions with a view to the economic development of Pacific Rim countries and regions. Sovereign states, including the United States, China, Japan, and Australia, and "regions" not considered states, participate (for a total of 21 members).[1] The most characteristic course of action in APEC is that of "open regionalism." The idea is not to conduct trade and investment as a block economy in a closed space, and, like a restaurant, not discriminate against trade (exports and imports of goods and services) and investment (establishment of factories and offices overseas by companies) from any country ("economy" in APEC). The idea is to create an integrated economic zone by applying equal tariff rates and, if possible, as low a tariff rate as possible.

In considering social justice, the consideration of philosophical and ideological perspectives is essential while thinking about APEC because it provides members of society with a worldview and a code of ethics. One perspective that I wish to focus on here is the position of Kawase (2021), who advocates liberal nationalism as it relates to the political management of the state.[2] It is a perspective that applies the two policy foci of liberalism and nationalism,[3] as two-in-one governing principles, and

---

[1] Specifically, Hong Kong is part of the nation of China, but is an independent APEC member, and Taiwan is also an independent APEC member, but as is well known, China considers Taiwan to be part of its own nation and does not recognize its national sovereignty. Therefore, in APEC, the word "country" is never used, but instead "economy" (economic zone) is used. In this chapter and wherever the context permits, "economy" is used in place of "country."

[2] In connection to this, Kawase (2021: 328) said, "a properly administered liberal democracy is necessary to maintain the nation-state that is strong and prosperous for a long time. And an autonomous nation-state is necessary for the just and effective maintenance of the system of egalitarian liberalism. It is this complementarity that is most important to liberal nationalism." he stated.

[3] The pre-war thinker Kanzo Uchimura developed the argument that, "truth is not in a circle (where only one focus exists), but in an ellipse (where two foci exist)" (Uchimura 1970). In nature, the

seems to echo the main principle of action that APEC has in "open regionalism," which is the principle of "openness" and "regionalism"—also two principles in one.

The Ideal of a Fair and Global Society Based on Immunity

Here, I would like to focus on the word "immunity," which is one of the terms that characterizes the COVID-19 crisis and applies it to the ideal of a global and just society. Tada (1993, 2001), while conducting scientific research on the function of immunity as a medical scientist, has at the same time developed a "semantics of immunity" that relates the philosophical meaning of immunity,[4] from the point of view of society. According to his observations,

- Immunity is an enigmatic mechanism for distinguishing between self and non-self.
- For a living organism with an immune system, the distinction between self and non-self is actually ambiguous.
- In fact, the essence of life is the desire for a "supersystem" (self-reference, self-organization, i.e., the transformation of the self and the rules surrounding the self by the internal and external relationships of the self) that goes beyond the "system."
- Society is also a "supersystem," and from the perspective that emphasizes the generative process itself, it is likely to have unexplained prin-

solar system has two foci, and the Earth orbits in an ellipse with the Sun as one focal point and is therefore said to be stable. According to Uchimura, there is a theory that the entire universe is also elliptical, including the governing principle of human society, and the point where attention should be focused on is sought from the two principles (focus) of being neither too close nor too distant is similar to Kawase's liberal nationalism and APEC's "open regionalism," which is what I am focusing on. This is an argument that can be understood as the fundamental problem of Western philosophy, which has struggled to integrate materialism and spiritualism.

[4] Regarding immunity, the philosopher Derrida and other philosophers were studied. For example, he introduced the concept of "auto-immunité" in his book, *Rogues* (Derrida 2009), in which he points out that democracy, "for the sake of what is good for democracy," destroys the very idea of democracy. However, Derrida continues his philosophical reflections on overcoming the situation with the concept of "autoimmunity."

ciples for its fair maintenance, stability, and growth, but at least an "immune" function that resolves the rules surrounding the self and non-self becomes essential.

As is well known, in the case of the COVID-19 crisis, much attention was paid to the argument that we should deal with the infections caused by COVID-19 by acquiring "immunity." The important issue in this chapter is that the mechanism of immunity, which distinguishes between "self" and "non-self," is consistent with Tada's discussion of society, and seems to overlap with the policy management that distinguishes between the internal and the external areas of a sovereign state (although in APEC it is not a state but an "economy"). The "open regionalism" of APEC has become a slogan with two foci (values), "open" (emphasizing extraterritoriality, i.e., non-self) and "regionalism" (emphasizing intra-regionalism, i.e., self), as mentioned above, but the relationship between APEC members has fluctuated over the two foci. Additionally, during the COVID-19 crisis, APEC, where the US and China coexist, is also joined by the "unilateralism" of the two countries, and the effectiveness of its values (open regionalism) and practical functions are being questioned in the struggle between them.

APEC is Open to Regionalism (Self) and Extraterritoriality (Non-Self)

APEC plays the role of incubator, that is, the parent body that creates regional integration. Specifically, APEC created the Trans-Pacific Partnership Agreement (TPP) negotiations in 2005 (12 APEC member economies participated in the negotiations). In September 2021 (with the exception of the United States, which has withdrawn from the TPP negotiations), 11 other members participating in the negotiations, including Japan, have entered into a "Comprehensive and Advanced Agreement on the Trans-Pacific Partnership (CPTPP)," which went into effect in 2020. China and Taiwan (referred to as Chinese Taipei in APEC) applied for participation at about the same time, and it is one of the highlights of the global trend regarding regional integration.

Promoting regional integration in a way that is open to oneself (APEC members) and non-self (non-members) means, specifically, applying tariffs on imports at the lowest possible level without discriminating between intra- and extra-regional tariffs [i.e., tariff measures based on most favored nation (MFN) treatment], which is also a major "implicit issue." The US, a key APEC member, has interpreted the current situation as "the promotion of free trade agreements (i.e., the application of low tariff rates only within the region) is the principal axis of APEC," in order to prioritize its own trade interests.

3 APEC's Response to the COVID-19 Crisis APEC Ministers Responsible for Trade Meeting, Summit Meeting, and Response to the COVID-19 Crisis

The APEC meeting in 2021 was chaired by New Zealand, with the overall theme of

> "Join, Work, Grow. Together" (or Haumi ē, Hui ē, Tāiki ē in the language of the Maori, the indigenous people of New Zealand), and in terms of social justice, the keyword is "together."

In July 2021, an informal summit was held in an online format and a joint statement was issued by the leaders that they will work to expand the supply and production of vaccines in response to the COVID-19 pandemic. In addition, discussions were held among the leaders on how to rebuild the economy damaged by the COVID-19 crisis, and the statement also included a commitment to work together on vaccinations. Furthermore, the joint statement said it would encourage the voluntary transfer of vaccine production technology "on mutually agreed terms" to prepare for future public health crises and stressed that the path for the safe resumption of cross-border travel should be paved "without compromising efforts to control the spread of infection." The joint statement continued, "the pandemic continues to have a devastating impact on the region's population and economy. Only by accelerating equitable access to safe, effective, quality-assured, affordable COVID-19 vaccines can we overcome this public health emergency."

The conference was attended by then Prime Minister Yoshihide Suga, US President Joe Biden, Russian President Vladimir Putin, and others, in addition to Xi Jinping, President of the People's Republic of China, who gave a video speech (instead of participating live), in which he announced that he would "donate funds to APEC and establish a fund for the fight against COVID-19 and for economic reconstruction." After the meeting, Prime Minister Jacinda Ardern of New Zealand, APEC chair, said, "this discussion moved away from vaccine nationalism and focused on all aspects—the production, sharing and use of vaccines—that will lead to global vaccine deployment." She said they had agreed that pandemic was not over and that it was important to prepare for the future.

Additionally, President Biden also stressed the importance of multilateral cooperation and a commitment to a free and open Indo-Pacific, arguing that "we must invest in improving the security of global public health in preparation for the next pandemic." Russian President Putin said that global barriers to vaccine production and distribution need to be removed.

Sovereignty Conflicts and Social Justice

The conflict between the United States and China (both members of APEC) has not been resolved, but rather the situation of conflict between the two countries can be seen in the daily news on the trade and security standoff between them, and the sovereignty conflict is far from the situation of "open regionalism" advocated by APEC. In the case of the COVID-19 crisis, APEC encourages the "voluntary" transfer of vaccine production technology (without distinction between domestic and international, intra- and extra-regional), but joint vaccine development between the US and China cannot be envisaged at present.

However, the "open regionalism" of APEC, in which both the US and China, the world's major economies (or major economies), participate, seems to have mitigated the clash between them to some extent. Even if the US and China do not meet on their own, both attend APEC meetings and certainly exchange views about cooperation.

As mentioned above, Tada has pointed out from immunological research that the self and non-self are extremely ambiguous, and even in the global confrontation between the two major powers, the United States and China, it is quite common for Americans of Chinese descent to occupy important positions in the US government. This seems to indicate the ambiguity of the distinction between self and non-self in society.

The values of social justice of APEC's "open regionalism" have been greatly shaken by the reality of the conflict between the United States and China. Nevertheless, APEC still seems to have its own reason for existence. Therefore, at the beginning of the next section, I would like to reexamine the values held by APEC.

4 APEC and Global Social Justice

APEC's Response to the Corona Disaster

The APEC meeting is held every year one; they speak of "open regionalism." Regarding COVID-19, they say, "let's voluntarily develop a vaccine." The idea is to make it voluntary, make it open to the outside world, and to export if possible. The 2021 APEC, which took place during the COVID-19 crisis, was chaired by New Zealand, as mentioned above, and policy efforts were made to embody "open regionalism." In APEC, there is also a policy that states that vaccines should be supplied in the supply chain as voluntarily as possible. In the ministerial meeting, the supply chain of vaccines is spoken of. Toward the end of 2021, an informal summit meeting was held online, and the leaders issued a joint statement to expand vaccine supply and production in response to the coronavirus pandemic. The statement also included discussions among the leaders on the way to rebuild the economy damaged by the coronavirus, and that they would cooperate in advancing vaccinations.

The joint statement also said it would encourage the voluntary transfer of vaccine manufacturing technology "on mutually agreed terms" to prepare for future public health crises and stressed that it should pave the way for the safe resumption of cross-border travel "without undermining efforts to control the spread of infection." "The pandemic continues to have a devastating impact on the region's population and economy. Only by accelerating equitable access to safe, effective, quality-assured, and affordable corona vaccines can this public health emergency be overcome," the joint statement said.

The meeting was attended by then-Prime Minister Yoshihide Suga, U.S. President Joe Biden, and Russian President Vladimir Putin, and Chinese President Xi Jinping also delivered a video speech (instead of a live performance), declaring that he would "donate funds to APEC and establish a fund for corona countermeasures and economic recovery." Prime Minister Jacinda Ardern of New Zealand, APEC Chair Economy, said after the meeting, "This discussion focused on moving away from vaccine nationalism and focusing on all aspects that will lead to global vaccine rollout, such as vaccine manufacturing, sharing and use." They said they agreed that the pandemic was not the end of the pandemic and that it was important to prepare for the future.

President Biden also stressed that "we should prepare for the next pandemic and invest in improving global public health safety" and emphasized the importance of multilateral cooperation and commitment to a free and open Indo-Pacific. Russian President Vladimir Putin pointed out the need to remove global barriers to vaccine production and distribution. However, this "multilateral cooperation" has not been realized in the true sense due to the conflict of sovereignty between the United States and China (both APEC members), and rather the situation of bilateral confrontation is reminiscent of the situation of the sovereignty of the two countries far from the situation of "open regionalism" advocated by APEC when we see the news of the trade and security struggle between the two countries in the daily media. In the wake of the coronavirus, APEC is encouraging the transfer of vaccine manufacturing technologies "voluntarily" (without making any distinction between Japan and overseas, inside and outside the region), but joint development of vaccines between the United States and China, for example, cannot be envisaged at this time. The "open regionalism" in APEC, in which the world's major countries (or major economies) of the United States and China participate, seems to have alleviated the clash between the two countries to some extent.

Even in situations where the U.S. and China alone do not hold meetings, both sides attend APEC meetings and certainly exchange views toward cooperation. On November 12, the APEC Economic Leaders' Meeting was held in the form of a video conference, at which discussions were held on recovery from the novel coronavirus toward the prosperity of all people and future generations, the Leaders' Declaration was issued as a summary, and the "Aotearoa Action Plan" was adopted to implement the "APEC Putrajaya Vision 2040."

In 2022, Thailand chaired the APEC meeting, and "Openness, Connection, and Balance" has already been raised as the theme of the APEC meeting. Specifically, the three main objectives are to reconnect the region in a safe and seamless manner, to stimulate trade and investment toward the realization of the Free Trade Area of the Asia-Pacific (FTAAP) initiative, and to revitalize the economies of the APEC region in order to ensure sustainable, balanced, inclusive and long-term growth, and these are the three main objectives, and these are APEC's "open regionalism." It reflects the values of that. In the Asia-Pacific region, where there are concerns about further divisions after the coronavirus, APEC has its own raison d'être.

APEC's Three APEC Priorities and Fairness in Thailand in 2022

In 2022 under Thailand's chair, APEC's priority issues were Open, Connect, and Balance. In the three simple-word expressions, it is intended to solve fundamental economic problems, namely, to make the economies of the Asia-Pacific region, which have been battered by the corona disaster, "open" to all opportunities, including trade and investment, and, more specifically, to promote open trade and investment while APEC continues to support the rules-based multilateral trading system centered on the World Trade Organization (WTO) in order to revitalize the economy (note that in APEC, the word "economy" is used instead of "country" in consideration of the debate over national sovereignty). The Government of Thailand also expressed its intention to improve the business environment, promote regional economic integration, and utilize digitalization and innovation.

In addition, the attitude of emphasizing "Balance" in all aspects, such as "Connect" in all aspects after breaking away from the disruption of logistics, income inequality and the relationship between the economy and the environment, has been set out, and logistics have not fully recovered even now, two years after the pandemic. The policy intention is to focus on restoring connectivity by reinvigorating the safe and seamless cross-border travel, tourism, and services functions at the Asia-Pacific region, promoting business liquidity, and increasing investment in health and security. He also pointed out that economic imbalances in the region have worsened due to the coronavirus, and said that APEC must integrate the goals of inclusiveness and sustainability in parallel with the economic goals. These all relate to the issue of fairness.

The "Principle of Being Open" as Two Focal Points

A diagrammatic representation of the two codes of conduct in APEC ("openness" and "regionalism") is shown in Fig. 10.1. It is not in strict correspondence with the principles of social governance, but it expresses the stability of governance in global society. In general, it is mathematically known that a collection of points where the sum of the distances from two points (the foci) is constant, is an ellipse. It is impossible for the real situation to coincide perfectly with these two foci, but if the sum of the distances from them is constant, then the real situation will be somewhat stable. It can be said that APEC is expected to function as a "super-system" (as described by Tada above) in which the actions (movements) of the members themselves create new value, while the actual management is carried out in such a way that the divergence from the two principles of

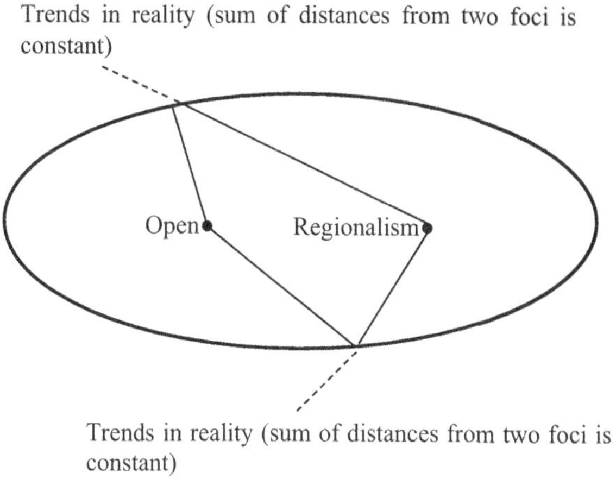

Fig. 10.1 Two foci and the trajectory of reality in APEC (represented by elliptical trajectories). (Source: Prepared by the author)

"openness" and "regionalism" (the "foci" of the community) remains constant. The statement that the self and the non-self are ambiguous is also a new value to be created, and the same kind of "value creation" is expected as at least part of social justice in the governing principles of global society. The statement that "truth is elliptical" (by Uchimura, above) may be a stabilizing measure for the existence of a community when its social justice is considered realistically (a single focus may easily destabilize and destroy the community). Thus, the values of the APEC community (open regionalism) could also be viewed from this perspective.

Tokyo Olympics and Paralympics, WTO, EU, and Social Justice

I would also like to make a few brief remarks on global actors other than APEC and social justice. In the Tokyo Olympics and Paralympics held in 2021 during the COVID-19 crisis, the importance of a "symbiotic society" (one which involves the peaceful coexistence of self and non-self) was raised as a value; at the same time, however, competition in the sporting event was an essential element. In other words, it is clearly stated that the

Olympic and Paralympic Games will be managed according to the two values of competition and symbiosis.

The World Trade Organization (WTO), which is constantly mentioned at APEC meetings, has two principles of action, "freedom" and "non-discrimination," in accordance with the purpose of its establishment (to avoid conflicts caused by block economies). The two may conflict in some ways (for example, the principle of non-discrimination can deny the existence of the strong and the weak in free competition), but its combination manages to keep the global trading system stable. In the wake of the COVID-19 crisis, it is important to reaffirm that global trade rules based on the WTO continue to uphold "freedom" (including competition), but also the principle of "non-discrimination" in the sense that they can support recovery from health and economic crises.

The concept of social justice held by the European Union (EU), which APEC is said to have modeled its philosophy on, cannot be examined in detail here, but it can be inferred that it is not a single concept, but rather is fair based on a complex set of values. Merkel (2018: 71–72) is a politician who served for a long time as Chancellor of Germany and has a deep knowledge of Christian thought, which continues to have a great influence on EU operations. She wrote a paper that points out that in the Old Testament, "justice" means "loyalty to the community" in the original language ("Tzedakah" in Hebrew), and the "complex" governing principle is also closely related to justice in the "subsidiarity principle." This is the principle of action of the EU community, meaning that decision-making should be made as close to the citizens as possible, and that the EU should act only if the actions of the regional and member states do not adequately achieve its objectives. Even in the regional integration of the European Union, where political and economic events dominate the media, it is important to consider the philosophical and ideological aspects, and the values are "complex although there is only one."

Even if we consider the global society from the economic point of view, there are limits to "resources" in a broad sense, such as human and natural resources, and land, so it is understandable that a certain range of "communities" such as nations ("nations" or "economies") need to be divided in fair distribution of vaccines and economic measures. However, it is desirable for social "immunity" to stabilize global society in an "open" manner, at least in principle, by not excluding other countries (others) as the junction of self (within the nation) and non-self (outside the nation). Since the actual development of vaccines naturally requires a competitive element, "competition" in an "open" manner should be realized as a form of social justice.

5 Conclusion

In a global society, there is no supranational organization that transcends national sovereignty, so there is an inherent limit to coercively giving instructions to countries. Under these circumstances, it is impossible to achieve social justice using supranational powers, and a different principle is needed. This chapter introduces the APEC concept of "open regionalism" as one such alternative and proposes that a composite (two foci) rather than a single governing principle for global society may be desirable.

If global society cannot be governed by coercion, some kind of "prompting" is necessary to achieve justice. Nobel laureate Richard Thaler's contribution of the "nudge," i.e., a form of "encouragement" by nudging rather than coercion, seems to be necessary as a fundamental principle for measures to realize a global and just society in the future. He prefers neither the principle of "laissez-faire" (libertarianism) nor governmental "imposition" (paternalism), but a "libertarian paternalism" that is positioned in between the two (Thaler and Sunstein 2009: 10). Intergovernmental discussions are sometimes referred to as "first track," whereas exchanges at the level of private citizens are sometimes referred to as "second track."

Of these two, the first track usually involves hard bargaining between governments, with many "requests" and "bans." In contrast, in the private sector (second track), bargaining over "profits" is common. For example, if the United States, China, and other countries jointly develop vaccines and therapeutics, it may be possible to develop them quickly and at low cost, but then a great deal of time and negotiation costs would be required due to profit-sharing and inter-state conflicts. It would be essential for

APEC to provide a soft "nudge" in this situation and to offer some benefit, or "peace dividend," if the US or China changed their behavior. Since APEC is a forum for first track (intergovernmental consultations) and at the same time an organization that plays the role of an incubator for regional integration, it should implement its own concept of justice in "open regionalism" and nudge the participating economies to avoid friction among them.

In my article in the companion volume of this book (Ishido 2021: 268), I pointed out that consideration of diversity, complexity, and humanity is essential for global social justice. In the COVID-19 crisis, economic cooperation in the "diverse" Asia-Pacific region should be "complex," and seen in terms of both the joint development of vaccines and therapeutic agents without over-emphasizing short-term profit and also the loss and strengthening of the trade "supply chain" for economic recovery. The "humanity" (humanitarian aspect) that does not excessively distinguish between the self and the non-self, that is, the inside and outside of the community [APEC, individual nations (economies)] should be emphasized. In addition, it is likely that fairness-oriented activities on the second track by researchers, including me, and private companies, will have an impact on the first track, and we will continue to monitor the trends in APEC's "open regionalism."

References

Derrida, Jacques. 2009. *Rogues*. Misuzu Shobo.

Ishido, Hikari. 2021. Regional Integration and a New Era of Social Justice: The Characteristics of Sovereign States and the Potential of APEC, Chapter 11. In *Visions of a Just Society: An Interdisciplinary Approach to Theory, Thought and Current Conditions*, ed. Jiro Mizushima, Chiyo Yonemura, and Masaya Kobayashi, 250–269. Akashi Shoten.

Kawase, Takayuki. 2021. *A Theory of Liberal Nationalism*. Horitsu Bunka Sha.

Merkel, Angela. 2018. *Watashi no Shinko: Kirisutosha toshite Koudou Suru* (in Japanese) (My Faith: Acting as a Christian), Shinkyo Publishing.

Mizushima, Jiro, Chiyo Yonemura, and Masaya Kobayashi. (Eds.). 2021. *Kouseishakai no Bijon: Gakusaiteki Apurochi niyoru Riron, Shisou, Genjoubunseki*

(in Japanese) (Visions of a Just Society: An Interdisciplinary Approach to Theory, Thought and Current Conditions), Akashi Shoten.
Tada, Tomio. 1993. *The Semantics of Immunity*. Seidosha.
———. 2001. *Immunity: The Science of 'Self' and 'Non-Self'*. NHK Books.
Thaler, Richard, and Cass Sunstein. 2009. *Practical Behavioral Economics: Improving Decisions About Money, Health, and The Environment*. Nikkei BP.
Uchimura, Kanzo. 1970. *Bible Studies Reprinted Edition*. Bible Studies Reprint Publication Society.

Part III

Thematic Issues

11

COVID-19 and Its Impact on Women and Gender

Afsana Begum

1 Introduction

Pandemics almost always stimulate both men and women, in essence, society at large. A society is not a constant entity; depending on its era and institutions, it evolves and fights all threats. However, in this era of skill and hyper-technological equipment, COVID-19 has proven to be an overpowering tremor, especially for homebound women who find themselves in an inferior structural position given the hierarchal inequality which is already identifiable in civil society. In a study by Grierson (2021), it was revealed that the COVID-19 pandemic has led to a significant surge in violence against women. Nevertheless, COVID-19 has proven a new-fangled catalyst to sustain those inequalities and strengthen the fragility of gender inequality. Although both men and women have suffered during the Pandemic, the range and categories are starkly different; in particular, violence against women increases during epidemics,

A. Begum (✉)
Graduate School of Humanities and Studies on Public Affairs, Chiba University, Chiba, Japan

H. Ishido et al. (eds.), *Social Fairness in a Post-Pandemic World*,
https://doi.org/10.1007/978-981-19-9654-2_11

natural disasters, and economic downturns (Peterman 2020). Herewith gender inequality is situated habitually and tends to entire vulnerability, which is also perceived in the transnational cycle of gendered vulnerability (Fineman 2008). As Fineman also stated, arguably, women are born defenseless and become more feeble in the long run. It is also shown that they panic (Distressed/anxious) about natural calamities and epidemics. This panic ensued in the past two years of epidemic tenure.

2 The Background of the Study for This Chapter

No matter how many months the world continues to lock down in countries to prevent the transmission of the novel coronavirus, there has been no lockdown on violence against women and girls. In this unprecedented situation, the home is considered the safest shelter; however, for many women, the house has not become the safest shelter. On the contrary it has meant that violence against girls, especially domestic violence, could not be prevented. Wherever conflicts, riots, wars, or natural disasters exist, it is women and children that are the most at risk. Violence has also been more prevalent during these pandemic-stricken years. The novel coronavirus epidemic did not save them from that misery. In times of emergency, criminals exploit this vulnerability, causing inattention and house arrest. Again, home is supposed to be the safest shelter for a woman or a child in difficult times. But capitalizing on this social distance during the epidemic has increased women's oppression rate. The men are counter to them. (Taking advantage of this social distance during the epidemic, there has been an escalation in the rate of women's oppression. Men have actively opposed women, exacerbating the situation). Sadly, most domestic violence incidents, especially in South Asia, are unreported. Domestic violence is perpetrated by the individuals closest to the family, the people next door, mainly by the most intimate partner. The majority of the stories of those regularly tortured are kept silent; the fear is not publicized outside the home. Domestic violence can also be manifested in a number of different ways: emotional, physical, sexual, and economical.

Some of the anti-feminist commentators have tried to create a new discourse around this Pandemic, that the breadwinner of the family has been forced to carry out household chores: they describe it as taking a new turn with regard to the gender relationships in the society, where emergency and staying at home has forced male members of the family to 'share' in household work. Firstly, it has been suggested that this creates a masculine crisis[1] which creates difficulties and violence, simultaneously evolving *emphasized femininity*, where women become the facilitator to sustain gender inequality in society. According to *Ain o Shalish Kendra*, 27% of violence cases filed during COVID-19 were from the in-laws and against intimate partners, especially women (Roy 2021). The second issue is about *sharing*, rather than participating in, household chores; somehow, it is presumed that traditionally household chores are women's work and men just sometimes *share* them (although the words "share" and "participating in" might be interchangeable in terms of semantics). This could normalize the dominant societal power over women by sharing a misleading positivity; this type of action in COVID strains to justify the inequality and sustain the classic societal patriarchy by women commonly subjecting to the highest male ascendant (Henry Maine 1861). Related literature explores the heterogeneity of gender disparity during the COVID-19 period. This chapter identifies the principal factors of gender inequalities and how an epidemic affects and increases associated incidents. To explore the COVID-19 and gender situation, the author conducted secondary data analysis and in-depth interviews with women victims from different parts of the world.

Melvin Lerner (1965) suggests that victims hold responsibility for their misfortune, and this notion has become a societal norm or truth; it is reinforced by practice. Given that this research is undertaken as part of research into Fare Society, it is noticeable that the Millennium Development Goals (MDGs) and Sustainable Development Goals (SDGs) are the fundamental goals of the society, which can resemble a

[1] An apparent 'crisis' in contemporary forms of masculinity, marked by uncertainties over social roles and identity, sexuality, work and personal relationships (R.W. Connell 2005).

fare society shortly, where all the 17 goals are connected. This chapter also makes an overview of SDGs and gender issues during the pandemic situation

3 Methodology

Both qualitative and quantitative data have been used in this study of COVID-19 and gender research. The study analyzed how COVID-19 affects women inside out. Enormous numbers and percentages have been used to authenticate the worldwide scale of large-scale violence. As it was small-span research, most of those entitlements and quantitative evaluations were derived from secondary data. A total of eight in-depth interviews have been conducted with women from Japan, Bangladesh, France, and India who have experienced different types of violence against women either within or after the COVID-19 state to examine the research from a qualitative perspective. From the newborn girl to the oldest women, none of them have escaped violent experiences, and the study target, therefore, has no age limit. As the research examines confidential information from the respondent, random selection was difficult; initially, therefore, one of the respondents was selected objectively in August 2021, and then a snowball procedure was followed. Based on the interviews, the remarks below might have a certain subjectivity, yet the author wishes to express them nonetheless.

4 Findings from the Analysis

'This year-long emergency made me a sex slave in my own house.' So remarked a respondent for this research on COVID-19 and gender, which ascertains how the recent Pandemic established the common experience of gender inequality. In the response of this interviewee, from Dhaka, Bangladesh, the women revealed that her husband stayed at home for several months during the emergency. Besides engaging in his work, he did not have any recreation; sex became his only source of entertainment and refreshment. That woman was bound to respond to her husband's sexual desire every time he claimed. This is one of the significant consequences of the long-standing gender inequality; in any particular situation, women's agency tends to be denied, and they become subalterns (Spivak 1988). Immediately, COVID-19 makes women a heterogeneous subject; marginal became more marginal, poor became the poorest.

The essential findings of this research concern violence against women during the coronavirus period, in both developed and poorer economies. In a comprehensive study conducted by Sena and Dalgic (2020), the impact of COVID-19 on gender inequalities was examined, shedding light on the specific challenges faced by women during the pandemic. The study highlighted the various socio-economic, health, and psychological difficulties experienced by women, emphasizing the need for targeted interventions and support systems. It is not that the case countries like Nepal or Bangladesh experienced the vulnerability of women whereas countries such as Japan and the USA marked themselves as safe from the Pandemic. The reality is that even in developed countries, women became increasingly vulnerable as women in the poorer economies can do any type of work with reduced or low salaries, while women from a developed economy count themselves as first-world women and mostly depend on third-world countries' women in such work fields as caregiving and nursing; most of them (the former in developed countries) are not supposed to carry out low-paid work. During the pandemic period and due to the lockdown, a disproportionate number of female workers in the developing world lost their jobs and became mere income consumers. Furthermore, employers tend to pay male employees more than female workers. Not only has there been an alarming rise in the rate of violence against women in Australia, Brazil, England, and the USA in March 2020 compared with March 2019, but there has also been a concerning increase in child abuse, particularly affecting young girls. Chakraborty (2017) brought attention to the persisting issue of gender-based violence and emphasized its exacerbation in the context of the coronavirus outbreak. The study shed light on the increased vulnerability of women to violence during this period, highlighting the urgent need for effective measures to address and prevent gender-based violence. Recently, in

India, some social influencers stated that pedophilia[2] is a sexual orientation, rather than a punishable disorder. There are many brothels where men can meet their sexual needs in the Indian subcontinent (as elsewhere in the world). Due to COVID-19, though, most of those brothels were closed; staying at home, women, even under-aged ones, were sexually abused at home. Women are taking triple burdens in their families. Some women lost their jobs, and others are doing remote office work with lower payment; so firstly, they are economically taking a load (while men are also working). Secondly, due to the Pandemic, daycare facilities and schools were closed for the first few months, so the care work burden for women also increased. Thirdly, the load of their reproductively and related sexual assaults increased: beating and marital rape also amplified and entailed pregnancy, specifically childhood pregnancy, which became problematic during the Pandemic.

Lastly, what could be termed the "Masculine Crisis" also grew in the household; for instance, some women in Japan are getting scholarships from the government and studying, some of whose husbands are dependent spouses. Before the Pandemic, they were working contractually. The problem is during the Pandemic, some of them lost their jobs, yet still, their wives were getting the scholarship, so here, when wives claim themselves as the breadwinner, the masculinity crises arise, which might, at times, worsen the marital relationship on side women as well.

Cases from different countries show different faces. A United Nations report shows how domestic violence has increased in multiple countries. Before the Pandemic, fewer than 40 percent[3] of women reported domestic violence or asked for help with regard to this issue. However, since the lockdown in Singapore, which is generally considered an advanced country, and one in women seem more confident, the number of violence reports and calls increased by 33 percent. The figure also increased by around 35 percent in Cyprus, France, and Argentina.

[2] Pedophilia is a psychiatric disorder in which an adult or older adolescent experience a primary or exclusive sexual attraction to prepubescent children.

[3] COVID-19 Responses, United Nations, retrieved at https://www.un.org/en/coronavirus/un-supporting-%E2%80%98trapped%E2%80%99-domestic-violence-victims-during-covid-19-pandemic

Statistics show that 743 million girls dropped out of their schools.[4] We can analyze the situation by drawing Michel Foucault's (1968) "power," that creates the reality and rituals of truth. In some countries (especially in South Asia, including India and Bangladesh), schools were closed for about half a year; after that, students, primarily boys, started to return to school; a large number of girls, on the other hand, were married off, or became a sexual enslaved personal money for the family. A girl from Kolkata, India, reported: "I am only 16 years old. According to the law in my country, I am underage to get married. But my parents bound me to get married to get rid of the burden of supporting me; this is due to the Pandemic. Also, my in-laws are not rich enough, so now they are torturing me for lack of dowry. Being a Hindu woman, I cannot ask for a divorce." It can be theorized that their family's behavioral change forced them to drop out, and with the act, their performance was troubled (Butler 1990). And they cannot become resistant by practicing their agency. Other statistics show that some 25 million migrants lost their jobs during the Pandemic;[5] in this situation, the migrant's bodies became docile (Foucault 1977). This led to the creation a new political economy which delineated women's life. Datta (2020) conducted research on the economic consequences of COVID-19 for women, revealing the alarming number of job losses among women during the pandemic. Most female migrants are involved in care work in different countries or some contractual jobs, which, while contributing to society, are not well-paid. Another impression (which is admittedly subjective) is that they stay dependent on their male family members; during the Pandemic, when as many as 25 million migrants lost their jobs during the pandemic-fabricated economic crisis, male members could still retain their migrant status with another visa; other dependents, including women and children, became vulnerable and returned to their native countries (Fig. 11.1).

In 2020 and 2021, 1.8 million women lost their jobs.[6] Chandra (2020) conducted a study on the effects of the pandemic on women's employ-

[4] UNESCO, COVID-19 School closer around the world will hit girls the hardest. Retrieved at https://www.unesco.org/en/articles/covid-19-school-closures-around-world-will-hit-girls-hardest.

[5] ILO, COVID-19: Protecting workers in the workplace, retrieved at https://www.ilo.org/global/about-the-ilo/newsroom/news/WCMS_738742/lang%2D%2Den/index.htm.

[6] Politico, retrieved at https://www.politico.com/news/2021/07/22/coronavirus-pandemic-women-workforce-500329.

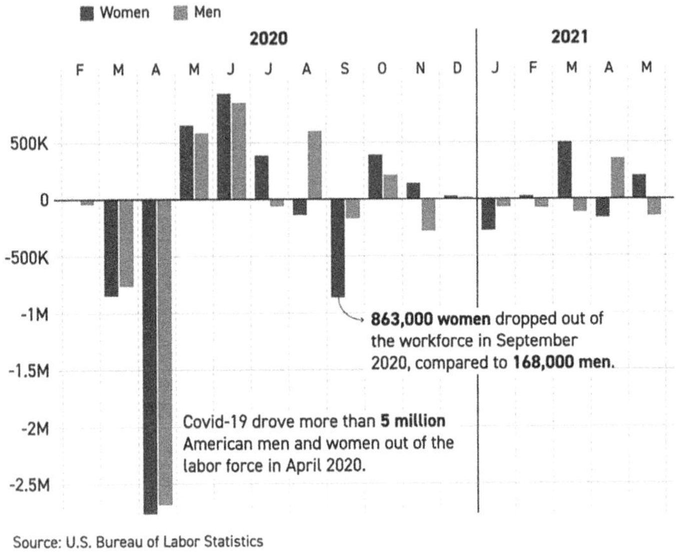

Fig. 11.1 Fall in the women's labour force in America

ment and found that a staggering 1.8 million women lost their jobs in 2020 and 2021. This highlights the devastating economic consequences of the pandemic for women, exacerbating existing gender inequalities in the workforce. The loss of jobs not only affects women's financial stability but also has long-term implications for their career progression and economic independence. The study respondent from Yokohama, Japan, expressed 'I work in a renowned Japanese Company. During Covid, my office allowed 40 percent of workers to come to the office. And the other 60 percent worked in their home office with less payment. I was among those 60 percent as a woman, and I don't feel like having a voice.' This situation is perceived as a delinquent process created by the central system. Because they are women, it is presumed that they have low work-related capacity and skills. Cutting them off from their job makes the company more robust, whereas influence almost defines masculinity (R.W. Connell 1995). COVID-19 situated women in the microphysics of power, where they became the target of a political tactic. (Chomsky 1980).

One issue to consider is that a significant number of women die during childbirth on a daily basis. With the emergence of the COVID-19 pandemic, many hospitals primarily focused on accepting and treating patients with coronavirus, resulting in other patients, including pregnant women, not receiving adequate prioritization for their non-COVID-related healthcare needs. Moreover, the increased demand to fulfill the sexual needs of men at home during this time potentially heightened the risk of unintended pregnancies. The mention of a higher number of male COVID-19 patients compared to pregnant women emphasizes the strain on healthcare resources and the importance of prioritizing care based on varying risks and vulnerabilities. Gallen (2018) explored the unequal distribution of caregiving responsibilities during the pandemic, emphasizing the disproportionate burden placed on women. A respondent from Dhaka, Bangladesh, stated, "I cannot even go to the hospital for treatment after being tortured at home, as hospitals are not taking any cases except COVID." It is true that just because of being pregnant does not mean that the (pregnant) woman is sick (Leifer 1980), yet this makes women more vulnerable, which is why the death rate in childbirth increased during the pandemic period.

There are a lot more statistics showing different situations in different countries. Studies conducted during the pandemic have shown a significant increase in violence against women. For instance, Albanesi and Stefania (2020) found that violence against women increased during the pandemic, highlighting the significant impact of COVID-19 on gender-based violence. This increase in violence poses a serious threat to the safety and well-being of women in various communities. In the Indian subcontinent, it has been suggested that half of the women are victims of domestic violence.[7] Since no one was out during the lockdown period, living with these violent family members became longer, with many family members facing fears of losing income, potential food insecurity, sudden economic downturns, minimal mobility, and constant reports of COVID-19 outbreaks. Panic was increasing day by day, and all of this provoked more violence.

---

[7] WHO, "Violence against Women" (March, 2021).

While all the family members stayed inside their houses almost 24 hours a day, mutual conflicts increased. Divorce cases have also increased. The leading British law firm Stewarts registered a 22 percent increase in inquiries between July and October 2020, compared with the same period in 2019. People in desperate situations seek legal advisors online to end their marital relationships. In the USA, a prominent legal contract creation site recently announced a 34 percent rise in its basic divorce agreements, with newlyweds married within the previous five months making up 20 percent of the sales. There has been a similar pattern in China, which experienced one of the world's strictest lockdowns at the start of the Pandemic. The same was also observed in Sweden, which initially applied voluntary guidelines to try and slow the spread of COVID-19.

The pandemic has cast its dark shadow on stereotyped work patterns as well. Initially observed in China, the novel coronavirus prompted a significant transformation in the involvement of women in income-generating economic activities, challenging societal structures. This shift revealed a different labor structure, one that deviated from the traditional gender-biased framework. In some hospitals in China, women took on frontline roles, while men assumed managerial positions, highlighting a gender disparity despite women actively participating in labor. Not limited to China alone, globally, approximately 80 percent of healthcare workers are women,[8] many of whom also bear the responsibilities of caring for their families alongside their jobs. As they juggle their professional and domestic duties, they face an increased risk of infection. However, it is important to note that the impact of the pandemic extends beyond hospital settings.

During times like these, all forms of violence, including domestic and sexual violence, tend to escalate. This is a broader consequence of the pandemic, illustrating the interconnectedness of various societal aspects. To address these issues comprehensively, it is crucial to consider the labor dynamics in hospitals alongside the wider implications of violence.

[8] WHO, National Health Workers Accounts for 91 countries (2019) (https://www.who.int/data/gho/publications/world-health-statistics).

Not in the hospitals only, when this type of Pandemic occurs: all forms of violence, including domestic and sexual violence, increase. Teenage pregnancies were also on the rise during this Pandemic. These give all the risks, covering economic, emotional, and psychological ones, to women. The biggest challenge to the corona disaster is that our limited communication and mobility may also limit healthcare and legal services for combating violence. If that happens, the level of risk for women will increase. In the United States, it is estimated that 65 percent of unpaid family care women and 80 percent of caregivers over 50 are under such a negative influence. Those women often act as primary caregivers at home, which can further increase the risk of exposure. In addition to the role of long-term care, women are overused in informal employment: In low- and middle-income countries, two-thirds of working-age women work as part of the informal economy, limiting access to healthcare for themselves and their families. Functional alternatives, such as closing daycare facilities for children and providing paid sick leave, can increase unnecessary exposure to illness and family vulnerability.

Concerning risk factors, coronavirus affected both developed and poor economies. Academic documents indicate that the loss of income from losing a job is exceptionally permanent (Stevens 1997) and much more severe when they occur in an economic recession (Davis and von Watcher 2011). Those who lost their jobs face this experience and are less likely to find secure employment in the future (Jarosch 2015). The consequences are not limited to those who lost their jobs, but those who did were also entering the labor market for the first time. COVID-19 seems to be an epidemic that appeared to lock humans in the domestic shelter where domestic violence was raised. Bradberry-Jones and Isham (2020) mention that with regard to all the social institutions such as family, workplace, education, and social media, COVID-19 has given abusers greater "freedom." Their report shows that domestic violence is on the rise in various countries. The author conducted interviews in different parts of the world. In Australia, the overall crime rate has decreased due to the lockdown, but domestic violence has increased by 5 percent. Some Australian charities have also expressed concern that perpetrators are further controlling and abusing victims of domestic violence by using false information on COVID-19. Domestic violence incidents in various states of the United States have reportedly increased by about 21–35 percent. The UK is also concerned about the growing number of domestic violence; the Refugee website recorded a 150 percent increase in calls on domestic violence.

An article in the *Indian Express* noted that most people in Mumbai had no access to domestic water. As summer temperatures rose, household water was in high demand; people spent more time at home during the lockdown, and there was an increased emphasis on hand washing (which itself is a sound practice). As a result, many women looked at the underground market, which is run under dark clothing. Also, women spend more time waiting for water and often come to need it early in the morning, experiencing both verbal and sexual harassment. Despite this increase in gender-based violence, the Delhi-based NGO Jagori has reduced its search for helpline numbers by 50 percent. Its director stated that this might be due to the fear of being found by criminals. Restricting access to phones, the Internet, and others has made it easier to implement abuse management strategies.

The violence cases in India are also worth mentioning in this context. In Uttar Pradesh, India, poor tribal families forcibly sent their 12–14-year-old girls to work in illegal mines. They had to agree to hand them over to those mining contractors and brokers. Even if they objected to this, not only are the girls threatened not to be employed, but they are also threatened with severe social consequences or being marginalized. In this way, the family takes away the girls' security first. Then the insolent society forces them to be the victims of sexual abuse at an early age. And it is difficult to count how many girls had already been forced into marriage and how many girls and women had been trafficked due to scarcity and poverty. According to Reuters, violence against women in India nearly doubled in the first week of the lockdown, with homicide rates also rising in Turkey after the government instructed citizens to stay home, with at least 90,000 allegations of gender-based violence reported in the first week of the lockdown in South Africa. During the pandemic the rate of online help requests to the Australian government rose by 75 percent.

Europe has witnessed similar patterns. In one week, domestic violence in France increased by about 32 percent. In another instance, the number of women victims of torture reported to government hotlines in the UK increased by 75 percent in 2020. Peterman (2020) shows that violence against women increases during epidemics, natural disasters, and economic downturns. For example, in a study of sexual harassment during the Ebola outbreak in Africa, Yasmin (2016) showed that sexual violence against women, including rape, increased during this period. According to Wenning (2020), the rate of violence against women in China, Australia, Brazil, England, and the United States in March 2020 increased compared with March 2019.

The *Guardian*[9] stated that the lockdown has led to increased violence against women, child abuse, and domestic violence in England. Meanwhile, in France, the Interior Minister Christophe Caste said that the number of complaints of domestic violence reported to police stations in France had risen by 30 percent since the lockdown. The United Nations reports that domestic violence may also increase in connection to relatively poor people in the least developed countries.

If we consider Bangladesh, the situation seems to have been worsening. As of this writing, though, no official report or information has been released by law enforcement or human rights organizations to the best of the author's knowledge. Therefore, from March 20 to April 20 (2021), the reports in five daily newspapers were reviewed. The incidents that were found to be more serious were rape, torture for inability to pay dowry, sexual harassment, domestic violence, and suicide. The rate of rape incidents is relatively high, and 70 percent of the victims are children. In addition, as reported in April 2020, 36 people were arrested for 26 cases of rape, torture for demanding dowry, sexual harassment, and kidnapping in a period of just ten days, from March 26 to April 4, in the Dhaka metropolitan area. There have been nine rape cases during this period. There have been six cases of torture in connection to dowry. However, this image of violence against women is nothing new in Bangladesh. The picture of violence against women in 2019 emerged in the report of the Legal Aid Sub-Council of Bangladesh Mahila Parishad. Analyzing the news, 14 dailies reported that there were no incidents of

[9] The *Guardian* (2021, March 23), "Calls to domestic abuse helpline in England up by 60% over past year" (Retrieved at: https://www.theguardian.com/society/2021/mar/23/domestic-abuse-covid-lockdown-women-refuge).

rape in that year. Under the COVID-19 disaster, the situation continued at the very least. For example, an activist of the Hasnabad Hingalganj Muslim Women's Organization, a non-governmental organization called Action Aid, said that in the North 24 Parganas of West Bengal, an unemployed father forcibly married his 13-year-old daughter. In another case, a seven-month-pregnant wife was driven out of the house by her unemployed husband.

It is seen that women have been subject to violence by their husbands, neighbors, elderly people above 60, pedestrians, and classmates. In terms of space, there were more incidents in rural areas and incidents of torture inside municipalities in urban areas. Class and class-based identity also arose in this violence. Lower middle-class or poor women, such as garment workers, housemaids, children, and marginal women, have been the victims of more violence. In different countries, suicide cases have also increased; these have included suicide due to attempted rape or harassment, suicide due to a quarrel with mother-in-law, and, exceptionally, the suicide of a 10-year-old child due to lack of food. Incidents such as harassment over requests for dowry and related murder by husbands are also recorded.

Case studies reveal the face of untold stories in different countries. A girl from Jharkhand, India, stated, "We did not have food at home; we are three sisters and two brothers. My father is always drunk. Due to the Pandemic, my mother lost her housekeeping job. So my father forcefully sends my two sisters and me to sex worker brokers." In this context, the objectification theory (Fredrickson and Roberts 1997) provides a framework for understanding the female experience in a sociocultural context. In a nutshell, the female body is sexually objectified. Women's body is primarily seen as an object; whenever there is nothing to sell for money other than the female body, this idea arises, making women and girls vulnerable in this Pandemic. Another case is from Grenoble, France: "My husband is working for the Atomic Energy Commission. Since the Corona pandemic broke out, he has been working from home. He became violent to me, and his behavior became more prominent. Domestic violence has increased by 32 percent these days." In this connection, we can see the household as the a domestic display of "panopticism." The panopticism[10] starts from the official authorities; they are surveilling what male employees are doing during the remote work; by the same token, a husband inside a home is surveilling his wife. This might well be seen as panopticism regarding the gender issue.

5 The Impact of COVID-19 and SDGs

Society is a cluster of all economic as well as political institutions. SDGs, as societal goals, have 17 key targets (goals), each of which has specific measuring of a country's status quo. These 17 goals are related to each other, and during the COVID-19 afflicted period, every aspect of the SDGs related to women were adversely affected. Due to COVID, it is also becoming apparent that it is impossible to secure the target of SDGs by 2030. Concerning the target of No Poverty, 193 million girls (together with a sizable number of boys, of course) live on less than US$1.9 a day. Women are relatively poorer in this global economy due partly to the loss of their jobs and dependency on male workers in the household; dropping out from school makes them even poorer over the long term because of the lack of educational credentials deemed necessary for well-paid jobs. It can be said that while girls are drop-outs in education, they engage in income-generating work for their households, even if it does involve the sale of their bodies. And in the process, they retain little money. They are doing this to serve their family in the absence of any other option. Then comes another set of goals under SDGs about Good Health and Well Being. Women dying from pregnancy and childbirth-related problems are examples of a minimal level of well-being not secured. Neither is quality education assured during this pandemic period.

Most importantly, SDG Goal 5, "Gender Equality," is an issue given the persistence of both sexual harassment and gender violence. Twelve million girls married before the age of 18. This shows the position of women in this Pandemic: they exist only to serve men in their families

[10] A Panopticon is a structure in the form of a circle, with an observation at the center; the purpose of the design of the Panopticon is to increase the security (often of a prison) through effective surveillance at the center. The Panopticon was conceptualized by philosopher Foucault in the sense outlined in the main text.

and, if anything happens, they become the object of sacrifice. This is how "discipline" and "punishment" (Foucault 1977) work in modern society. Finally, with regard to SDG's targets concerning Clean Water and Sanitation: 300 million women and girls lack menstrual hygiene management. Even in Japan, a developed country, women's menstrual concerns are not given sufficient attention. The law stipulates that women can take paid leave every month for menstrual crumbs or pain. But less than 1 percent of women do actually take such leave. This is for fear of losing their jobs; that means the rule cannot be implemented; if so, there is a heightened consequence of women workers being stressed and harassed. This is because women are not stepping into positions of legislative power. In my view, the problems women face during COVID-19 are seldom resolved or explained by top politicians and law practitioners (mostly male). And it seems that they are serving and thinking mainly of men. In need of making a "Fare Society," we should be connected through the global partnership, in which SDGs will create a bridge to connect one goal, issue, or problem to another goal; indeed, the burden of responding to the immediate and long-term impacts of the Pandemic should not threaten women's involvement in politics in the long term.

6 Conclusion

Society is a complete structure, including all its institutions, starting from the family—pandemic crates crisis in migrants and masculinity, which lead to vulnerability towards women.

Covid-19 is a symbolic image that shows how pandemics create risks in women's lives. Again, there is an urgent need to adopt gender lenses to study epidemics and their effects, including policies and measures implemented at the global, national, and local levels. This can be especially important for disadvantaged people in resource-poor communities, where women are particularly vulnerable. While focusing on containing the epidemic, the public health community must also ensure that existing health and social services help women maintain their unique needs. In addition, special care needs to be taken to ensure that informal caregivers are supported, informed, and protected. To establish a fair society, the visibility of womanhood, aka sisterhood, which is possible through the international platform, is of utmost concern for reducing gender stereotyping and discrimination.

References

Albanesi and Stefania. 2020. *Changing Business Cycles: The Role of Women's Employment,* NBER Working Paper.

Bradberry-Jones, C., and Isham, A. 2020. Domestic Violence During the COVID-19 Pandemic: Risk and Recourse. *British Journal of Community Nursing* 25 (6): 280–285.

Butler, J. 1990. *Gender Trouble: Feminism and the Subversion of Identity.* New York: Routledge.

Chakraborty, C. 2017. *Mapping South Asian Masculinities: Men and Political Crisis*, pp. 166–172.

Chandra, J. 2020. COVID-19 Lockdown Rise in Domestic Violence, Police Apathy: NCW. *The Hindu*; (April 2). https://www.thehindu.com/news/national/covid-19/lockdown-spike-in-domestic-violence-says-ncw/article31238659.ece.

Chomsky, N. 1980. *Rules and Representation.* Cambridge University Press.

Connell, R.W. 1995. *Masculinities*, pp. 122–127.

———. 2005. *Masculinities* (2nd ed.). Berkeley, CA: University of California Press.

Datta, A. 2020. Patriarchal Bargains and a Triple Bind: On Writing Geographies of Gender in India. Handbook on Gender in Asia, pp. 14–15.

Davis, S., and T. Von Wachter. 2011. Recessions and the Costs of Job Loss. *Brookings Paper on Economic Activity* 2011 (2, Fall): 1–72. https://doi.org/10.1353/eca.2011.0016.

Fineman, M.A. 2008. *The vulnerable subject: Anchoring equality in the human condition*. Yale Journal of Law & Feminism, 20(1): 1–23.

Foucault, M. 1968. *Biopolitics and Biopower*, pp. 142–144.

———. M. 1977. *Discipline and Punish: the Birth of the Prison.* New York: Pantheon Books.

Fredrickson, B. L., and Roberts, T. 1997. Objectification Theory: Toward Understanding Women's Lived Experiences and Mental Health Risks. *Psychology of Women Quarterly* 21 (2): 173–206.

Gallen, Y. 2018. *Motherhood and the Gender Productivity Gap*. Unpublished Manuscript, The University of Chicago.
Grierson, J. 2021. Calls to Domestic Abuse Helpline in England Up by 60% Over Past Year This Article Is More Than 11 Months Old. *The Guardian*, Accessed 23 March. https://www.theguardian.com/society/2021/mar/23/domestic-abuse-covid-lockdown-women-refuge.
Jarosch, G. 2015. Job Security Perceptions and the Employer–Employee Relationship in Germany. *Journal of Economic Psychology* 46: 39–51.
Leifer, G. 1980. The Psychological Effects of Women's Reproductive Events: A Discussion of Current Research. In *Psychological Aspects of Women's Health Care: The Interface Between Psychiatry and Obstetrics and Gynecology* 53–70. New York: Springer.
Lerner, M.J. 1965. Evaluation of Performance as a Function of Performer's Reward and Attractiveness. *Journal of Personality and Social Psychology* 1: 355–360.
Maine, H. 1861. *Ancient Law: Its Connection with the Early History of Society, and Its Relation to Modern Ideas*. London: John Murray.
Peterman, A. 2020. *Epidemics and Violence Against Women*. Washington, DC: Center for Global Development.
Roy, U. 2021, July 9. 'Korona kalin nari o shishu nirjaton bereche' [In Bangla] [VAW increased in Covid 19]. Desh Rupantar.
Sena, C., and H. Dalgic. 2020. *The Emergence of Procyclical Fertility: The Role of Gender Differences in Employment Risk*. CRC TR 224 Discussion Paper Series No. 142.
Spivak, G. 1988. *Can the Subaltern Speak?* New York, NY: Columbia University Press.
Stevens, A. H. 1997. The Dynamics of Poverty Spells: Updating Bane and Ellwood. *The American Economic Review* 87 (2): 34–38.
Yasmin, S. 2016. Sexual Violence Against Women in Ebola-Affected Countries. *The Lancet* 388 (10041): 2279–2280.
Wenning, R. J. 2020. Gendered Patterns of Violence and Vulnerability During the COVID-19 Pandemic: An Analysis of Police Incident Reports in Philadelphia from 2015 to 2020. *Feminist Criminology* 16 (4): 427–454.

12

Modern Japanese Literature and Infectious Diseases: Representations of Infectious Diseases and Social Fairness in Literary Works

Yongjiao Zhang

1 Introduction

Tracing the History of Infectious Diseases Through Literature

Looking back at the history of infectious disease outbreaks in Japan, recurring outbreaks of smallpox, measles, leprosy epidemics, among other diseases, can all be identified before the modern era. The smallpox epidemic is mentioned in *Nihon Shoki* (*Chronicles of Japan*), Japan's first official history, and there is also a poem about smallpox in *Manyoshu*, Japan's oldest-surviving anthology of poetry. *The Tale of Genji*, *Hojoki*, *Tsurezuregusa*, and many other classical works also contain descriptions of infectious disease epidemics.

Y. Zhang (✉)
School of Foreign Languages, Shanghai University, Shanghai, China
e-mail: yongjiaoz@shu.edu.cn

H. Ishido et al. (eds.), *Social Fairness in a Post-Pandemic World*,
https://doi.org/10.1007/978-981-19-9654-2_12

The history of compiling statistics on infectious diseases began in the early Meiji era. In 1874, the Medical Affairs Bureau of the Ministry of Education took charge of medical administration in the country[1] and issued the "Medical Code", which established the obligation to notify patients of infectious diseases. Later, with the promulgation of the "Regulations for the Prevention of Infectious Diseases" in 1880, the information was compiled as a weekly report of infectious diseases by the Ministry of Home Affairs. On April 1, 1897, the "Infectious Disease Prevention Act" (Act No. 36 of 1897) was enacted. The act designated the eight "infectious diseases" as cholera, dysentery, typhoid fever, smallpox, typhus, scarlet fever, diphtheria, and plague. Table 12.1 displays the data for six infectious diseases from 1897 to 1945; it selects only the highest incidence rates from the whole data pool. While pulmonary tuberculosis is not even included in the legally designated infectious diseases, this table still presents a tremendous number of deaths as well as high mortality rates.

With the introduction of the mandatory notification of patients with infectious disease, it has become possible to obtain statistical data on the spread of infectious diseases since the Meiji era. Behind the numbers, however, are those suffering from the "legally designated infectious diseases". They suffer both physical pain and legal restrictions. In addition, leprosy and pulmonary tuberculosis, although not "legally designated infectious diseases", were perceived as filthy, sinful, heretical, or viewed through an otherwise discriminatory and exclusionary lens. Furthermore, the influenza known as the Spanish flu arrived in Japan around the spring of 1918, and by 1921, there had been 23.8 million cases and 380,000 deaths (Ogawa and Suzuki 2021: 182).

Thus, the spread of infectious diseases in modern Japan coincided with the establishment of a modern health administration system. The deaths of the many infected people also began to be recorded. When an unknown infectious disease emerged, statistical data reflected its prevalence to some extent, but of course there were limitations in considering the psychological impact it had on society and individuals. As shown in Table 12.2,

---

[1] Ministry of Education, 1874, "Medical Code", August 18, 1874, Documents Related to Toshimichi Okubo (collection), https://dl.ndl.go.jp/info:ndljp/pid/11444432 (Retrieved on July 19, 2023).

Table 12.1 Number of Infectious Disease Patients, Deaths, Morbidity rate, Death rate (per 100,000 individuals), by type of infectious disease, the year 1897–1945

	Cholera		Dysentery		Typhoid		Smallpox		Plague		Tuberculosis	
	Patient count	Morbidity rate	Patient count	Morbidity rate	Patient count	Morbidity rate	Patient count	Morbidity rate	Patient count	Morbidity rate	Deaths	Death rate
1897 (Meiji 30)	894	…	91,077	…	26,998	…	41,946	…	1	…	–	–
1899 (Meiji 32)	829	…	108,713	…	27,673	…	1215	…	62	…	–	–
1901 (Meiji 34)	101	0.2	49,384	109.9	24,052	53.5	92	0.2	3	0.0	76,614	172.7
1903 (Meiji 36)	172	0.4	30,304	65.7	18,820	40.8	72	0.2	58	0.1	85,132	186.9
1907 (Meiji 40)	3632	7.6	24,940	51.9	25,916	54.0	1034	2.2	646	0.9	96,584	203.7
1909 (Meiji 42)	328	0.7	28,005	56.9	25,101	50.8	90	0.2	389	0.8	113,622	234.0
1910 (Meiji 43)	2849	5.7	31,958	63.9	35,378	70.8	80	0.2	49	0.1	113,203	230.2
1912 (Taisho 1)	2614	5.1	25,666	49.7	31,519	61.0	14	0.0	–	–	114,197	225.8
1914 (Taisho 3)	5	0.0	26,121	49.2	35,368	66.6	485	0.9	83	0.2	113,341	217.8
1916 (Taisho 5)	10,371	19.0	22,449	41.1	41,846	76.3	264	0.5	77	0.1	121,810	227.7
1918 (Taisho 7)	–	–	13,997	25.4	43,072	78.2	1467	2.7	1	0.0	140,747	257.1
1920 (Taisho 9)	407	0.7	12,891	23.3	54,595	98.6	4054	7.3	3	0.0	125,165	223.7
1922 (Taisho 11)	743	1.3	15,101	26.6	52,287	92.0	679	1.2	118	0.2	125,506	218.7
1925 (Taisho 14)	624	1.1	14,720	24.9	45,768	77.3	430	0.7	–	–	115,956	194.1
1926 (Showa 1)	25	0.0	17,135	28.5	43,938	73.0	1256	2.1	8	0.0	113,045	186.1
1928 (Showa 3)	1	0.0	25,196	40.6	41,996	67.7	723	1.2	–	–	119,632	191.1
1930 (Showa 5)	–	–	29,672	46.5	41,367	64.8	7	0.0	–	–	119,635	185.6
1932 (Showa 7)	4	0.0	32,249	49.0	35,437	53.8	305	0.5	–	–	119,196	179.4
1934 (Showa 9)	–	–	42,939	63.4	42,420	62.6	320	0.5	–	–	131,525	192.5
1936 (Showa11)	–	–	52,053	74.9	36,799	52.9	178	0.3	–	–	145,160	207.0
1938 (Showa 13)	18	0.0	80,221	113.9	42,074	59.7	60	0.1	–	–	148,827	209.6
1940 (Showa 15)	–	–	83,689	117.3	40,706	57.0	575	0.8	–	–	153,154	212.9
1942 (Showa 17)	–	–	55,785	77.7	35,589	49.6	381	0.5	–	–	161,484	223.1

(continued)

Table 12.1 (continued)

	Cholera		Dysentery		Typhoid		Smallpox		Plague		Tuberculosis	
	Patient count	Morbidity rate	Patient count	Morbidity rate	Patient count	Morbidity rate	Patient count	Morbidity rate	Patient count	Morbidity rate	Deaths	Death rate
1944 (Showa 19)	–	–	55,196	76.2	57,488	79.3	311	0.4	–	–	–	–
1945 (Showa 20)	–	–	96,462	134.0	57,933	80.5	1614	2.2	–	–	–	–

Notes: The survey data is based on "Infectious Disease Statistics" (November 15, Showa 50, Policy Umbrella Issue No. 408).The morbidity rate is calculated according to the following formula. Annual morbidity rate = number of patients in the current year/statistical population on October 1 of the current year *100,000. Death rate refers to the number of deaths per 100,000 people.

Identification sign: No count "–", very small rate (less than 0.05) "0.0". The data is unknown or the data cannot be accurately identified "…".

Source: Made by the author based on Health and Welfare Statistics Association (ed.) (2009) and Ikeda Isao (2002).

Table 12.2 Modern Japanese Writers and Infectious Disease

Writer	Year of birth & death	Literary work	Initial public offering	Publication Information	Related infectious diseases	The occurrence and countermeasures of infectious diseases in Japan at the time of publication
Higuchi Ichiyo	1872~1896	*Takekurabe*	1895~1896	*Bungakukai* (magazine)	variola	In 1895, cholera broke out in the Japanese army and spread throughout the country, killing 40,154 people. Meanwhile, 12,959 people died of dysentery and 8401 died of typhoid.
Ozaki Koyo	1868~1903	*Aobudo*	1895	*Yomiuri Shimbun* (newspaper)	cholera	In 1896, Japan had an epidemic of dysentery, which killed 22,356 people. In addition, 9174 people died of typhoid fever.
Tokutomi Roka	1868~1927	*Hototogisu*	1898~1899	*Kokumin Shimbun* (newspaper)	tuberculosis	The first national survey of tuberculosis deaths was carried out in Japan in 1899. The death toll was 66,408. That's 153 deaths per 100,000 people. It accounted for 7.12% of the total deaths.

(*continued*)

Table 12.2 (continued)

Writer	Year of birth & death	Literary work	Initial public offering	Publication Information	Related infectious diseases	The occurrence and countermeasures of infectious diseases in Japan at the time of publication
Masaoka Shiki	1867~1902	*Byosho Rokushaku*	1902	*Nihon* (newspaper)	tuberculosis	Kyushu was hit by a cholera epidemic in 1902. "*Proposals for the control of lepers*" was Proposed. The first Japan Association Medical Association meeting was held in Tokyo, and Kitasato Shibasaburo gave a speech on the prevention and eradication of tuberculosis at the meeting.
Natsume Soseki	1867~1916	*Wagahai Wa Neko Dearu*	1905~1906	*Hototogisu* (magazine)	variola	The plague was prevalent in 1905. "*Infectious Disease Prevention law*" was amended. Vaccinia manufacturing Institute and Serum Medicine Department were placed under the control of the Infectious Disease Institute.

Tayama Katai	1872~1930	*Inaka Kyoshi*	1909	Sakura Syobou (bookstore)	tuberculosis	In 1909, Japan set up five public leper sanatoriums. Japan promulgated the "*Vaccination Law*" and began to implement on January 1, 1910.
Ishikawa Takuboku	1886~1912	*Ichiaku No Suna*	December 1910	Shinonomedou Syoten (bookstore)	tuberculosis	In 1911, the Japanese White Cross Society, as a civil tuberculosis prevention group, was founded. The Universal Congress on Tuberculosis opened in Rome, Italy.
Nagai Kafu	1879~1959	*Dan Chiyo Tei Nichi Jyo*	Written after 1917	*Kafu Zensyuu* (portfolio)	Spanish influenza	In 1917, the cities of Kyoto, Yokohama, and Nagoya were ordered to set up tuberculosis sanatorium. Tokensan Sanatorium of Osaka City was opened, and it was the first public tuberculosis sanatorium in Japan.
Yosano Akiko	1878~1942	*Kanbou No Yuka Kara*	November 10, 1918	*Yokohama Boueki Shinpou* (newspaper)	Spanish influenza	Around the spring of 1918, the Spanish flu landed in Japan. By 1921, 23.8 million people got infected, and the death toll went as high as 380,000. A freeze-dry smallpox vaccine was developed.

(*continued*)

Table 12.2 (continued)

Writer	Year of birth & death	Literary work	Initial public offering	Publication Information	Related infectious diseases	The occurrence and countermeasures of infectious diseases in Japan at the time of publication
Shiga Naoya	1883~1971	*Ryuukou Kanbou*	April 1919	*Shirakaba* (magazine)	Spanish influenza	In 1919, the "*Tuberculosis Prevention Law*" was enacted, And the "*School Infectious Disease Prevention Regulations*" was formulated. A minor outbreak of meningitis occurred in Nagano and Niigata. It spread in Tokyo and Osaka around the spring of 1920. The death toll stands at 1,392.
Tanizaki Jun'ichiro	1886~1965	*Tozyou*	January 1920	*Kaizou* (magazine)	Spanish influenza	In 1920, there was an epidemic of Japanese influenza and cholera. Tokyo Tuberculosis Sanatorium opened. The League of Nations Health Agency was established in Geneva, Switzerland.
Kikuchi Kan	1888~1948	*Masuku*	July 1920	*Kaizou* (magazine)	Spanish influenza	In 1921, the "*Guidelines for the Prevention of Influenza*" was published. The Ministry of Education in Japan set up a school hygiene section. The Health Department of the Ministry of the Interior established a Preparedness section.

Sasaki Kuni	1883~1964	*Zyosei*	1925	*Syufu No Tomo* (magazine)	Spanish influenza	"*Keimusyo Experience of Infectious diseases prevention*" was released in 1925. Forty-eight countries signed or acceded to the Geneva Protocol, banning the use of chemical and biological weapons in warfare.
Kishida Kunio	1890~1954	*Kaze Issoku*	January 1929	*Jiji Shinpou* (newspaper)	Spanish influenza	In 1929, the "*Leprosy Prevention Law*" was amended. Japanese Parasitic Society was founded. Osaka Imperial University established the Osaka Institute of Dermatology and began to study leprosy.
Miyazawa Kenji	1896~1933	*Me Nite Iu*	October 1946	*Gunzou* (magazine)	tuberculosis	There was an epidemic of influenza in Tokyo in 1931. At the end of January, 833,284 people got infected. As one of the prevention strategies of tuberculosis, the first public tuberculosis counseling center in Japan opened in Tokyo.

(*continued*)

Table 12.2 (continued)

Writer	Year of birth & death	Literary work	Initial public offering	Publication Information	Related infectious diseases	The occurrence and countermeasures of infectious diseases in Japan at the time of publication
Kajii Motojiro	1901~1932	*Nonki Na Kanja*	January 1932	*Tyuuou Kouron* (magazine)	tuberculosis	In 1932, the Ministry of Internal Affairs issued a notice about the establishment of tuberculosis prevention counseling. The Ministry of Internal Affairs issued the "*Code of practicing the Parasitic Diseases Prevention Law*", it goes into effect on August 1.
Hojo Tamio	1914~1937	*Inochi No Shoya*	February 1936	*Bungakukai* (magazine)	Leprosy	In 1936, a meeting was held by the Ministry of Internal Affairs of Japan, the director of the Government leprosy sanatorium, the director of the prefectural Health section, and developed "*20-year Leprosy Eradication Program*". The rise of tuberculosis became a social problem.

Hori Tatsuo	1904~1953	*Kazetachinu*	April 1938	Noda Syobou (bookstore)	tuberculosis	In 1938, the Protection Institute for the Wounded of Japan opened 25 nationwide sanatoriums for disabled soldiers with tuberculosis. When Japan established the Ministry of Health, Labor and Welfare, Public health centers established under the jurisdiction of this ministry.

Source: Made by the author based on the information from Tachikawa Shoji (1989) and Ogawa Shuji, Suzuki Mizuho (eds.) (2021). The author also made references to the chronologies and complete works of the writers listed in the Table.

there were many literary figures who suffered from infectious diseases in modern Japan, including Ichiyo Higuchi, Shiki Masaoka, Soseki Natsume, Takuboku Ishikawa, Kafu Nagai, Naoya Shiga, Kan Kikuchi, Kenji Miyazawa, Motojiro Kajii, and Tatsuo Hori. In addition to enriching the sensibilities of these literati, the disease is thought to have deepened their thinking about social issues and the human mind. A comparison of these literary figures and their literary texts with the current situation of the spread of infectious diseases could be a good source and perspective for reconsidering the impact of infectious diseases and social fairness.

In the face of the ongoing COVID-19 crisis, people are becoming increasingly interested in how society and people have responded to pandemics in the modern era, and what kind of enlightenment the history of infectious diseases has left for people today. For example, if we focus on the Spanish flu, which had a great impact in the Taisho era, we can find not only works by modern writers about the Spanish flu, but also works derived from them, such as *Writers and the Spanish Flu* (2021) and *Writers and Infectious Diseases: How the Spanish Flu Was Written About 100 Years Ago* (2021). In her seminal work on the representation of infectious diseases in literary works, Susan Sontag (1978) examined the use of diseases such as tuberculosis, syphilis, cancer, and insanity as metaphors. While touching on literary works from eighteenth-century Romanticism to modern science fiction, she discusses the role and prejudices carried by various diseases in the historical sense. Mahito Fukuda (1995) organized the images of pulmonary tuberculosis in modern Japanese literature, proposing that the migration and concentration of population due to modernization, urbanization and industrialization seeded the soil for the spread of tuberculosis and developed an argument to replace the "myth of genius" and "romantic image" associated with tuberculosis.

Among the latest studies, Masami Ishii (2021: 187), in "Infectious Disease Literature as Historical Documents", discusses the historical meanings of words about infectious diseases from the perspective of literary studies. In addition, there are *Japanese Classics and Infectious Diseases* (edited by Robert Campbell, 2021), a collection of essays focusing on the representation of infectious diseases in classical literature such as the *Manyoshu* and *The Tale of Genji*, and *Epidemics and Japanese Literature* (edited by Yoshitaka Hibi, 2021), which traces novels, haiku, and works related to infectious diseases from ancient to modern times. The emergence of these collections of works and essays also points to the need to examine the COVID-19 crisis and the future of social fairness from the perspective of the humanities and social sciences. In literary works, what happens historically is often combined into the story from the point of view of the writer who lived through this disease. When a writer presents an infectious disease as a subject or part of a literary work, their individual experience with disease is woven into the work, and it becomes possible to examine the infectious disease explosion in the same period. In addition, there is room to explore ideological issues such as the attitudes of others and society toward an infected person and their self-awareness. This chapter will focus on the modern era, when various infectious diseases were spreading explosively, and at the same time modern medical care and health administration were being developed. This was done by reading the literary works in terms of being a mirror that reflects the social conditions of the times and listening to the voices of the people who actually existed behind the data, in an attempt to approach a place of understanding.

2 Representations of Infectious Diseases in Modern Japanese Literature

When considering the infectious diseases as represented in literary works, the objects of analysis can be divided into two main categories. One is that the writers themselves are victims of infectious diseases, and their literary works are to some extent based on their own experience of infection. This category includes works by Ichiyo Higuchi, Shiki Masaoka, Soseki Natsume, Takuboku Ishikawa, Tatsuo Hori, Kenji Miyazawa, etc. They have left many poems, diaries, novels, and children's stories related to infectious diseases. The other type is where the writers themselves are not infected, but where the subjects of their work are the social psychological changes and phenomena such as discrimination, exclusion, and upset caused by the pandemic. In this type of work, various social phenomena and psychological changes of individuals caused by infectious diseases and injuries are written as fictional stories as well as direct records. Cholera in Koyo Ozaki's *Aobudo* (*The Green Grapes*) (1896), and representations of tuberculosis in Roka Tokutomi's *Hototogisu* (*The Cuckoo*) (1900) and Wakizo Hosoi's *Zyokouaisi* (*The Sorrowful History of Female Factory Workers*) (1925) are representative works.

Spread of Infectious Disease and War in Modern Times

If we trace the axis of time, it can be seen that the spread of infectious diseases has had a great impact on modern Japanese society, and infectious diseases themselves have left a strong imprint on modern Japanese literature. Soseki Natsume, the most representative writer of the Meiji era, is said to have died from a stomach ulcer, but suffered from infectious diseases like smallpox and tuberculosis prior to his death. This experience of infection is also reflected in the characters that appear in his works. In *Wagahai Wa Neko Dearu* (*I Am a Cat*), Teacher Kusyami had smallpox scars on his face.

> My master is pockmarked. Though I hear that pockmarked faces were well regarded in the days before the restoration of the emperor, in these enlightened times of the Anglo-Japanese Alliance, such cratered features look distinctly out of date. The decline of the pockmark began precisely when the birthrate started to climb, so one may confidently expect that it will soon become extinct. This conclusion is an inescapable deduction from medical statistics; these, being thus scientifically established, even a cat, a creature as penetrating critical as myself, would not dare cast doubt upon it. (Natsume 1906: 174)[2]

Smallpox was also mentioned in the *Nihon Shoki*, indicating that it was a recurring epidemic throughout history[3] (Iguchi 1929). Natsume's

---

[2] English translation from Soseki Natsume (author), Aiko Ito (translator), Graeme Wilson (translator). 1993, *I Am a Cat*. Tuttle Publishing.

[3] In the modern era, smallpox saw nationwide outbreaks in 1870, 1874, and 1876. From 1892 to 1894, there was a local epidemic north of Tokyo, with 88,095 patients and 3603 deaths recorded. Later, in the Taisho and Showa eras, the disease continued to sporadically infect people throughout the country. Iguchi, Jokai, 1929, *Smallpox and Vaccination Theory*, Bunkodo Shoten, 5–16.

works often depict historical situations related to infectious diseases, such as the spread of smallpox, the conclusion of the Anglo-Japanese Alliance in 1902 and the advancement of medicine. In the era when Natsume lived, the Sino-Japanese and Russo-Japanese wars broke out over interests in the Korean Peninsula and Manchuria (now known as Northeast China). Furthermore, these foreign wars were inextricably linked to the spread of infectious diseases in the country. For example, in Soseki Natsume's *Kokoro* (1914), the cause of death of "Sensei's" (teacher's) parents is explained to the young man in the text as follows:

> I was not yet twenty when I lost both my parents. My wife told you, I remember, that they died of the same illness. You were astonished when she said they died at virtually the same time. The fact is that my father contracted the dreaded typhoid fever, and my mother became infected through nursing him. (Natsume 1914: 220)[4]

The story is narrated by "Sensei", who came to Tokyo and lived in a boarding house after the sudden death of his parents due to infection; that is when the story of Sensei's wife and K unfolds. Thus, the representation of infectious diseases is also a major aspect in the development of the fictional story. Also, as Yoichi Komori (2020: 62–72) argues, typhoid fever broke out in Japan because wounded soldiers infected with typhoid bacilli during the Sino-Japanese and Russo-Japanese Wars returned from the battlefields and the infection spread during their treatment. In the turbulent process of modernization, the outbreak of the Sino-Japanese War, the Russo-Japanese War, World War I, the Siberian Intervention, and finally World War II, among others, promoted the flow of population, which provided a major opportunity for a global pandemic of infectious diseases.

[4] English translation from Soseki Natsume (author), Meredith McKinney (editing, preface, translator). 2010, *Kokoro*, Penguin Classics.

The Spread of Infectious Diseases and Industrialization in Modern Times

One of the most important causes of the spread of infectious diseases during the war is that the "army", which is an organization of communal living, was forcibly created through conscription. This is because the maintenance of medical systems in the military and on the battlefield could not be guaranteed at all. In a newspaper report dated July 22, 1933, "Tuberculosis among Soldiers" (*The Asahi Shimbun*, Morning Edition, Tokyo 1933: 3), more than 2000 soldiers in the Army and Navy contracted pulmonary tuberculosis every year, and that the number of deaths each year was close to the number of those killed in the Manchurian Incident. Undeniably, a "group" is one of the conditions that favors the spread of infectious diseases. In modern Japan, in addition to the military, factories, schools, villages, and households also became the collective nuclei for the spread of infectious diseases, and Spanish flu, cholera, typhoid, tuberculosis, and other infectious diseases spread there.

In the process of laying the foundations of capitalism from the early Meiji period, lung disease among factory women was even positioned as a disease that was an occupational curse and not hereditary (Hosoi 1925: 382). In modern Japan, tuberculosis was once referred to as the national disease and the "disease of the exiled". The combination of various conditions, such as the increase in population, the progress of urbanization and the widening gap between the rich and the poor, and the development of industry and the accompanying changes in working conditions, provided the perfect soil for the spread of tuberculosis (Fukuda 1995: 7). The spread of tuberculosis among female workers in textile factories was particularly serious. In *Zyokouaisi* (*The Sorrowful History of Female Factory Workers*), Wakizo Hosoi wrote, "Looking at those who returned home from sickness, 703 out of 1000 who died after returning home had tuberculosis or suspected tuberculosis. They endure the work for as long as they can, and when they realize they can take no more and return to their hometown, the deaths are as high as 70%" (Hosoi 1925: 383–384). The living environment of the female workers in the textile factories is said to have had a very high rate of pulmonary tuberculosis infection and mortality due to various factors such as dense population, poor ventilation, poor eating and drinking conditions, and long working hours. In addition, female workers suspected of being infected were sent back to their hometowns, opening a pathway for the spread of infectious diseases throughout the city and countryside. There were also many cases in which people from rural areas had gone to Tokyo for higher education but returned to their hometowns to recuperate from infectious diseases. Thus, even though groups such as the army, factories, and schools increased the risk of the spread of infectious diseases through their movement, there was no adequate system in place to control it at the time. Therefore, Dr. Paula Fujiwara, scientific director of the International Union Against Tuberculosis and Lung Disease, points out that tuberculosis, which has not been eradicated even today, is a disease of poverty, a social disease with medical implications (Senthilingam 2020). It is a common issue today that more attention should be paid to the poor in the spread of infectious diseases.

3 Impact of the Spread of Infectious Diseases as Seen in Literary Works

Feelings of Guilt and a Frenzy to Differentiate and Exclude

Specifically, when looking at modern descriptions of measures to prevent the spread of infectious diseases, we often find expressions in which sickness is considered to be a "sin" and patients are represented or self-identified as "sinners". In Koyo Ozaki's *Aobudo* (*The Green Grapes*) (1896), the protagonist talks about his own self-identification as a sinner when he is suspected to have contracted cholera.

> When I think about it, I am a sinner. I am a great sinner who is hated by my neighbors dozens of times more than I hate police officers. The owner of a house that has a contagious disease that not only causes trouble for society, but trouble for the government, I am a great sinner! (Ozaki 1896: 153)

According to the regulations of that time, households with infected people had to write the name of the disease on the front of their gates. With regard to the prevention of cholera mentioned in the work, the "Provisional Regulations for the Prevention of Cholera", Proclamation No. 32 of August 1879, was issued. In Article XI of the proclamation, it is stipulated that "the names of those who have contracted cholera shall be written in large letters and posted on the doors of their houses. After healing or death, for one week, except for in unforeseen circumstances, there must not be any communication with other people".[5] The infected person in *The Green Grapes* had to face this kind of scrutiny because of the provision that "the name of the disease should be written in large letters and posted on the doors of their houses". Cholera patients were integrated with the families to which they belonged, and that house was required to put up a placard with the name of the disease in large letters. The public announcement of the name of the disease and the disinfection method were not limited to individuals, but extended to the entire family, and at the same time, fear and discrimination against that family were magnified. The above rules were removed with the implementation of the "Infectious Disease Prevention Act"[6] on March 30, 1897, but the law kept infectious patients and their families under the surveillance of authorities at all levels.

When the government of the time intervened in the treatment and prevention of infectious diseases, frank and violent measures were always taken. Under such laws, infected people, who should have been seen as victims, ended up with condemning themselves as sinners. It can be said that the social mechanism that is supposed to play a role in protecting the vulnerable, instead turned into a system that brings the

---

[5] Kobe Court Compilation 1880, "Provisional Regulations for the Prevention of Cholera", *Complete Book of Regulations and Punishment Examples, Volume 5*, Kobe Court, 33.

[6] Article 4 of the law stipulates that "any patient with a contagious disease or suspected contagious disease, or any household of a person who has died, shall be immediately examined or autopsied by a physician, or shall notify the local police officer, mayor of the municipality, mayor of a ward, mayor of a town, quarantine committee, or prevention committee". Prepared by the Cabinet 1897, "Infectious Disease Prevention Act Enacted, Regulations for the Prevention of Infectious Diseases Repealed, Original Signature, 1897, Law No. 36". https://www.digital.archives.go.jp/img/155206 (Retrieved on July 19, 2023).

vulnerable out into the world in which they may suffer humiliation and public judgement.

Exclusion From the Group

The infected person's perception of themselves as a sinner is not just about the contagiousness of the disease. In Japan around the twentieth century, forced conscription and the promotion of foreign wars made the realization of people's values a national-level responsibility. The loss of an individual was also seen as a loss of the nation's human resources. By not being able to participate in the compulsory military draft or foreign wars, the infected and sick were burdened with mental guilt as well as illness. In Katai Tayama's *Inaka Kyoshi* (*The Country Teacher*), the protagonist Seizo, who is suffering from pulmonary tuberculosis, laments, "if I were really strong, I would go to war!" He then expresses his feelings that "it's really shameful to be lying down useless like this because of illness" (Tayama 1909: 523). Seizo thinks it is shameful that he cannot participate in the nation's foreign war (the Russo-Japanese War) due to his illness. A psychological inferiority complex emerges, where the connection to the nation is severed by physical illness. In times of war, there is a mechanism by which human beings are nationalized. Furthermore, their bodies are nationalized, which brings their minds under the control of the state. Thus, individuals who are excluded from the system of national community, because of physical illness, are made to feel inferior.

Amid this intersection of war and infectious disease, there is the discussion of *Tuberculosis and Social Problems* by Sakura Ujihara. Ujihara cites "the case of a young man who had been sent to the army and came back home with tuberculosis, and then infected his family and relatives, resulting in the tragic death of the whole family" and states that "expelling the patient without any treatment should not escape the criticism that it is a measure to avoid responsibility" (Ujihara 1914: 87). People infected with COVID-19 today are forced to stay at home to recuperate, which has led to many deaths; this is reminiscent of those pandemics that happened 100 years ago.

Infectious Diseases and Gender Inequality

In Japan around the turn of the twentieth century, where infectious diseases such as smallpox and pulmonary tuberculosis were widespread, the attitudes of families and the society toward infected patients of different genders also differed, providing a glimpse of gender injustice at that time. Ichiyo Higuchi's *Takekurabe* (*Child's Play*) (1896) also weaves in descriptions of "smallpox and scabies" and shows a clearer disdain for women's skin diseases and scars, in comparison to the male Soseki's Teacher Kusyami. In contrast to "beautiful wives", Shotaro of Tanakaya refers to women with smallpox scars or scabies scars on their faces as ugly women, and says, "if a woman should come in with a face like Ofuku of the rice shop full of pox scars, or a woman with a forehead that protrudes like the one of the firewood shop, I would drive her out immediately and not let her in" (Higuchi 1896: 165–166). In those days, it was very common for men to boast about women's physical appearances. In other words, whether beautiful or ugly, a "woman" will always be subject to a "man's" gaze. But the skin infections that left scars on the body brought more scorn to women than men. For men, physical features such as scars caused by infections are merely fodder for momentary self-mockery and criticism, while women's physical flaws are a source of ridicule and rejection. This kind of positional relationship between men as the viewer and women as the object of being viewed certainly existed in those days. In a sense, beauty and health become the criteria for evaluating the existence and body of the "bride", and the ugly and unhealthy infected person would naturally be the target of discrimination and exclusion.

This societal system of evaluating the physical representation of women makes it clear that women's role in the family system is to bear healthy offspring. Therefore, when a woman loses this physical value, she is cut off and excluded from the family system. Roka Tokutomi's *Hototogisu* (*The Cuckoo*) can also be seen as a story about society and family's attitude toward women who were infected. In the story, when Nami contracts pulmonary tuberculosis, she is divorced on the grounds that it is detrimental to the survival of the family. Nami's mother-in-law persuades her son, "it's not only Nami, but you would also be infected, you would have children and the children would be infected. Both you and your precious children would get tuberculosis and die. The House of Kawashima would be destroyed" (Tokutomi 1900: 186). The existence of an infectious disease foregrounds the character of the infected person, Nami, as a mother's body spreading disease germs rather than as a human being. Infection is not only a problem in Nami's body, but also manifests itself through her contact with her husband, Takeo, as a bad body that would infect him. She must be eliminated as a negative influence on the family, as well as one that would infect the children in the household. In this way, the infection expands the problem not only to the sick person but also to the survival of the family. The female body is cast out of the home because it cannot fulfill its role of nurturing healthy children.

Later, in 1904, the Ministry of the Interior issued Ministerial Order No. 1, stipulating the control measures for preventing pulmonary tuberculosis and prohibiting the marriage of pulmonary tuberculosis patients under the national law. The fictional story becomes even more realistic because an infectious disease can be a catalyst to trigger a reaction not only in the infected person's body, but also in the institution of family, the system of society, and the power of the state. In this way, infectious diseases bring to light the subordinate status of women in the family system, at the time, and their role in performing a negative function for the survival of the family system.

4 Attitudes Toward Infectious Diseases Suggested by Literati

Phenomena such as exclusion, discrimination, feelings of guilt, and gender inequality arose during the spread of infectious diseases and were various expressions of social injustice. In modern Japanese literature, there are some works that accurately depict such social injustice and distortions, and do not condone them. Therefore, it is believed that such literary texts may contain elements that will make us reconsider and reconstruct the new social transformations of today's post-pandemic world.

From the Image of Death to the Hope of Living

This study has traced the cases in modern Japanese literature where the infected people in the story were looked at differently by those around them and were regarded as heretics in the group. This phenomenon of the group excluding infected individuals was particularly pronounced in the early stages of the explosion in infectious disease. When a carrier of an unknown pathogen appears, the psychology of differentiation, demonization, and even exclusion of foreign substances is at work within the group. In such cases, people consciously or unconsciously try to protect themselves in groups, succumb to peer pressure, and even join the frenzy of exclusion. It is a social phenomenon that is often seen in any country at any time. However, it would be extremely difficult to prevent this social psychology of the othering of the unknown. It is true that it is important to accurately recognize what an infectious disease is and to come into contact with infected people based on that understanding, but the gaps until that point may have been supplemented by literary works that foreshadowed the theme of infectious diseases.

In Roka Tokutomi's *Hototogisu* (*The Cuckoo*), there is a description that "there is not a single person who has fully recovered from pulmonary tuberculosis" (Tokutomi 1900: 185), which gives the impression that the infection of pulmonary tuberculosis at that time means death. This kind of recognition is also mentioned in Ishikawa Takuboku's *Ichiaku No Suna* (*A Handful of Sand*), just as the verse "the lung has a disease/ there is the man who will go die soon", and "the number of lung diseases increases every year" (Ishikawa 1910: 114). On the other hand, there are works that reverse the negative impression of infectious diseases and create hope and courage for "living" through understanding and love for the sick. Tatsuo Hori, who also suffered from pulmonary tuberculosis, distanced himself from the context of exclusion and discrimination, and depicted the isolation of tuberculosis in *Kazetachinu* (*The Wind Has Risen*). When her father sends the protagonist's fiancée, Setsuko, to the "Sanatorium of F", the protagonist responds: "If so, I can go together." There was warm understanding, sympathy, and love between the two people, who were both infected, and his words made Setsuko feel vibrant and eager to live: "I, somehow, suddenly feel like I want to live...." She added in a whispered voice that may or may not have been heard: "Because of you..." (Hori 1938: 28–40).

Rather than the eyes of the people around him and the cruelty of the social system, Tatsuo Hori focuses on the "sympathy" and "love" of the infected people. This is what gives humans the power to live. Therefore, the sentences, "The wind has risen, and it is time to live. ... The days that preceded my life were livelier than life itself, and even more sadly joyful...", contain the warm feeling of life that reverses discrimination and exclusion, and the sadness and joy of living are clearly shown.

Becoming Free from the Gaze of Others

Like Tatsuo Hori, Kenji Miyazawa is a writer who has contracted pulmonary tuberculosis and has talked about infectious diseases head-on. In his posthumous manuscript, which he is said to have written while recovering from a pulmonary illness that began in August 1928 and lasted until the end of 1930, he describes in *Me Nite Iu* (*Speaking with My Eyes*): "from your perspective, it may be a miserable scene/ but from my perspective, all I see is a beautiful blue sky and a clear wind" (Miyazawa 1946: 77–78). After the 3/11 earthquake disaster, Yo Henmi proposed that the words that were needed were not slogan-like inspirational words such as "hang in there, revival, unity, and unyielding spirit...", but rather words that went a step deeper, such as the content in the above "*Me Nite Iu* (*Speaking with My Eyes*)" (Yo Henmi 2021: 20–21). As the title of the manuscript, "*Me Nite Iu* (*Speaking with My Eyes*)" suggests, these words are the true feelings of the infected person as expressed by the sick body. When someone is infected, they are placed in a subordinate position, and they should resist being exposed to the eyes of others. They should always maintain the view of "my perspective" rather than "your perspective", and even if they are experiencing pulmonary hemorrhage, they will only see the "blue sky" and "wind". While seeking fairness, truth, and equality, as Henmi proposed, people affected by disasters continue to crave "words" that have a deeper meaning than slogans.

In *Me Nite Iu* (*Speaking with My Eyes*) one can learn about the importance of shifting one's gaze to the inner world of the self or to the natural landscape as a way of freeing oneself from the excessive gaze of others. This is done without being bound by the ideology created by the group or the established image of the artist. In addition, the words written in "*Me Nite Iu* (*Speaking with My Eyes*)" make suggestions to those who live in the midst of peer pressure and self-oppression in the COVID-19 crisis. Rather than being overly conscious of the existence of others (your perspective), it is more important to carry out deeper self-reflection (my perspective), to think about what we can see and what we can feel with our bodies, to live at this moment and in this place, and to be in contact with nature as a living body.

5 Conclusion

Pandemics of Infectious Diseases and the Future of Social Fairness

Literary works are records approaching history. It is important to read works by writers who experienced infectious diseases from a social perspective, regarding them as a kind of earnest voice of people living with infectious diseases. Through their literary works, modern literary scholars have told the story of the individual's experience of infection and desire for life, while at the same time recording the function and ineffectiveness of social institutions such as the "medical community", "family", "school", and "religion". The spread of infectious diseases in the modern era must have been the result of a multilayered effect of various factors. Industrialization, urbanization, population densification and migration associated with modernization, and especially war, have been cited as important causes, and there are records of infectious diseases such as tuberculosis and influenza spreading among workers, both in schools and in the military. This chapter focuses on the story of the individual "patient" in modern Japanese literature and the relationship between the individual and others/groups when an infectious disease is present, and attempts to organize various social responses to the spread of infectious diseases.

Koyo Ozaki's *Aobudo* (*The Green Grapes*) shockingly depicts how infected people were considered sinners and were differentiated along with the name of the disease. It also shows the social system that functioned in the background, allowing this to happen. Infectious diseases are highly contagious, so the prevention of them goes beyond the scope of medical care and is linked to issues of social security, political policy, and international relations. As can be seen from the ordinances and laws for the prevention of infectious diseases in modern Japan, when political powers became involved in the dynamics of exclusion against those who suffered from infectious diseases, the voices of patients were suppressed and reduced to insignificance by strong power systems.

In *Inaka Kyoshi* (*The Country Teacher*) by Katai Tayama, the dynamics of the exclusion of infected people by the nation and the military are depicted, and in *Hototogisu* (*The Cuckoo*) by Roka Tokutomi and *Takekurabe* (*Child's Play*) by Ichiyo Higuchi, there are depictions of the exclusion of infected women in some households. On the other hand, the image of death related to the incurable pulmonary tuberculosis in Takuboku's *Ichiaku No Suna* (*A Handful of Sand*), is reversed in some works such as *Kazetachinu* (*The Wind Has Risen*) by Tatsuo Hori, which describes the will to live based on the sympathy and love. In response to the stereotypical and discriminatory gazes of others, Kenji Miyazawa suggested the importance of shifting one's gaze and focusing on one's inner self in *Me Nite Iu* (*Speaking with My Eyes*).

Due to the contagious nature of infectious diseases, the infected people not only suffer physical pain caused by the diseases and tolerate the strange looks from the people around them, but also are cut off social activities. It is a common social phenomenon that the physical isolation of infected people evolves into a dynamic of exclusion. This is not just because of the objective existence of germs, but cultural codes such as impurity, sin, and filth are also attached. This is where the subjective and negative evaluation of the body and thoughts of the human being–the host of the bacteria–comes from. Moreover, the subjects of this evaluation system are extended beyond specific blood relations to local, national, and racial levels, as happened during the COVID-19 pandemic. From this, in addition to physical pain, the effects of infectious diseases are transformed into social sanctions such as discrimination, aggression, and violence. But rather than suppressing and eliminating the infected, it is necessary to make the group function in a way that gives them hope for life.

By unraveling the history of infectious diseases through literary works and delving into the responses and records from those times, rather than just focusing on slogans and big data, we have an opportunity to look at the vulnerable and listen to the voices of people living in the present. As a result, we will continue to search for ways to realize the vision of constructing a society that respects life itself and is based on fairness, truth, and equality in a post-pandemic world.

Acknowledgement This chapter is a substantially revised version of a paper presented at the Symposium of The Covid-19 Pandemic and the Future of Global Social Fairness, held by Chiba University Leading Research Promotion Program "Chiba Studies on Global Fair Society: A Multidisciplinary Approach" (online symposium, September 28, 2021). I would like to express my sincere gratitude to Dr. Jiro Mizushima, Dr. Yuji Ohara, Dr. Teiji Kenjo, Dr. Tomeko Misaki, Dr. Xi Cheng, Dr. Xiaofang Zhang, and the participants in the conference for their valuable comments on the paper and report.

References

Fukuda, Mahito. 1995. *Cultural History of Tuberculosis: Image of the Disease in Modern Japan*. Nagoya University Press.

Health and Welfare Statistics Association, ed. 2009. *Annual Trends in the Number of Reported Infectious Disease Patients 2009*. Health and Welfare Statistics Association.

Henmi, Yo. 2021. *Words from the Rubble to My Dead*. NHK Publishing.

Higuchi, Ichiyo. 1896, *Takekurabe* (*Child's Play*), *Bungei Kurabu*, 2 (5). (Reproduced in 2001, *The Collected Works of Higuchi Ichiyo*, Iwanami Shoten, 127–181.)

Hori, Tatsuo. 1938. *Kazetachinu* (*The Wind Has Risen*), Noda Shobo. (Reprint: 1978, *New Selection of Complete Works of Famous Books: Modern Literature Museum, Kazetachinu* (*The Wind Has Risen*), The Museum of Modern Japanese Literature.)

Hosoi, Wakizo. 1925. *Zyokouaisi (The Sorrowful History of Female Factory Workers)*. Kaizosha.

Iguchi, Jokai. 1929. *Smallpox and Vaccination Theory*. Bunkodo Shoten.
Ikeda, Isao. 2002. Japanese Modern Literature and Tuberculosis: A Genealogy of Negative Youth Literature. *Bulletin of the Institute for Research in Humanities*. Meiji University, 51, Institute for Research in Humanities, Meiji University.
Ishii, Masami. 2021. *Introduction to the Theory of Infectious Disease Literature: How the Great Writers Wrote*. Kawade Shobo.
Ishikawa, Takuboku. 1910. *Ichiaku No Suna (A Handful of Sand)*. Toundo Shoten.
Kobe Court Compilation. 1880. Provisional Regulations for the Prevention of Cholera. *Complete Book of Regulations and Punishment Examples, Volume 5*. Kobe Court.
Komori, Yoichi. 2020. *Rereading Soseki Natsume's Kokoro: Sickness and Humanity under the COVID-19 Crisis*. Kamogawa Publishing.
Miyazawa, Kenji. 1946. *Me Nite Iu (Speaking with My Eyes)*. *Gunzo* 1 (1): 76–79. (Reprinted in 1995, [New] *The Complete Works of Kenji Miyazawa*, Volume 5: Poems IV, Compilation, Chikuma Shobo, 140–141.)
Natsume, Soseki. 1906. *Wagahai Wa Neko Dearu (I Am a Cat) Part II*. Okura Shoten.
———. 1914. *Kokoro*. Iwanami Shoten.
——— (author), Aiko Ito (translator), Graeme Wilson (translator). 1993. *I Am a Cat*. Tuttle Publishing.
——— (author), Meredith McKinney (editing, preface, translator). 2010. *Kokoro*. Penguin Classics.
Ogawa, Shuji, and Suzuki, Mizuho, eds. 2021. *Encyclopedia of Topics on the Medical History of Infectious Diseases 1347–2020*. Nichigai Associates.
Ozaki, Koyo. 1896. *Aobudo (The Green Grapes)*. Shunyodo.
Prepared by the Cabinet. 1897. Infectious Disease Prevention Act Enacted, Regulations for the Prevention of Infectious Diseases Repealed, Original Signature, 1897, Law No. 36.
Senthilingam, Meera. 2020. *Outbreaks and Epidemics: Battling Infection from Measles to Coronavirus*. London: Icon Books. (Translated by Chiaki Ishiguro, 2021, *Humanity Lives with Infectious Diseases: A Modern History of Pandemics and Vaccines Not Taught in Schools*, Yodosha.)
Susan, Sontag. 1978. *Illness as Metaphor*. New York: Farrar, Straus and Giroux. (Translated by Takao Tomiyama, 1982, Misuzu Shobo.)
Tachikawa, Shoji. 1989. *Human History of Disease: The Meiji, Taisho and Showa Eras*. Shinchosha.
Tayama, Katai. 1909. *Inaka Kyoshi (The Country Teacher)*. Sakura Shobo.
Tokutomi, Roka. 1900. *Hototogisu (The Cuckoo)*. Minyusha.
Ujihara, Sakura. 1914. *Tuberculosis and Social Problems*. Ikai Jihosha.

13

Interim Conclusion

Hikari Ishido and Masaya Kobayashi

1 Global Multi-Layered Analysis on Fairness

Based on the preceding discussions, these concluding pages address what could be done for a fair society through the experience of COVID-19. It seems that the era of COVID-19 is almost over (as at the timing of writing, i.e., middle of 2023), without a clear-cut transition towards a "post" pandemic period, but its impact still persists. The pandemic indeed continues to affect countries, developed and developing (emerging) alike, yet it clearly affects developing countries disproportionately (Saasa and James 2020). That said, there would be a need to conclude our discussions so

H. Ishido (✉)
Graduate School of Global and Transdisciplinary Studies, Chiba University, Chiba, Japan
e-mail: ishido@faculty.chiba-u.jp

M. Kobayashi
Graduate School of Social Sciences, Chiba University, Chiba, Japan
e-mail: masaya_kobayashi@nifty.com

H. Ishido et al. (eds.), *Social Fairness in a Post-Pandemic World*,
https://doi.org/10.1007/978-981-19-9654-2_13

far, and of course make a proposal toward the development of a fair (or fairer) society after the pandemic, while noting that this attempt remains interim in nature.

The criteria to be excluded for a fair society has been clear to some extent, but the values to be realized and the specific vision is as yet unclear: when it comes to inequality of income, for example, it is reasonable to judge that it is unjust for the national regime of the time to arbitrarily give favors to its own close associates, as in the case of patronage, cronyism, and the patrimonial state. However, there is no uniform guideline as to what kind of welfare policies should be implemented to correct inequalities, and how well they should be funded. This is because disparities that emerge as a result of competition in the market are not necessarily unfair, as long as the principle of "fair and equal opportunity," in the terms of Rawls (1971), is achieved. Although Rawls himself justifies the correction of excessive inequality through the difference principle, others do not necessarily include this principle in their own "fairness principle." Hence, the contention that the fairness principle should correct the consequential inequality cannot necessarily be drawn.

The philosophical liberal theory of fairness, including Rawls' theory (see Introduction), is certainly important in that it provides rules, laws, and policies that should eliminate arbitrariness, bias, and the like. Through the experience of COVID-19, however, we learned that the provision of essential goods and services cannot be secured through present liberal trade regimes, with the World Trade Organization (WTO) at the center, for example (in a business/economic dimension). So then, it is important to examine various issues concerning COVID-19 from the philosophical and theoretical perspective introduced in the Introduction.

On the basis of the multi-dimensional fairness theory, let us indicate the cardinal points regarding the fairness of each chapter in this book. In the following, the term "the four-dimensional fairness" is used in the cases where these dimensions are kept in mind either explicitly or implicitly; the word "comprehensive fairness" is used in the meaning of composite vectors described in the Introduction (Figure 1.2); the word 'overall fairness' indicates the cases the four-dimensional fairness is analyzed without isolating these four dimensions.

The discussion in Chap. 2 (Fairness in the Global Allocation System for the COVID-19 Vaccine COVAX: Limits to Affected Parties Participation in Decision-Making) reveals that there are limitations in the global vaccine allocation system which centered on the actions of sovereign nation states (yet vaccines as products are being manufactured by private pharmaceutical firms); here indeed, the four elements of fairness, i.e., rule-compliance (e.g., with national regulations by pharmaceutical firms; with restrictions on socioeconomic life by citizens), equal impartiality (e.g., income-supporting measures for business companies and households, depending on the degree of economic hardship), ethical fidelity (sincere and agile implementation of policies and regulations) and benefit reciprocity (fair trade, i.e., exporting and importing, especially of essential items with mutually beneficial prices among the trading countries), all cohere; even when inter-state coordination, e.g., the Group of 20 (G20), cannot effectively function, with the outbreak of COVID-19 (Bernes 2020), some private companies (in the economic dimension) could voluntarily secure some doses of free-of-charge vaccines for citizens, especially in developing Asian and African countries.

Chapter 3 (Environment and Economy in the Post-COVID-19 Era: Focusing on Global Warming Issues) analyzes global-level comprehensive fairness, especially in terms of the biosphere and economy, by utilizing the conception of '"environmental fairness" based on the four-dimensional fairness; in this case also, national-level decision making, sometimes in parallel with non-governmental associations movements, has a big impact on the course of global environmental governance (and sub-national family as well as individuals are influenced by the movements).

While this chapter explicitly analyses fairness from the theoretical perspective in the Introduction, most of the other chapters give a general analysis of fairness. For example, citizens are supposed to comprehend fairness comprehensively, that is, including the four dimensions.

Chapter 4 (Philosophy and Case Studies of Regional Integrations and COVID-19) makes a comparative assessment of the European Union and the Association of South East Asian Nations. In all of these chapters, the citizens' differing attitudes toward overall fairness in political economy have idiosyncratic influences on the way in which the regional (inter-national) governance is carried out.

Chapter 5 (Challenges and Possibilities for Global Economic Cooperation after COVID-19—Focus on East Asia) considers the hitherto stagnant inter-state linkage between China, Japan and Korea and aspires for a post-pandemic cooperation in political, economic and cultural dimensions; a change in mood is actually taking place as of this writing in the middle of 2023: e.g., Japan–Korea collaboration in a forward-looking manner has been explicitly featured in the media, with historical and geopolitical "fairness" clearly in view. With these relationships, primarily inter-state in nature, the constituent citizens (i.e., family and individuals) both directly (official representation of politicians as a result of elections) and indirectly (e.g., through opinion polls and social media postings) influence the economic fairness (in particular, reciprocal fairness) of those inter-state relationships through the EU, APEC, ASEAN or unofficial regional linkages (e.g., between China, Japan and Korea).

Chapter 6 (Social Justice and the Response to the COVID-19 Crisis in European Countries) highlights, in relation to the societal community system, the impact of social control (peer-to-peer monitoring and advocation to comply with social norms, including wearing masks in the face of the pandemic). Chapter 7 (Well-being and Fairness in the COVID-19 Crisis: Insights from Positive Political Psychology) directly shows the interlinkage between personal well-being and overall societal fairness; the COVID-19 related attitudes of citizens both influence, and are under the influence of, the dominant political party at the subnational and local levels, with regard to political rule-compliance in Chapter 8 (Coping with COVID-19: Policy Response and Citizens' Well-Being in Australia).

Chapter 9 (Mexico Facing the COVID-19 Pandemic: Slow and Ineffective Societal and Governmental Responses in a Country with a High Level of Socioeconomic Inequality and a Precarious Health System) highlights the pandemic-related socioeconomic situation of Mexico, concerning aspects such as the economic unfairness of equal impartiality and rule-compliance, which experiences serious infection, the healthcare crisis, and the aggravation of poverty. Chapter 10 (APEC's Response to the COVID-19 Crisis and Social Justice) addresses the "open regionalism," i.e., inter-state interactions in an non-discriminatory manner, while noting the emerging conflicts between "self" and "non-self" of rivalling multiple nation states, regarding the economic fairness of equal impartiality and ethical fidelity and in the face of the pandemic with truly cross-border facets.

Chapter 11 (COVID-19 and its Impact on Women and Gender) highlights an unfair aspect of the human system in terms of gender, and this relates to the surrounding political/economic circumstances of those who are suffering from four-dimensional sociocultural unfairness concerning all forms of gender biases. Finally, Chapter 12 (Modern Japanese Literature and Infectious Diseases: Representations of Infectious Diseases and Social Fairness in Literary Works) seems to make a contribution to the sociocultural fairness concerning all of the four fairness-related components as "transcending" the stagnant status quo in terms of, e.g., economic indicators, and proposing a new (at least literary) value in the pandemic-hit society. This is, in a sense, an equity-oriented fairness: the human system which had been hit by the pandemic on a global scale, needs something positive (i.e., literary works), to counterbalance the negative "value" created by the pandemic. And this sort of value creation is expected to emerge more clearly, in a post-pandemic "new" culture (beyond national borders) of societal thriving and coping.

2 The Prospect of Fair Societies through the COVID-19 Crisis

Based on the findings from each of the chapters in this book, the importance of a "relational" consideration emerges: a matching of the four elements of fairness and four dimensions of human system would be applicable. Importantly, the boundaries between the fairness elements and the observed dimensions are ambiguous, thereby influencing one another in an intricate, yet realistic manner. During the pandemic-stricken period, these ambiguous or hazy boundaries have been observed, and this trend will be further intensified in the post-pandemic era. That is, albeit distinguished conceptually, these elements and dimensions are inter-related among themselves. This is one of the reasons why several of the chapters do not necessarily concentrate on specific elements of fairness.

While restrictions on the rights to free movement have become a matter for social discussion (Rubenstein and Decamp 2020), the new custom of telework (with the support from carefully handled digital technologies (Kaminski and Jennifer 2021; Margetts 2022)) has now become almost a business norm, with "workation" (vacation-like work, or work-while-having-vacation, especially in rural areas) gaining popularity among citizens across the globe. All told, the fairness vector (introduced in Introduction) seems linear in form, and yet in some aspects it is, actually, significantly nonlinear, with each components of fairness and dimensions intrinsically connected with each other. In other words, the demarcation among the fairness elements (vertical direction in table 1.1 presented in the Introduction in this volume) and among the dimensions (horizontal direction in the same table) has become rather hazy. This sort of "hazy-boundary" situation could be addressed in the past-pandemic era. In other words, fairness is, so to speak, "one in essence," yet "multi-dimensional in practical applications," i.e., "quadrinity" of practical fairness-related measurements is in place. With the outbreak of the pandemic, the "one-in-essence" feature seems to have been revealed, since this core value (fairness) is really intrinsic to human existence, which stands out more in the face of pandemic-stricken, "life or death" situations.

If this development was addressed then the decentralized emergence, rather than the top-down grand design, of a new society could be envisioned, with citizens always attempting to make the level and dimension they face fairer (in terms of rule-compliance, equal impartiality, ethical fidelity and benefit reciprocity), in a small-step and piecemeal manner. This could particularly be the case when multiple elements are intricately connected beyond one entity's planning for improvements; ecological, political and economic dimensions might then be connected intrinsically, since the citizens' very cultural activities (e.g., their "ecological life", and "ethical consumption") involve all of these dimensions.

In this spirit, Table 13.1 places each chapter in terms of the matching of fairness elements and dimensions, always bearing in mind that the boundaries between the cells remain rather hazy and ambiguous.

Table 13.1 The place of each chapter in the four fairness elements and four dimensions

	Ecological ⟺	Political ⟺	Economic ⟺	Societal-cultural
Rule-Compliance ↕	Chapter 3 (Global warming)	Chapter 2 (Vaccine allocation) Chapter 6 (Europe) Chapter 8 (Australia)	Chapter 9 (Mexico)	Chapter 12 (Japanese literature)
Equal Impartiality ↕	Chapter 3	Chapter 2 Chapter 6	Chapter 9 Chapter 10 (APEC)	Chapter 12
Ethical Fidelity ↕	Chapter 3	Chapter 2 Chapter 6	Chapter 3 Chapter 10	Chapter 12
Benefit Reciprocity	Chapter 3	Chapter 2 Chapter 6	Chapter 5(East Asia)	Chapter 12
All of the above fairness		Chapter 4 (Regional Integration)	Chapter 4	Chapter 7 (Japan)
	Chapter 1 (Introduction) Chapter 11 (gender)			

Notes: Multiple cells are chosen for some chapters, based on the relevance; the arrows indicate intrinsic interactions among the elements and dimensions
Source: Made by the editors, based on Kobayashi (2021)

How we can secure these elements of fairness is a crucial issue for the achievement of a fairer society. While theories of fairness differ in some details, there is commonality at their core. They all hold that in order to maintain a system, such as a nation-state, composed of free and equal people cooperating with each other, it is necessary for them to assume the political responsibility of doing things they would not necessarily be willing to do voluntarily, and that the principle of fairness is called for, as a social fairness on a global scale (Kolm 2004; Wellman, C. 2005).

Klosko (2004) developed liberal theories of political responsibility for achieving social good (or welfare). For excludable, private goods (including vaccines for COVID-19), it is possible to prevent those who do not fulfill their duties from enjoying the benefits of goods; it is, however, not possible to exclude those non-contributing people or entities for the case of non-excludable goods (i.e., goods that cannot be prevented from being consumed by those who do not pay the price) such as air, water and a high hygienic standard suppressing pandemics, and public goods (goods that cannot be prevented by those who do not pay the price), including government functions, e.g., putting pandemics in check at the national border. This creates the problem of free-riders, where cooperating parties who carry out their duties provide resources and labor and receive benefits, while non-cooperating parties receive only benefits and do not bear the burden. To avoid this problem, in a cooperative scheme, a political obligation is imposed to provide people with public, non-excludable goods, such as physical security, if the following three conditions are met. That is, (1) the benefits are worth the costs of the obligation, (2) the benefits are presumptive benefits, and (3) the overall distribution of benefits and burdens in a cooperative scheme can be accepted as fair. The global magnitude of COVID-19 would merit a serious and practical discussion on these conditions. We all have the right (with at least long-term benefits) and obligation to contribute to the social fairness.

It would cost trust (Rescher 2002) as well as some economic sacrifice for leading countries to commit to global political responsibilities in connection to the pandemic; the sacrifice, however, might, meaningfully enough (in terms of fairness elements), mitigate potential (and bigger) impacts of the human system at the economic and cultural dimensions (McMahon 2016; Barnett 2020; Markowitz 2021; Qing et al. 2021; Liu et al. 2021). COVID-19 strokes at society's neglected areas, exposing unnoticed issues, such as disparities across gender and income. Cross-elements and cross-dimensional efforts to achieve a fairer society "after" (arguably, depending on its definition) the pandemic, hence an interdisciplinary publication like the present one.

References

Barnett, Michael. 2020. COVID-19 and the Sacrificial International Order. Published online by Cambridge University Press. https://www.cambridge.org/core/journals/international-organization/article/covid19-and-the-sacrificial-international-order/7D64519B3541BD20C77D4DE82702243F.

Bernes, Tom. 2020. COVID-19: The Failure of G20. Research Report Open Access. https://www.jstor.org/stable/resrep24934.3?searchText=fairness%2C+COVID-19&searchUri=%2Faction%2FdoBasicSearch%3FQuery%3Dfairness%252C%2BCOVID-19%26so%3Drel&ab_segments=0%2FSYC-6451%2Ftest&refreqid=fastly-default%3A9513c14d6a6c744033cbb5d67ce56088&seq=2#metadata_info_tab_contents.

Kaminski, Margot E., and M. Urban Jennifer. 2021. The Right to Contest AI. *Columbia Law Review* 121 (7, Nov.): 1957–2048.

Klosko, George. 2004. *The Principle of Fairness and Political Obligation*. New ed. Lanham, MD: Rowman & Littlefield Publishers.

Kobayashi, Masaya. 2021. Chapter 3 Tajigenteki na Tougouteki Kousei Shakai Riron: Kyouryokuteki Kokyo Sisutemu niokeru Kihanteki 4 Kijun (in Japanese) (Multidimensional Theory of Integrated Fair Society: Four Normative Criteria in a Cooperative Public System). In *Kouseishakai no bijon: Gakusaiteki Apurochi niyoru Riron, Shisou, Genjou Bunseki* (in Japanese) (Vision for a Fair Society: Theory, Thought and the Analysis of Status Quo through Interdisciplinary Approaches), eds. Jiro Mizushima, Chiyo Yonemura and Masaya Kobayashi. Tokyo: Akashi Shoten.

Kolm, Serge-Christophe. 2004. *Macrojustice: The Political Economy of Fairness*. New York: Cambridge University Press.

Liu, Jia, Yasir Shahab, and Hafiz Hoque. 2021. Government Response Measures and Public Trust during the COVID-19 Pandemic: Evidence from Around the World. *British Journal of Management* 33 (2): 571–602.

Margetts, Helen. 2022. Rethinking AI for Good Governance. *Daedalus*, 151 (2), AI & Society (Spring 2022): 360–371.

Markowitz, M. 2021. Prosocial Responses to COVID-19: Examining the Role of Gratitude, Fairness and Legacy Motives. *Personality and Individual Differences* 171 (Mar.): 110488.

McMahon, C. 2016. *Reasonableness and Fairness: A Historical Theory*. New York: Cambridge University Press.

Qing, Han, Bang Zheng, Mioara Cristea, Maximilian Agostini, Jocelyn J. Bélanger, Ben Gützkow, N. Jannis Kreienkamp, Pontus Leander, and PsyCorona Collaboration. 2021. Trust in Government Regarding COVID-19 and Its Associations with Preventive Health Behaviour and Prosocial Behaviour During the Pandemic: A Cross-Sectional and Longitudinal Study. *Psychological Medicine* 26: 1–11.

Rawls, John. 1971. *A Theory of Justice*. Cambridge, MA: The Belknap Press of Harvard University Press.

Rescher, N. 2002. *Fairness: Theory & Practice of Distributive Justice*. London: Routledge.

Rubenstein, Leonard, and Matthew Decamp. 2020. Revisiting Restrictions of Rights after COVID-19. *Health and Human Rights* 22 (2), Special Section: Big Data, Technology, Artificial Intelligence and the Right to Health: 321–324.

Saasa, Sherinah, and Spencer James. 2020. COVID-19 in Zambia. *Journal of Comparative Family Studies* 51 (3/4), Special Issue: Global Family Perspectives on COVID-19: 347–359.

Wellman, C. 2005. Samaritanism and the Duty to Obey the Law? In *Is There a Duty to Obey the Law?* ed. C.H. Wellman and A.J. Simmons, 1–90. New York: Cambridge University Press.

Index[1]

[1] Note: Page numbers followed by 'n' refer to notes.

H. Ishido et al. (eds.), *Social Fairness in a Post-Pandemic World*,
https://doi.org/10.1007/978-981-19-9654-2

The manufacturer's authorised representative in the EU is Springer Nature Customer Service Centre GmbH, Europaplatz 3, 69115 Heidelberg, Germany. If you have any concerns regarding our products, please contact ProductSafety@springernature.com

Printed and bound by CPI Group (UK) Ltd, Croydon, CR0 4YY
30/09/2026
02225243-0004